About Island Press

Island Press is the only nonprofit organization in the United States whose principal purpose is the publication of books on environmental issues and natural resource management. We provide solutions-oriented information to professionals, public officials, business and community leaders, and concerned citizens who are shaping responses to environmental problems.

In 2002, Island Press celebrates its eighteenth anniversary as the leading provider of timely and practical books that take a multidisciplinary approach to critical environmental concerns. Our growing list of titles reflects our commitment to bringing the best of an expanding body of literature to the environmental community throughout North America and the world.

Support for Island Press is provided by The Bullitt Foundation, The Mary Flagler Cary Charitable Trust, The Nathan Cummings Foundation, Geraldine R. Dodge Foundation, Doris Duke Charitable Foundation, The Charles Engelhard Foundation, The Ford Foundation, The George Gund Foundation, The Vira I. Heinz Endowment, The William and Flora Hewlett Foundation, W. Alton Jones Foundation, The Henry Luce Foundation, The John D. and Catherine T. MacArthur Foundation, The Andrew W. Mellon Foundation, The Charles Stewart Mott Foundation, The Curtis and Edith Munson Foundation, National Fish and Wildlife Foundation, The New-Land Foundation, Oak Foundation, The Overbrook Foundation, The David and Lucile Packard Foundation, The Pew Charitable Trusts, Rockefeller Brothers Fund, The Winslow Foundation, and other generous donors.

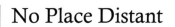

No Place Distant

For Spense and Val—

*extraordinary parents, teachers,
and companions*

No Place Distant

Roads and Motorized Recreation on America's Public Lands

David G. Havlick

Foreword by Mike Dombeck

ISLAND PRESS

Washington • Covelo • London

ISLAND PRESS is a trademark of The Center for Resource Economics.

Library of Congress Cataloging-in-Publication Data
Havlick, David G.
No place distant : roads and motorized recreation on America's public
lands / David G. Havlick.
    p. cm.
Includes bibliographical references (p.   ) and index.
  ISBN 1-55963-844-3 — ISBN 1-55963-845-1 (pbk.)
  1. Public land roads—United States. I. Title.
HE336.P82 H38 2002
388.1'2—dc21   2001006979

British Cataloguing-in-Publication data also available.

Printed on recycled, acid-free paper.

Manufactured in the United States of America
09 08 07 06 05 04 03 02   8 7 6 5 4 3 2 1

Contents

Foreword

Every American is affected in some way by roads on public lands. Roads affect our pocketbooks, our recreation experiences, the quality of the water we drink, and much more. Over one-half million miles of roads have been constructed on the lands that you and I, as citizens of the United States, own. In other words, we have built enough roads to circle the Earth twenty times on less than one-quarter of the total land base of the United States.

As a young boy growing up in northern Wisconsin's Chequamegon National Forest, I observed on more than one occasion the after-effects of a road built into a vast acreage of forest—usually for the purpose of timber harvesting. No longer could I hike in those areas and enjoy the solitude and wilderness that I once imagined Davy Crockett, Daniel Boone, and the ancestors of our neighboring Chippewa Indians experienced. No longer were they the magical, distant places far from the growl of a Jeep or the whine of a snowmobile. Spring ponds, with native brook trout bigger than a twelve-year old could imagine, soon became fishing holes littered with beer cans and candy wrappers, their banks chewed up by vehicle tracks. The character of the lands was altered, perhaps irrevocably.

The author of this book, David Havlick, also has experienced firsthand the overwhelming changes brought about by the building of new roads and trails in the backcountry. Havlick has been deeply involved in virtually all aspects of the public lands off-road vehicle and roads issues for years. The depth of his knowledge on the subject and his love of the land are clearly demonstrated by his coverage of the issues at hand. He writes in a crisp and easily readable style about how the character of the land is altered by human impact. *No Place Distant: Roads and Motorized Recreation on America's Public Lands* provides a timely, factual, and thought-provoking basis for an informed debate concerning the crucial public-land conservation challenges of this century.

We readily acknowledge that vehicular access to the land is necessary to our lifestyle in today's world, but must we be allowed to go everywhere, simply because we are able to get there? Public lands are the last remaining parcels of our frontier heritage. There has to be a balance between our need for access and our ability to preserve what truly wild land remains. The pressing issue today is determining what that balance is and what proportion of our wild lands should remain wild.

The United States today comprises 2.3 billion acres of land, ranging from the wildest and most remote 104 million acres of federally designated wilderness areas to millions more acres of highly developed and urbanized metropolitan areas. Between these extremes are ranches and farms, rural subdivisions, and small communities. Urban sprawl and land development are occurring at an unprecedented pace. An average of 3.2 million acres per year of forest, wetland, farmland, and open space were converted to more urban uses between 1992 and 1997—that is over 8,700 acres per day, each year—more than double the rate of development the previous decade, though the population remained relatively constant. This brings real meaning to the familiar quote, "buy land, they ain't makin' it any more."

Roads have had a significant influence on how humans interact with and use the land, as well as a profound and lasting impact on the land itself. Once a road or trail is etched on the land, more than just physical changes occur; our attitudes also change. We become accustomed to traveling along its route. Soon we perceive it to be our "right" to travel that route, regardless of the impact. This "I have the right" mind-set is much more pervasive on public lands. Though many citizens are very respectful of public lands, others are not. Certainly, I know of no private landowners who allow anyone to go anywhere at anytime on their land with any kind of motorized or even non-motorized vehicle.

Today, we can go to more places easier and faster than at any other time in history. In recent years, our ability to reach even the most remote areas has only increased. Traditional impediments to distant places—water, ice, snow, desert, or mountains-are no longer barriers to access. We are producing bigger and better off-road vehicles in larger numbers than ever before. Just a few decades ago the Jeep and snowcat were cutting edge, owned only by a very few. Now we invade the wild lands en masse on off-road vehicles, dirt bikes, snowmobiles, and jet skis.

Privately owned tracts of wild land and ranches are increasingly posted "no trespassing." Thus, a growing number of people have no other recourse than to use the declining acres of remote public land for their leisure activities. Sadly, the Americans whose recreation opportunities are becoming more limited are those who can least afford to pay for access to private land or belong to a hunting or fishing club. Will the opportunity to take pleasure in solitude become more and more restricted, available only to those who can meet the expense of traveling hundreds or thousands of miles to far-away places?

What about the ecosystem health of wild places? Wild lands are immensely important for their high-quality, undisturbed soil, water, and air. These three key resources are the foundation of ecosystem and watershed function, upon which long-term sustainability and all other resource values and uses depend. Healthy, functioning watersheds catch, store, and release water over time. They reduce the downstream effects of flooding, providing clean water for domestic, agricultural, and industrial uses, help maintain abundant and healthy fish and wildlife populations. Undeveloped wild lands serve as biological strongholds for threatened and endangered species and are essential to their long-term survival.

Another critical purpose of a watershed is to keep water on the land longer. The porous, vegetated topsoil of undisturbed watersheds acts as a sponge, soaking up moisture to replenish groundwater tables and aquifers. By contrast, when land is disturbed or has poorly maintained dirt roads, torrents of runoff can erode stream banks and roadways and carry tons of rich topsoil and silt downstream or downslope. Maintaining these areas relatively intact ultimately saves downstream communities millions of dollars in water-filtration costs.

Pristine areas are far more likely than roaded and developed areas to support healthy ecosystem function, including the diversity of native plants and animals. And areas of higher biological diversity are more resilient in response to such natural disturbances as storm events or drought. Unspoiled areas are more resistant to the proliferation of exotic invasive species, which is a major and growing problem throughout the country. Many species, such as the grizzly bear, elk, and wolf, are dependent on large, undisturbed areas of land for their survival. Roads and trails, especially those that are poorly maintained, are major sources of sediment, which adversely impacts aquatic species.

The body of knowledge about the long-term effects of management activities on landscapes is limited, so it follows that large, undisturbed areas are important outdoor laboratories. They provide the scientific data and information base for both the biotic and physical properties of what the land once was and perhaps could be again. It makes good sense to maintain remnants of the genetic library of life and physical character of the land. Future generations will want and need this information.

If we do not develop the land with utmost care, we erase nature's notebook of our own culture and history as a people and a nation. Undisturbed lands keep the record of prehistoric people's advance across North America. They contain many archaeological and sacred sites of Native Americans. We should not put at risk the few remaining remnants of the very frontier that shaped the American character. Elsewhere around the world, countries have temples and relics that stand as testaments to their cultural history, but it is our wild frontier that has defined the spirit of our American way of life.

During my tenure as chief of the U.S. Forest Service, many forest supervisors and rangers reported to me that they regard off-road vehicle management as the most challenging, land-damaging, resource issue that they face professionally. Developing scientifically based, off-road vehicle-use guidelines was high on my list of priorities, along with the need to protect roadless areas and old-growth forests. I believe that off-road vehicles have their place on public lands, but they must not be allowed to degrade the land or impair its long-term sustainability or ecosystem function.

David Havlick's book will help us understand the choices that we as Americans face in preserving important remaining parts of our natural and cultural heritage. Opportunities to enjoy nature by hiking, camping, picnicking, wildlife viewing, hunting, fishing, cross-country skiing, and canoeing must never be lost. Opportunities to pursue scientific and cultural studies must never be lost. Opportunities to experience firsthand the solitude of undisturbed landscapes must never be lost. As Wallace Stegner said in "Coda: Wilderness Letter," published in *The Sound of Mountain Water* (Doubleday, 1969):

> Something will have gone out of us as a people if we ever let the remaining wilderness be destroyed; if we permit the last virgin forests to be turned into comic books and plastic cigarette cases; if we drive the few remaining members of the wild species into zoos or to extinction; if we pollute the last clear air and dirty the last clean streams and push our paved roads through the last of the silence, so that never again will Americans be free in their own country from the noise, the exhausts, the stinks of human and automotive waste.

MIKE DOMBECK
Former chief, U.S. Forest Service, and acting director,
Bureau of Land Management
Pioneer Professor of Global Environmental Management,
University of Wisconsin–Stevens Point

Acknowledgments

Many people contributed in many different ways to this book. I hope that a broad, "Thank you!" will suffice for any whose names I fail to include here.

Tom Platt and Tom Skeele first dropped me into the thick of national forest roads by bringing me on to work for Predator Conservation Alliance's Roads Scholar Project. In that effort, Tim Bechtold, Bill Haskins, Keith Stockmann, and others at The Ecology Center in Missoula helped me out on more occasions than I can count. I remain grateful.

This book springs largely from the years I spent with the Roads Scholar Project inventorying roads in the field, meeting with land managers, and working on geographic information system maps. For much of this time, Bethanie Walder at Wildlands Center for Preventing Roads has been a loyal friend, colleague, critic, supporter, and resource. Having ready access to Wildlands CPR's library, staff, and contacts around the country has proven, time and again, to be of inestimable value. Jacob Smith, Tommy Petersen, and Marnie Criley at Wildlands CPR have also given excellent suggestions and enthusiastic support when I've come looking.

Barbara Dean at Island Press gave me encouragement and critical feedback when all I had was an idea, and her support and guidance throughout the process of writing this book have helped to keep me on track even when I tried to veer off-road. I feel fortunate to have worked with her. In the later stages of the process, Barbara Youngblood and Laura Carrithers also proved to be great help and constant sources of good cheer.

A number of people took the time and effort to review chapters or parts of the budding manuscript. I was consistently impressed by their wisdom and insight, some of which I hope remain in the final text. Any lingering mistakes are, of course, my own. Thank you to Dan Flores, Meg Hahr, Doug Hawes-Davis, Marion Hourdequin, Bart Miller, Reed Noss, Tom Platt, Tom Power, Mike Schwartz, Jacob Smith, Joseph Sax, Paul Sutter, and Bethanie Walder.

Without help at critical junctures I would have struggled simply to keep food on the table during the long off-seasons between paid work and our backyard garden's produce. I am particularly grateful to the Mountaineers Foundation for their support of my writing and research. Wildlands CPR offered its fiscal sponsorship for grantwriting, and Tommy Petersen and Bethanie Walder both worked with me on grant proposals. Tom Roy at the University of Montana Environmental Studies Program and Barbara Dean were also kind enough to write letters of support. Wildlands CPR funded a challenge grant that Predator Conservation Alliance and the Pacific Rivers Council both responded to generously: I accepted their *quid* and offered no *pro quo*.

I benefited from a number of interviews and shared information throughout my research. Thank you to Howard Wilshire, both for answering my questions and for years of important research on the impacts of off-road vehicles. Land managers from federal agencies consistently took time out to meet with me, provide me with information, or enlist the help of their colleagues on my behalf. Though I do not always stifle my criticisms, I do appreciate the efforts these public servants make, day in and day out, to manage our public lands. To name but a few: Jim Amenta from the Federal Highway Administration; Jake Cebula on the Uwharrie National Forest; Dom Ciccone and Ed Loth of the U.S. Fish and Wildlife Service (and many individual refuge managers); Anne Connor on the Clearwater National Forest; Theresa Ely from the National Park Service; Charlie Sells at the Forest Service's Northern Region; and Jim Howard, Meredith Manning, Terry Spreiter, and Neal Youngblood at Redwood National Park went out of their way to help me and provide me with information, interviews, lunch food, or photos. A special thanks to Mike Sanders at Redwood National Park, who gave me the grand tour in and around the park and, with Andrea McManus, made me feel most welcome in Arcata.

Jim Amenta; John Bissonnette; T.J. Brown; Meg Hahr; Don Mazzola at Predator Conservation Alliance; Nicky Phear; Mike Schwartz; Tryg Sletteland; Diane Kelly at the Southern Utah Wilderness Alliance; Wildlands CPR; my parents; and others were also kind enough to send me books, articles, slides, or reprints that helped with my research.

A number of Wild Rockies Field Institute students and instructors helped to shape my ideas and prod me to consider new perspectives. I appreciate their active minds and persistent questioning.

Friends in Missoula and elsewhere have proven to be a constant source of encouragement and assistance. Thanks, especially, to Townsend Zwart and Bart Miller, who helped me leave roads behind for half a year. And, more recently, to Doug Hawes-Davis who never failed to believe in me as a writer.

My family has been immensely supportive, from Scott's legal advice and comments early on to Jenny's positive reviews. Had my nephew Spenser learned to read or talk just a little bit earlier, I'm confident that he, too, would have helped. My parents, Spense and Val, have been my most ardent supporters and teachers for as long as I can recall, and this project was no exception. Thank you for reading chapters, sending photos and maps, coaxing me along, sponsoring the redwoods visit, and for impressing upon me the value of the written word. Thanks, as well, to Kris, Ian, Miles, Mary and Jim, Peter and Jaime for their interest and support.

Finally, Marion Hourdequin has been my beacon throughout this process. The whole thing may even have been her idea. I have been privileged to have her as a reader and resident expert on ecology and ethics, and for ready conversation day and night. Above all, she kept me on-task by doling out lavish praise on those odd days when she came home to find me with pen or keyboard in hand.

No Place Distant

Roads go ever ever on,
Over rock and under tree,
By caves where never sun has shone,
By streams that never find the sea. . . .

—J.R.R. Tolkien, *The Hobbit*

1 | Introduction

In 1975, my parents took the whole family to our first big concert in Colorado. It was John Denver, live, and he was in his prime. Smoke machines pulsed during the rowdier songs, and even from our seats high in the arena we could see an occasional glint of laser light flashing off the singer's round glasses. On our way home that night, and many times later on family trips, we broke into one of our favorite tunes from the concert: "Country roads, take me home, to the place I beloooong . . . " and right about there our voices cracked on the high note and we collapsed into a pile of whoops and laughter.

Like most American kids, I grew up surrounded by roads. I walked down a road to get to school, bicycled to swim practice on roads, and, nestled in my family's car, cruised along glorious highway miles to go to the mountains, visit national parks, or vacation for the summer. Roads were part of the background, an essential feature of my daily life, and I rarely thought much about them.

Years later, I hiked with two friends through the Rocky Mountains. We walked for six months, from Mexico to Canada, into some of the wildest country remaining in the continental United States, but some of my clearest memories of the entire trip come from those times we had to cross or hike on roads. For the first time in my life, I had managed to get away from roads long enough to notice them.

More and more people are starting to notice certain kinds of roads—those found on our nation's public lands—and a good deal of what we are discovering is troublesome. This book is about roads on public lands. These are generally not the roads we drive home on each day or the interstate highways that speed us across the country (though these deserve attention too). Public land roads tend to be modest in size, consisting of gravel or dirt or two lanes of pavement, but they are vast in number. Criss-crossing our national parks, national forests, national wildlife refuges, and other federal lands, these public land roads cover more than half a million miles—enough to drive to the moon and back.

If you have ever visited the Great Smokies, Yellowstone, or other national parks, you have driven on public land roads. In national forests, you can scarcely miss them. The national forests, alone, are laced with enough roads to wrap around the earth more than eighteen times at the equator.

By comparison, the interstate highway system runs through most major U.S. cities and every state. At 43,000 miles it has been called the largest public works program in the history of the world, dwarfing the Panama Canal, Egypt's pyramids, and the Great Wall of China.[1] Public land roads span nearly thirteen times the length of all the interstate highways.

This book examines the 550,000 miles of public land roads. Unlike the interstate highway system, most of these roads are not multi-lane thoroughfares and many are no longer even passable by high-clearance automobiles. To date, few people have considered the road system on public lands in any comprehensive way. Lacking this overarching view, we have put roads in many places without sound planning or a long-term vision and without considering the overall consequences or cumulative impacts.

Found most abundantly in the millions of acres of public land in the western United States, roads on our public domain vary in their characteristics and impacts but they all have one feature in common: they need to be noticed. These roads, and the surging industry of motorized recreation, now threaten to undermine many of the fundamental features that Americans have valued in their public lands for more than a century.

The Public Lands

To understand the roads, their impacts, and their possible futures, we first need to understand public lands. The lands discussed in this book are part of the U.S. public domain, owned by the citizens of the entire nation and managed purposefully by four different federal agencies. These agencies—the National Park Service, U.S. Fish and Wildlife Service, Bureau of Land Management, and U.S. Forest Service—employ more than 70,000 engineers, biologists, landscape architects, law enforcement officers, rangers, foresters, planners, and administrators to tend to the daily and long-term management of more than 600 million acres of land.[2]

Some of these lands are well-known, include outstanding natural features or wildlife, and attract millions of visitors each year. The national parks, in particular, have gained fame throughout the world. Many countries have created their own park systems after the U.S. model, which further contributes to the conservation and enjoyment of natural places. National parks such as Acadia, the Everglades, the Grand Canyon, Yosemite, and Glacier are as varied as they are treasured. In all, there are more than 89 million acres dedicated in the national park system. These lands are to be managed for the conservation of natural scenery and wildlife, as well as for the lasting enjoyment of human visitors. And visit we do: in 2000 more than 287 million people came to at least one of the 384 units of the national park system.[3] With highways intentionally linking one park to another, and scenic routes prominently constructed through their midsts, the way we visit most of these parks is on roads.

Though slightly less famous, the national forests cover more area, attract more annual visitors, and generate a steadier stream of controversy over their management than do their sibling parks. At 191 million acres, the national forests would appear plenty large—and some of them are—but they are pledged to a multiple-use agenda for management that frequently pits timber harvest against wildlife habitat, mining claims against water quality, and motorized recreation against wilderness protection. Roads flow through this mix like muddy water, providing access to hunters, for instance, even while degrading habitat needed for their prey. And with more than 345 million visitor days each year (a visitor day equals one person visiting for a 12-hour period), the national forest system in many places is struggling to keep pace with public demands.[4]

Although President Theodore Roosevelt protected the first national wildlife refuge in 1903, just a few years after the first national forest reserves were set aside and before all but a handful of national park designations, most refuges have dodged the mixed blessing of popularity felt by the national parks and national forests. The majority of the national wildlife refuge system's 92 million acres are in Alaska, which makes them seem remote and inaccessible to many Americans. However, the refuges of the lower forty-eight states are the public lands most likely to exist within an hour's drive from a major city.[5] Whether for egrets or bison, alligators, elk, or humans, the U.S. Fish and Wildlife Service manages the national wildlife refuge system to preserve fish and wildlife habitat for future generations. Despite often spectacular settings and many units' proximity to human populations, the national wildlife refuge remains the least attended of the four main public land types, with 35 million visitors each year.[6]

The final and largest chunk of public lands is managed, fittingly, by the Bureau of Land Management (BLM). Comprising some 236 million acres, BLM lands include large parcels of western lands that were never claimed for other private or public uses such as homesteads, railroads, national parks, state lands, Indian reservations, or military sites. Many of these lands developed a reputation primarily as range for cattle grazing. Though BLM lands in southern Utah, Nevada, California, Idaho, and Montana are increasingly being "discovered" for their spectacular canyons, desert ecosystems, or recreational opportunities, these lands still struggle to shed their reputation as the lands that nobody wanted. More than 70 million visitors each year demonstrate that BLM lands are not, in fact, ignored, but these lands continue to receive some of the most liberal use and hardest impacts—from off-road vehicles (ORVs), cattle grazing, or mining—of any of our public lands.[7]

The BLM manages more than 80,000 miles of road on its lands, which ranks it a distant second to the Forest Service for having the greatest number of roads. At its latest count, the Forest Service recognized more than 386,000 miles of constructed road, as well as more than 60,000 miles of unplanned or illegal roads created by ORVs and other forest uses.[8] The national wildlife refuges and national parks have relatively few roads of their own, checking in at slightly less than 10,000 miles each. In addition to the roads managed and administered by these federal agencies, another 115,000 miles of state, local, or private roads cross federal public lands. Although this book will focus on the 550,000 road miles under federal jurisdiction, many of the ecological, economic, and social impacts discussed should be applied to the entire network of nearly 700,000 miles. Table 1-1 itemizes road miles on the four types of federal land discussed in depth in this book.[9]

There are a few other categories of public land that are not much covered in this book. The Department of Energy and Department of Defense manage a number of areas for bombing ranges, missile tests, military maneuvers and training, and other purposes, but these are typically not open to the public and often have impacts other than roads or ORVs with which to contend, including undetonated explosives or radioactive wastes. The Bureau of Reclamation and Army Corps of Engineers also manage federal lands, primarily for flood control and hydroelectric projects, and again these fall outside the focus of this book. The total federal land base is approximately 634 million acres, including Bureau of Reclamation, Department of Defense, and Department of Energy lands.[10]

Public Land Roads

As Americans recognized public lands with special features, it rarely took long for people to clamor for access. Within five years of the first national

Table 1-1.
Road Miles on Federal Public Lands

Agency	Paved	Unpaved	Other	Total
U.S. Forest Service	28,000 (21,400)	357,570[a] (29,200)	60,450[b] (26,470)[a]	446,020 (77,070)[a]
U.S. Fish and Wildlife Service	500	5,400	3,100[c] (34,000)[d]	9,000 (34,000)[d]
National Park Service	5,140	2,990	n/a	8,130
Bureau of Land Management	1,700 (3,600)	81,300 (3,600)	n/a	83,000 (7,200)
Total Agency Road	**35,340**	**447,260**	**63,550**	**546,150**
Total All Road	**60,340**	**480,060**	**124,020**	**664,420**

Numbers in parentheses represent public and private road miles that cross federal lands but are not under the jurisdiction of the respective federal agencies. Unless otherwise noted, information comes from *1999 Status of the Nation's Highways, Bridges, and Transit: Conditions and Performance Report to Congress*, Appendix E—Conditions and Performance of the Transportation System Serving Federal and Indian Lands, Exhibit E-2, Federal Highway Administration, 1999.

[a] Total reported in Forest Service Roadless Area Conservation Final Environmental Impact Statement, U.S. Forest Service, November 2000, Table 3-5, p. 3-25.

[b] Unclassified roads, reported in Forest Service Roadless Area Conservation, Table 3-5, p. 3-25.

[c] Administrative roads not necessarily open for public travel.

[d] Personal communication with Thomas Hawkins, Realty Specialist, U.S. Fish and Wildlife Service, Division of Realty, Washington Office, August 11, 1999.

park designation of Yellowstone in 1872 and more than two decades before the Duryea brothers built America's first automobile, federal land managers set out to build roads that would allow people to see the geyser basins, wildlife, forests, and mountains of Yellowstone for themselves.[11]

Similarly, the national forests had scarcely reached their adolescence in the 1920s and '30s before the proliferation of roads caused agency employees such as Aldo Leopold and Bob Marshall to sound the alarm: America was losing many of its natural treasures to "mechanized man."[12]

Other public lands, including many of those now managed by the U.S. Fish and Wildlife Service and BLM, were roaded even before their designation as refuges or resource lands. In some cases, the road building has barely faltered since.

Roads on our public lands have been a mixed success. We have unquestionably been able to reach and utilize more raw materials from our nation's forests, mineral reserves, grasslands, and waters thanks to roads. We now have easy motorized access to lands that once seemed unimaginably distant or difficult, from the summit of Pikes Peak to the dunes of Death Valley. As a case in point, some 300,000 motor tourists drive to the 14,110 foot crest of Pikes Peak every summer, but sedimentation and erosion problems caused by the road were recently the focus of a successful Sierra Club lawsuit.[13] In other words, many people enjoy and make use of this road, even as others—and the courts—recognize that it generates unacceptably high impacts to the surrounding environment.

The financial ledger for roads is also cluttered with both liabilities and benefits. The wealth of our nation has often come rolling into market on public land roads. Driving the other direction, countless Americans have learned to value and appreciate natural beauty and our nation's heritage by coming to visit and learn about public lands. Roads helped national parks, especially, become well visited and well loved. Early National Park Service director Stephen Mather falls off some lists of conservationists' heroes for just this reason: Mather pushed for roads in many places as a way to boost the country's support for national parks. Managers in some of these same parks are now trying to eliminate cars or remove roads to salvage the air and water quality, wildlife habitat, and natural experiences to be found there.

There is surely some merit to the idea that in order to appreciate a place it helps to know it, and the best way to know a place is to visit. Had I never been able to visit Yosemite or Rocky Mountain National Park as a boy tucked in my parents' car, I might never have cared enough to walk away from these same roads on later family outings or as an adult. Yet there are many of us who also place tremendous value on lands that we will never see in Alaska or the Amazon or Antarctica, in part because they are so difficult to reach and have so few roads. Clearly we do not need to drive to an area to appreciate it, and for some places the fact that we cannot drive there makes it all the more precious.

Beyond the environmental effects or financial spreadsheets, the way we view roads on public lands is inextricably linked to our values as a nation and our values as citizens. In the end, our ideas about how public lands ought to be managed will dictate how we decide to treat roads and motorized access on our public domain.

Like Leopold, Marshall, or even Mather, I come to roads with a certain mix of appreciation and apprehension. I am grateful that millions of us can drive each year to visit our public lands, while I am also genuinely relieved that we cannot drive everywhere on these same lands. This book, then, is not written to convince anyone that all roads are bad; I don't believe they are, and many roads provide a great service with relatively little harm. Rather, I contend that many roads—and especially certain types of roads—are causing problems for no particular good. By most measures, we currently have too many roads causing too many problems on our public lands.

Appropriate Access?

Roads on public lands, and elsewhere, continue to prove controversial because they represent so many things to so many people. If the benefit of a road could be isolated to one purpose covering a specific place and time, then we might be able to evaluate with relative ease its costs and the appropriate response of building it, maintaining it, or removing it. Unfortunately, roads and the equations we are left with which to evaluate them are far more complex.

For example, a single road will often cross many different environments as it connects point A with point B. The ecological impacts of the road will be different when it runs along a riverbank, cuts across a steep slope, drops down a gentle swale, or splits through a forest. Similarly, depending on the type and frequency of use, a road will vary in both its impacts and its usefulness. At different times of year, a road may be used for activities as varied as timber harvest, berry picking, hunting access, or winter recreation, or as a travel corridor by certain kinds of wildlife.

Depending upon your leanings for or against maintaining the current network of public land roads, you might point to firsthand experience (or scientific studies) to indicate that roads are good or bad for wildlife. In the 1990s, I attended a number of public hearings in Montana about roads and motorized access. There were always some people opposed to restrictions of any type. Pro-access citizens often mentioned that they had seen bear tracks, bear scat, and even live grizzlies on the very roads the agencies proposed closing. If these roads were so damaging to bears, then why were the critters using them on a regular basis?

I, too, have seen tracks, scat, and bears on roads. I have also seen roadside bears that have grown dangerously habituated to humans and cars, as well as dead bears that paid a dear price for their familiarity with roads. Grizzly bears use or avoid roads differently, depending upon the time of year, the sex of the animal, the availability of food, and the types of activities that occur in the area.[14] The confounding truth is that for bears and many other animals, roads both kill and attract them. While some animals make use of roads for ease of travel, forage, or lack of competition, others cross roads simply because they have little choice. Still other animals will not cross a road even at the expense of breeding.

Different kinds of roads and road uses also create different effects. Busy roads tend to be far deadlier than little-used roads or routes closed to motorized traffic. Thousands of animals die each day from vehicle collisions on roads, while road salts and roadside carrion bring other animals near.[15]

As with many questions of values, Americans hold diverse views about roads. Some road and motorized recreation advocates contend that having easy motorized access to every part of the public lands is simply our right as Americans. Other folks, more inclined toward wildlife protection or human restraint, would like to see roads removed from public lands and motorized access strictly curtailed. Opinion polls as recently as 2000 showed that the majority of the American public favors increased protection for public lands that are currently roadless.[16] And when we take the time to look at the ecological, economic, political, and ethical consequences of roads and motorized recreation on our public lands—as we will in this book—the ready conclusion is that a good number of our national forest and BLM roads, especially, are causing significant harm for very little good. Despite their ongoing costs, many of the roads causing adverse impacts are not even passable because of their deteriorated condition, lack of maintenance funds, or planned closures.

Although it may be tempting to cast difficult land management policies to a shoulder-shrugging middle ground of indecision, Americans have in fact established a deep tradition of managing our public lands for very specific uses. Most of us readily accept prohibitions against hunting in national parks, mining without a claim on BLM lands, or building shopping malls in national wildlife refuges.[17] We make such accommodations in most aspects of our lives, where we recognize that a restriction in one circumstance is appropriate and just, while in another setting it might be unfair. In this manner, we recognize the value of free speech even as we refrain from shouting "Fire!" in movie theatres, or accept that if we drink too much alcohol we are not legally able to drive. These rules are not indiscriminate prohibitions against free speech or alcohol, rather they protect public interests from private lapses of judgment (or criminal intent).

Similarly, we have little cause to view road and motorized access limitations on public lands as unfair government interference or "locking out" the public. There are many good reasons for restricting motorized access on many public land areas. In even the most carefully managed wilderness areas, people are still allowed to visit, they simply need to leave their machines behind.

Motorized Recreation: Off-Road Vehicles

A few years ago in the mountains of southwest Montana, I came upon a crew working on a national forest trail where I had hiked regularly each summer. Unlike trail crews I had encountered in other places, I heard and smelled this group long before I saw them. When I finally reached their work site, I discovered that two of them were driving motorized all-terrain vehicles (ATVs) and another was operating a bulldozer and backhoe rig. The noise and smoke of the vehicles easily obscured the sound of Red Canyon Creek and the scent of pine and fir.

The crew was busy converting the thin, rocky trail I'd hiked to a 5-foot-wide, smooth path that fit the four balloon tires of the ATVs. Even though the trail passed through a specially designated wildlife management area, including prime habitat for elk, moose, and grizzly bears, ATVs were allowed on it between July 15 and October 30, and snowmobiles had free license. This trail had been historically used by hikers, horse packers, and the occasional motorcyclist, but had been off-limits to others due to its narrowness and steepness. It was now being opened up to easy ATV and snowmobile access.

Trail widening projects such as this are not isolated events so much as they are part of a growing revolution in the way people recreate on public lands. Promoted at times by agency planners, as well as by vehicle manufacturers and users, recreation on public lands is making more and more noise in recent years. With wider trails and more powerful engines appearing every year, motorized vehicles are leading the recreation charge.

Motorized recreation and ORVs mimic the impacts of roads in too many ways to ignore in a book about roads. ORVs are now powerful and reliable enough to render nearly all backcountry, roadless lands vulnerable to the impacts of motorized access.* They include a wide array of machines designed to travel across snow, water, land, or air.

Along with increases in power and performance, ORVs have become increasingly popular. Four-wheeled ATVs are comfortable and easy to use and can carry plenty of gear for picnicking, fishing, or camping. This has allowed their sales to outpace that of motorcycles, which require more skill and have narrower appeal. Marketing campaigns by vehicle manufacturers such as Yamaha, Polaris, Kawasaki, and Arctic Cat have helped trigger the boom and have also played a role in motorized recreationists banding together to form vocal constituencies for greater motorized access.

Some slightly quieter changes in land management priorities have also supported the surge in motorized recreation. Traditional extractive industries such as logging, mining, and grazing are no longer the undisputed champions of local economies, and in many places their popular luster has grown increasingly tarnished by a legacy of clear-cuts, contaminated waters, and devastated range. A declaration of extractive industry's demise would be premature in America at the turn of the twenty-first century—much of western politics is still dominated by livestock, mining, and timber associations—but federal land management agencies are increasingly

---

*Some agencies, publications, and user groups refer to off-road vehicles as "off-highway vehicles" or OHVs. To represent more accurately the nature of these vehicles, which typically are not street-legal and are specifically designed to perform on rugged terrain, I will use "off-road vehicle" or "ORV" throughout the book, unless quoting directly from a source that uses "OHV."

changing to new revenue streams for their sustenance. To many, recreation of all types promises to be the cash cow of the future.

The Lay of the Land

The following seven chapters cover a range of topics that bear on the subject of roads, and to varying degrees, motorized recreation. Taken together, these topics challenge us to address the cumulative impacts of roads on our public lands, our values, and our lives. In order to place the profusion of public land roads in its historical context, Chapter 2 charts the development of roads in national parks, national forests, national wildlife refuges, and BLM lands. The history of public land roads illustrates that the four agencies have had different incentives, or disincentives, for building roads at different stages of their development. For this reason, most road miles in national parks, for example, are paved and offer scenic views, while the majority of national forest roads are narrower dirt routes that wind through logged-over forests.

The historical overview also connects broader trends in society, such as the mass production of the automobile or the post–World War II housing boom, with the development of roads and roads policy on our public lands.

Chapter 3 offers an overview of the ecological effects of roads, generally, and public land roads more specifically. To evaluate what we ought to do about roads, we should first gain some understanding of how these roads affect us and the lands, waters, and wildlife of our nation. As mentioned above, roads built for different purposes come in different forms and places, and these differences also create a variety of ecological impacts. Roads affect their surroundings in two broad classes of impacts: those caused simply by the *existence* of the road, and those created by human and vehicular *use* of the road. Ecological effects of roads also extend beyond the land and soils to impact the flow, quality, quantity, and character of water; plant and animal life; air; and ecological processes. Most ecological effects of roads that scientists have identified are considered negative influences on biodiversity or ecosystem health, but in some cases there are also unexpected positive or ambiguous impacts from road systems.

Most roads have come to our public lands by intent rather than by chance, and Chapter 4 explores the policies, politics, and economics that have allowed this. From the first large federal road allocation in 1916, to the multibillion-dollar Transportation Equity Act for the Twenty-First Century, the United States has changed its position dramatically since James Madison declared federal road funding unconstitutional in the early 1800s.[18] Changes continue to occur, as attempts to reform timber road programs have cleared some congressional and administrative hurdles. As we explore the federal programs that have helped spur road building on public lands, we must also consider our own role as citizens in this system. This chapter includes an appraisal of the costs and benefits of roads on public lands, which lends support to road removal—not continued road building—as a net economic gain.

With Chapter 5 we broach the contentious topic of motorized recreation, focusing on the two types of ORV that are most abundant on public lands: four-wheeled ATVs and snowmobiles. This examination of ORVs and their growing popularity offers a microcosmic view of many of the issues that also apply to roads: the social and political pressures that influence recreation programs, the economics of motorized recreation, and a philosophical look at their propriety on public lands. This chapter also examines the government's program to charge recreation user fees as a way to boost agency budgets, and questions whether this comes as needed relief to cash-poor land managers or is the inappropriate commercialization of a public good.

In spite of dollar amounts or scientific studies, most decisions regarding roads and motorized recreation boil down to a matter of values. Policy makers and others may strive for balance and objectivity, but personal values and environmental ethics ultimately dictate many of the decisions we make for public lands. Controversies about roads and motorized access on public lands across the country highlight the fact that people care about these lands, how we get to them, and how we use them. Chapter 6 arrives at an appropriate policy for roads and motorized recreation on public lands, and shows how ethics, laws, and values have changed over time to guide us in this direction. Considering road policies as part of the public trust is another approach that may help us recognize the need for reform and for the development of a new set of land management ethics that we can apply to roads and motorized recreation. Many existing laws also highlight a steady shift in American attitudes toward public lands, from one of utility and resource extraction to one of public involvement and conservation.

As new access management plans spark debate from coast to coast, each month brings new reminders that the management of roads and motorized vehicles on public lands is undergoing change. Whether for swamp buggies in the Big Cypress National Preserve in Florida, snowmobiles in Yellowstone, or cars in the Yosemite valley, we are now questioning and changing decades-old habits. Chapter 7 looks at a number of these changing landscapes for motorized access, including how land management agencies, citizens, conservation groups, motorized users, politicians, and local communities are playing a role in the unfolding drama. New technologies such as geographic information systems (GIS), satellite imagery, and global positioning systems (GPS) have transformed our ability to monitor roads and their condition. Relatively new fields such as restoration ecology and conservation biology have also affected the way we apply science to problems caused by motorized access and roads. In this chapter we visit several sites where restoration ecologists and land managers have removed roads and are bringing degraded lands back to a healthier, less roaded condition. Many of these changes emphasize that we have the ability to dramatically alter the pattern of past road policies.

While the challenge of managing people and their competing desires for access may prove long and difficult on public lands, many remedies already exist for the ecological and economic ailments documented in this book. Roads serve essential functions in many aspects of our lives and have a place in the landscapes in which we live, as well as some of those we visit, but as with any technology roads must have limits if they are to be beneficial.

Chapter 8 continues with the idea that removing roads can be just as important to American progress as road building once was. In this final chapter, I point to signs of this progress and propose a number of actions for land managers and policy makers to adopt, for educators and students to consider, and for conservationists and citizens to promote. Working with sound information and policies, we can maintain a network of roads on our public lands that is relatively benign environmentally, that is functional and in good condition, that has acceptable costs, and that provides a variety of opportunities to access the places that remain so integral to our national heritage.

If we are able to think about public land roads as a dominant feature of many of our landscapes, then we may also find ourselves pressed to think carefully about how we manage public lands in general. For many of us, public lands and our treatment of them reflect public values. This is ultimately a book about values—those intrinsic to public lands and those we hold as Americans.

Ours is so much an age of technology and the machine that machines come to be loved for their own sake rather than used for other ends. Instead, for instance, of valuing the automobile because it may take one to a national park, the park comes to be valued because it is a place the automobile may be used to reach.

—Joseph Wood Krutch,
American Forests, April 1957

2 | From Bicycles to Board Feet: A History of Public Land Roads

When the first car rolled out of the Ford Motor Company's Detroit plant in 1903, the public lands we know today were but a twinkle in the nation's eyes. The U.S. Forest Service was two years shy of its birth, the National Park Service would arrive in thirteen years, and the other major land managing agencies would not emerge for nearly half a century.[1] But even then the public lands had roads.

Long before the advent of the automobile, Americans relied on roads for travel, whether by foot, by horse, by cart, or by bicycle. Roads relieved the rural American's sense of isolation and made for easier, faster travel than ever before. Roads could be useful for moving supplies and mobilizing troops as the nation pushed its boundaries westward. Roads linked neighbors and small towns, creating stronger communities and greater prosperity. Even without cars, eighteenth- and nineteenth-century Americans thought good roads were a great thing. It was an idea that would prove difficult to shake.

Although the twentieth century will surely be remembered by Americans in a variety of ways—for its Great Depression and New Deal, World Wars, television, atomic bomb, moon launches, and Internet—few events have been as dramatic, as linked, or as transformative as the widespread emergence of roads and cars onto the American landscape.

On public lands, roads came for many reasons. Many national parks arrived with initial support from railroads. As tourists abandoned the trains for cars, the parks also shifted their attention to court the automobile. The Forest Service wanted to bring visitors and popular support to the nation's forests, but also wanted roads to transport timber and fight fires. By the time the Fish and Wildlife Service and Bureau of Land Management (BLM) finally appeared, they came to a nation already captivated by the automobile.

In the West, far from the halls of power, roads and public lands developed an early affinity for each other. In 1883, eleven years after the creation of Yellowstone National Park, army engineers began the first systematic road construction in what would become the flagship of America's public lands.[2] In just over two decades, Yellowstone would feature 300 miles of road looping through some of the most remote reaches of northwest Wyoming.[3] Early national parks supporters calculated that in order to create a constituency for land reserves, people needed to have easy access. Though it would take several decades for the horse and railroad to give way to the automobile, roads were still the key to bringing visitors.

Whether motivated by easier rural access to goods and services, opening the hinterlands to extraction, or simply to create routes for pleasure driving, Americans have found reasons to build roads for several centuries. By looking at the history of roads on our public lands—how and why we built so many miles to so many places—we may better understand our current desires for access. The historical perspective will not resolve all of the decisions and disputes we continue to face, but insights from the past can at least help us frame today's questions and tomorrow's answers more strategically.

In 1900, Americans owned 8,000 automobiles. Thirty years later cars and trucks numbered 40 million.[4] At the close of the twentieth century, Americans had more than 200 million registered automobiles and we continue to buy another 15 million each year.[5] The demand for roads, in other words, has not diminished. At a glance, it makes perfect sense that with the number of cars (and drivers) increasing, road miles should too. The history of road building on public lands, however, does not always reflect the idea that cars need roads.

The Good Roads Movement

The early roads movement had more to do with bicyclists, farmers, and railroads than it did with automobiles. The League of American Wheelmen was formed in 1880 to lobby for the needs of bicyclists in the United States.[6] By 1900, when bicycles outnumbered automobiles by more than 500 to 1, the League's membership crested 150,000.[7] Cyclists made a formidable political constituency, but rough roads, full of potholes, could quickly bring a day's ride to a crashing halt. What cyclists wanted were firm, smooth roads. In 1893, the League of American Wheelmen successfully petitioned Congress to form the Office of Road Inquiry within the U.S. Department of Agriculture. The following year *Harper's Weekly* reported that 90 percent of the nation's highway builders belonged to the bicyclists' League of American Wheelmen.[8]

Farmers, meanwhile, wanted roads to connect their homes and businesses to neighbors, markets, and railroads. A better road system promised rural residents more connections to the outside world, and bicyclists were not shy about courting the support of farmers for the roads cause. In a persuasive book published in 1891, *The Gospel of Good Roads: A Letter to the American Farmer,* a civil engineer and bicyclist touted the cost savings farmers would enjoy with better roads.[9] The advent of Rural Free Delivery mail service brought another incentive for good rural roads.

In 1899, the federal Post Office Department announced that it would establish free rural delivery routes only where roads were "usable year around."[10] With farmers eager to reduce their isolation from broader society—and increase their commercial opportunities—the call for road improvements shifted in tone from one of desirability to one of urgency. Within a decade, many states had joined in the effort to help improve local routes.[11]

While railroad companies were not as directly dependent upon roads as bicyclists or farmers, they expected that more road access to railroad depots would lead to increased revenues. Railroads were one of the most powerful lobbies in the nation in the late 1800s and dominated interstate shipping and transportation. Cyclists and farmers naturally enlisted their support for what became known as the Good Roads Movement.

The Good Roads Movement spread quickly across the United States. Even as the private automobile was still a rare sight and largely a privilege of the very rich, Good Roads boosters and automobile clubs became common. In the late 1800s, the League of American Wheelmen published a monthly journal, *Good Roads Magazine.*[12] In 1900, Port Huron, Michigan, hosted the First International Good Roads Congress.[13] Oregon's first Good Roads Association formed in 1902.[14] By 1912, North Carolina, alone, claimed 65 good roads associations.[15]

As the network of good roads expanded, cross-country motoring trips became a source of adventure and grew popular among travel writers. The "horseless carriage" quickly drew converts who fondly remembered the days before the railroad. Despite their unreliability and the lack of good roads, early automobiles attracted flocks of wealthy Americans eager to experience the life of the "motorized gypsy."[16] Unlike the train, cars offered a mode of transport that allowed people to travel freely and on their own schedules. And unlike the horse, cars were technological marvels that seemed neither to eat nor leave droppings.

With roads and drivers becoming more common, good roads advocates increasingly began to disagree about which types of roads they wanted. Locals continued to support rural and farm-to-market roads, but other boosters lobbied for regional highways to stimulate long-distance travel. As these factions emerged, so did state and federal funding programs for roads. In concert, these factors ultimately led to the demise of the Good Roads Movement.[17] Despite its relatively short life, the roads movement had a deep and lasting impact: it awakened state and federal government to a whole new class of public works.

The Good Roads Movement also helped spawn what would become an early motto of the national parks: See America First. Pitching tourism as an act of patriotism, the See America First League offered the natural splendor of the western United States as a virtuous domestic alternative to the European Alps or cities of the East Coast.[18] With the onset of World War I and a publicity campaign launched by both the Great Northern Railroad and the National Park Service, the call to See America First helped drive tourists to visit Glacier and other western national parks. A domestic automobile tour quickly emerged as a way to support America, experience nature, and create a vibrant economy at home.

Federal Road Building

The Good Roads Movement and the See America First League played key roles in bringing government road projects back to life. Though now commonplace, federally funded roads had a controversial first century in the United States. A number of early presidents and congressmen considered federally funded internal improvements—including roads—illegal and unconstitutional.[19] James Monroe and Andrew Jackson granted federal support only to projects assigned for common defense and the national interest. When Thomas Jefferson threw his administration's support behind the Cumberland National Pike, which was eventually built from

Washington, D.C., and Baltimore to St. Louis, construction required $7 million and thirty-eight years, and failed to convince the nation to embrace many similar road projects.[20]

The Early Days of Federal Roads: 1850 to 1916

Although good roads and automobiles quickly captured the fancy of twentieth-century Americans privileged enough to own a car or drive along scenic routes, the federal government took some time to rouse from its road-building slumber. Despite the overruns of the Cumberland "National Road," federal road projects continued through the mid-1800s at a steady pace, dodging controversy by using the label of "military" roads. Often following the dozens of existing trails used by Native Americans, some of these early routes did in fact link military outposts and forts. Construction duties went to the War Department's Army Corps of Engineers and Topographical Bureau. Most of the War Department's roads played an important role in opening western lands up to settlement, with or without military clashes. By the mid-1850s, the thirty-fourth Congress no longer balked at the constitutionality of federal road projects and in 1857 the Department of the Interior opened a Pacific Wagon Roads Office. Congress approved more than $1.3 million to wagon road projects west of the Mississippi in the decade before the Civil War, which then diverted funding, labor, and the nation's attention.[21]

One of the first clear signs of a federal road building revival came in 1905 when the government combined the Office of Public Road Inquiry with the Bureau of Chemistry's Division of Tests to form the Bureau of Public Roads.[22] Eleven years later when the first Federal Highway Act became law, federal road building appropriations started in earnest. Worries of constitutionality and secession dormant at last, by 1916 the Bureau of Public Roads had money to pursue its mission of funding and building roads. Within a year, every state in the Union had a highway department putting federal funds to use.[23]

Land Management Agencies and Roads Programs: United at Birth

For reasons of both technology and culture, the modern era of federal road programs meshes closely with the genesis of the two most prominent land management agencies. In 1905, Congress created the Bureau of Public Roads and the U.S. Forest Service.[24] Little more than a decade later, 1916 saw the passage of the National Park Service Act and the inaugural Federal Highway Act.[25] Virtually united at birth, roads and these public lands have in many ways been characterized—for better and for worse—by their common bond ever since.

Beginning with Yellowstone in 1872, we created national parks most famously in response to tawdry commercial developments springing up in scenic natural areas across the country.[26] American altruism seldom strays far from capitalism, however, and Yellowstone and many of the subsequent national parks proved to be no exception. The Northern Pacific Railroad Company planned a route across the Dakota and Montana Territories and had a clear financial interest in attracting tourists to the Yellowstone region. To this end, the Northern Pacific promoted the 1870 Washburn–Doane Expedition from which the Yellowstone National Park idea first emerged. The next year, the Northern Pacific sponsored artist Thomas Moran's place in the Hayden Expedition, whose paintings and reports led to the successful passage of the Yellowstone legislation in Congress.[27] Much as its promoters hoped, Yellowstone's designation as a national park created an attraction for hundreds of thousands of visitors in the years ahead.

From the Yellowstone Park Act of 1872 to the National Park Act of 1916 and on to the present, national parks have been guided by what sounds like a challenging dual mission: *"to conserve* the scenery and the natural and historic objects and the wild life . . . as will leave them unimpaired *for the enjoyment* of future generations (emphasis added)."[28] With that charge, Congress established the National Park Service both to preserve lands and to make them available for human use. The disparate prongs of this mission statement have created a history of national park planning that fosters tourism while at the same time preserving scenic beauty. For its first two decades the National Park Service was staffed predominantly by engineers and landscape architects, with wildlife biologists, for example, notably absent.[29] The general agency philosophy concerning roads was that they should be built, but they should be built sparingly and handsomely.

Though the National Park Service had ample incentive to build roads that offered scenic and enjoyable experiences to park visitors, lurking in the background of the early planning and park developments was the shadow of a competing senior agency: the U.S. Forest Service. Whereas the national park system limped into place piece by piece, with each park requiring its own legislative act by Congress, the Forest Service strode into creation with 63 million acres of forest reserves already in its care.[30] Thanks in large part to President Theodore Roosevelt's fondness for conservation and, at the time, his power to designate forest reserves by proclamation, the national forest system swelled to more than 151 million acres before the National Park Service even existed.[31]

With only fourteen national parks designated on about 5 million acres in 1916, the Park Service might have been understandably daunted by its agency counterpart.[32] The surest way to secure its own bureaucratic tenure was to create a large constituency of public support. At the end of World War I, with an expanding leisure class, the patriotic call to See America First, and a newly affordable and widely available Ford Model T, Park Service planners knew right where to turn: roads and motor tourists.

The Forest Service took to roads a bit more slowly. Recreational tourism was tangential, at best, to the agency's mission of securing favorable water flow and providing a continuous supply of timber to a growing nation.[33] Staffed primarily by trained foresters, the Forest Service dedicated itself early on to controlling fires and to a management philosophy of sustainably using the natural resources of the country's forests. A handful of roads already existed on national forest lands at the time of their designations—and the agency built or improved more roads each year—but in its early days the Forest Service generally lacked the incentive to build a great number of smooth, easily traveled roads.[34] In the agency's view, roads served utilitarian purposes and little more. It would build roads on a limited basis, as foresters needed them to access timber or to help manage sprawling administrative units.

By the early 1920s, however, motorized travelers had so overwhelmed roadsides and private lands that car camping tourists were spilling into the national forests.[35] In 1912, a dozen stalwart motorists managed to drive across the country; by 1921, transcontinental motor trips numbered 20,000.[36] By 1922, the *New York Times* estimated that of the 10.8 million cars registered in the United States, 5 million would be used for camping.[37] The Forest Service soon realized that recreational demand of its lands required some response.

In 1920, Forest Service chief Henry S. Graves published an article in *American Forestry* entitled, "A Crisis in National Recreation."[38] Written at the close of his tenure with the Forest Service, Graves's article partially reflected his agency's growing concern over the newly formed National Park Service. The crisis he identified, though, was the exodus of urban automobile tourists pouring into national forests and parks. To Graves, the subsequent commercialization of national park lands—and by extension, the blurring of lines between parks and national forest lands—presented an alarming trend. In Graves's view, national forests were the proper storehouse for the country's natural resources, and recreation was becoming just that: a valuable resource. Five million car-camping tourists represented money and power too great to ignore. National parks, on the other hand, ought to be kept apart from commercial exploitation.[39] In other words, national forests should be used, whether for recreation or timber extraction, and national parks should be preserved.

Regardless of Graves's concern as a "friend of the National Park System," both agencies would find cause for further road building on their lands. The Forest Service could capitalize on the recreation resource, while the Park Service wanted to boost its constituency and provide roads for the enjoyment of visitors.

Graves's article is noteworthy for more than its whispers of agency rivalry. It represents one of the first acknowledgments that the Forest Service would concern itself with recreation. And significantly, according to Graves, recreation was intimately linked with roads: "[R]ecreation has an important place in the demand for a large program of road improvement and extension."[40] Later in the same *American Forestry* article, Graves wrote, "Roadbuilding is an important feature of the development of our public forests and parks for recreation."[41]

Several things happened close on the heels of Graves's 1920 article to reveal a growing interest in recreation on public lands. First, Congress appropriated more money for forest roads, and the Forest Service responded with a more directed road building program than it ever had before. The 1916 Highway Act had directed $10 million to the Forest Service for road building over the next ten years. In 1921, Congress boosted this with an additional $5.5 million for "forest development" roads, such as those used for fire control and administrative use, and $9.5 million for "forest highways" to supplement state road systems.[42] With the passage of the Post Office Appropriations Act in 1919, Congress also granted $9 million to develop and administer roads on national forest lands. The latter amount, prompted originally by rural free delivery mail service and the desire to connect rural lands, effectively shifted a portion of road development out of the farmlands and into the woods. In 1916 there were only 2,795 miles of road on national forest lands; by 1939 the Forest Service reported nearly 140,000 miles.[43]

Within a year of Graves's article, the Forest Service also redrafted its manual to recognize recreation as a value of the Forests to be managed in coordination with timber, water, and forage.[44]

The new crush of motor tourists and roads spurred Forest Service employees Aldo Leopold and Arthur Carhart to press for a new type of land classification, which Leopold called "wilderness." The simmering interagency rivalry may have played a role in the Forest Service's willingness to move in a new direction for managing lands. By designating wilderness and primitive areas, the Forest Service could take land preservation a step further than the National Park Service and preserve lands without the trappings of commercial development and penetrating road systems that already characterized national parks.[45] But both Leopold and Carhart made it clear that the threat of roads and motorized recreation, not agency competition, lay at the heart of what moved them to protect lands in a primitive, undeveloped condition.[46]

Carhart's interest in a different and less intrusive management of forest lands came most directly from his concern over shoreline development at Trapper's Lake, high in the mountains of western Colorado. Since 1915, the Term Permit Act had allowed recreational developments on national forest lands.[47] These permits were typically operated under thirty-year leases and most commonly came in the form of lakeside lodges, cabins, and developed camps. What troubled Carhart about the arrangement, though, was that public lands were being developed and built upon, rendered into commercial goods, and effectively removed from free public access.[48] Carhart favored leaving lands, such as Trapper's Lake, undeveloped in a primitive condition as a means of protecting public access equitably. Thus lands would remain a public good instead of being parceled out to the privileged, permitted few (and their paying clients).

Leopold, meanwhile, came to a similar position—that certain lands should be protected from roading and development—but from a slightly different slant. To Leopold in the 1920s, as with many conservationists today, wild undeveloped lands offered an antidote to the consumerism of outdoor recreationists and society at large.[49] Whereas Carhart spoke against development in order to ensure equal access to public lands, Leopold sought more simply to protect lands from the menace of "automobility"; that is, motorized access and the roads and crowds that invariably accompanied it.[50]

Though much has changed in the ensuing years, we need only to look at private partnership agreements and fee programs on public lands today to see that Carhart's fears may still be realized. Many of Leopold's concerns over automobility have also reemerged, as motorized off-road vehicles such as motorcycles, all-terrain vehicles, and snowmachines once again threaten to bring a surge of humanity into remote areas known and valued for their solitude.

National Park Roads and Tourism

At the time of the stock market crash of 1929, the National Park Service managed a total of 1,298 miles of road and more than three times that many miles of trail.[51] During the 1920s, Park Service director Stephen Mather occasionally lashed out at the U.S. Forest Service for its "commercial exploitation of natural resources."[52] At the same time, Mather had pressed for more hotel and road development in the national parks to provide for visitor services and enjoyment. Writing in 1920, Mather declared "the road problem," which he defined as the need for more and better roads, "one of the most important issues before the [Park] Service."[53]

In fact, Mather's words during this time highlight the challenge of trying to balance the Park Service's directives of preservation and tourism. Differing somewhat from his contemporaries Aldo Leopold and Arthur Carhart in the Forest Service, Stephen Mather and the National Park Service stopped short of labeling roads and associated developments a means of ruining wild country. Rather, roads and hotels could be essential services that enabled Americans to appreciate, value, and visit the natural beauty of the national parks.

With that understood, Mather and others described a very specific and limited role for roads in national parks: one major road should bring tourists to the core of each large park, but roads should not be overbuilt or overabundant.[54] In his 1923 *Report of the Director*, Mather wrote, "We must guard against the intrusion of roads into sections [of parks] that should forever be kept for quiet contemplation and accessible only by horseback or hiking."[55]

In 1927, Congress granted the Park Service $51 million to improve and build roads over a ten-year span. At about the same time, though, a gathering of national park superintendents agreed that they should restrict themselves to a ratio of 1 mile of road to every 10 miles of trail to avoid the "cheapening effect of easy accessiblity" from auto tourists.[56] Even in its early years, then, the Park Service clearly struggled to preserve lands while also making them available to the American public.

One striking exception to the National Park Service's philosophy of limiting road access appeared at about the time of the Depression and its New Deal programs: the Park Service called it a "Parkway." Shortly after Americans had finally gained widespread access to affordable cars, the New Deal established a massive labor force for federally funded projects. Between 1933 and 1940, the federal government poured $1.8 billion into road construction.[57] The New Deal's Civilian Conservation Corps crews were a natural jumpstart for the National Park Service's two decades of building national parkways.[58]

These ribbons of national park roads—the George Washington, Blue Ridge, Natchez Trace and others—were typically identified, created, and built solely to accommodate motor tourists. Designated as elongated parks, national parkways such as the Blue Ridge in some aspects epitomize the roaded extreme of American public lands: a corridor of asphalt buffered by 1,000 feet of natural, forested right-of-way. Understandably, the parkways came under attack as a departure from Park Service ideals. The National Parks Association, for instance, complained in an article titled, "Park Service Leader Abandons National Park Standards," that "Some persons even go so far as to assert that [the agency's] proper function is to stimulate and direct recreational travel throughout the country."[59]

The parks and parkways of the Appalachian Mountains actually provide an interesting perspective on the paradox of the National Park Service's mission. Indeed, the dual charge to protect lands unimpaired for future generations *and* provide for people's enjoyment has proven daunting from its inception. To some, parkways could combine these two goals admirably: a smooth, scenic road offers comfortable access to visitors, while the "beauty strip" of protected lands lining the parkway preserves land in a natural state. This rationale would scarcely work for the larger parks such as Yellowstone, Yosemite, or Grand Canyon, which were primarily wildlands at the time of park designation, but in Appalachia by the 1920s, 60 percent of the Smoky Mountains' forests had already been clear-cut.[60] The call for parkways (and a Great Smoky Mountains National Park) rang out not just from conservationists interested in protecting what remained of the region's forest and mountain scenery, but also from civic boosters looking for an economic boon in cities such as Asheville, North Carolina; Knoxville, Tennessee; and Roanoke, Virginia. Much like the sponsors of Yellowstone National Park a half century earlier, Appalachian park supporters were interested both in preserving nature and in promoting the economy.

Parkways differed from most highways in that they were built not to move people from one point to another with great expediency, but rather to provide an opportunity for pleasurable driving.[61] And although the scenic parkways differed in many respects from interstate expressways built in the decades that followed, one troubling feature was present in both: local residents, homes, and entire towns were bulldozed or relocated to make way for the incoming roads. The lands of the wealthy were characteristically spared, while those of the poor were plowed under or condemned.[62] The roads, in other words, took precedence over the individuals affected by the roads.

The overwhelming popularity of national parkways aptly reflects the powerful role that automobiles and roads have played in the development of American culture and its public lands. When parts of Skyline Drive in Shenandoah National Park opened in Virginia in 1934, nearly 50,000 drivers cruised its asphalt curves in the first five weeks.[63] To this day, the national parkways still rank high on the list of the most visited units of the National Park System: the Blue Ridge Parkway notches first place with more than 18 million visits each year, while the Natchez Trace and George Washington Parkways also appear in the top ten with nearly 6 million visitors annually. By comparison, Yosemite National Park in California, although infamous among the large scenic parks for its summer hordes, attracts fewer than 4 million visitors a year.[64]

The Civilian Conservation Corps, 1933 to 1942

Along with parkways, the Depression and its subsequent New Deal programs brought other threats that would alarm people like Aldo Leopold and chip away at the roadless forest lands that he prized. Faced with massive unemployment and widespread depression, President Franklin Roosevelt sent Americans to work "in nature" for their economic and societal therapy.[65] The most visible result of this push, the Civilian Conservation Corps (CCC), was active for only ten years, from 1933 to 1942. During that time, however, the CCC managed to pour more than 3 million laborers into work camps on federal and state lands.[66]

In addition to employing and training Americans by the millions, the CCC also greatly increased the amount of roads and motorized access on federal lands. By some estimates, the CCC crews built in ten years what otherwise would have taken fifty to accomplish.[67] By 1942, CCC crews had constructed 126,000 miles of roads and "truck trails" on public lands.[68]

Of these latter, some commentators could not keep their criticisms quiet. In one of her many pamphlets, conservationist Rosalie Edge noted, "C.C.C. camps are established in hundreds in the National Forests and the Forests are being honeycombed with roads. Roads in the Forests, if not surfaced with asphalt, are called 'truck trails.' The word *trail* presents to the mind a picture of a narrow woodland path wending its way beneath the trees. Actually, the so-called trail is a graded swath, usually following a stream up a narrow valley, over which may be transported machinery to cut huge trees. . . . Surely *trail* is a misnomer for a road wide enough for the motor truck."[69]

In the Forest Service's annual report for 1942, the chief estimated that CCC workers contributed some 730,000 "man years" to national forests over the course of the program.[70] With America's entry into World War II, enrollment in the CCC quickly dissipated. In 1942 it was terminated by Congress. The roads, bridges, fire trails, and other major works of the CCC, however, would remain for years to come. The CCC effort worked wonders for the economy and morale of a struggling nation, but it also left its mark on an increasingly fractured landscape.

Forest Roads: Getting the Wood Out, 1946 to 1960

Although recreational visits to national parks surged after World War II, from 11.7 million visits in 1945 to 25.5 million in 1947 and nearly 50 million by 1954, few new roads have been built in the national parks in the latter half of the twentieth century.[71] The Park Service focused, instead, on road maintenance and improvements rather than major new construction.

Conversely, after World War II the Forest Service finally kicked its road building machinery into high gear. As production dwindled from heavily cutover private timberlands, the wood products industry increasingly turned to national forests to feed the demand of a booming nation.[72] Road miles in the national forests doubled in the two decades following World War II, with an increase of 100,000 miles from 1946 to 1969.[73] The vast majority of these roads were built to access timber.

Photo 2-1: Roads often facilitate logging and other extractive industries.

In 1946, former U.S. Forest Service Chief William Greeley wrote that the logging industry was operating at only 60 percent of its potential in national forests in the Pacific Northwest for one basic reason: limited road access.[74] Although at the time Greeley was working for the West Coast Lumberman's Association and was no longer affiliated with the Forest Service, his message still carried considerable weight with Congress. Furthermore, the word from the agency was almost verbatim.

That same year, 1946, Ira J. Mason was head of the Forest Service's timber operations. Mason proposed a $260 million, 26,000-mile road building program in order to access timber.[75] With the price of wood on the rise, demand also rose with a burst of post-war construction. Forest Service timber sale receipts increased more than tenfold from 1946 to 1956.[76] To get the wood out of the forests, the Forest Service needed roads (see photo 2-1).

Logging operations required a variety of road types to access timber. Depending on the terrain, the species of tree, soils, the logging method, and other factors, the Forest Service built a different combination of roads. Arterials were high-volume roads, often two-lane and paved. They were also fairly rare, even today comprising just 5 percent of the agency's system roads. Another 20 percent came in the form of collector roads, which carried a mix of logging and other traffic. Collector roads were typically wide enough for vehicles to pass each other safely and made of dirt or gravel. The remaining 75 percent of national forest roads, the local roads, were single-purpose and usually built to harvest timber (they were also occasionally used to access administrative sites or trailheads).[77]

In addition to these main road types, which persist to this day, logging operations typically created a network of "skid trails," or wide tracks cleared for logs as they were dragged or "skidded" from their stumps to the roadside truck-loading platforms. Skid trails were not often driveable by passenger cars, but in recent years have become increasingly used— even developed and maintained—by off-road vehicle drivers for motorcycle or all-terrain vehicle (ATV) routes.

Roads proved to be so important and so closely linked to timber operations that some logged areas now have more than 10 miles of road for every square mile of land. In some cases, such as the towering redwoods of California, which are both extremely valuable and extremely brittle, loggers may build road spurs to access individual trees.

Even with thousands of miles of new roads, by 1952 Forest Service Chief Richard McArdle determined road access was still limiting his agency's timber harvest to 70 percent below its potential. In his annual report that year, McArdle wrote, "Millions of acres of wild forest land must await an adequate road system before they will return their full worth in forest products and growing capacity."[78] To respond to this, the Forest Service requested $112 million from Congress for road construction.[79] The agency received more than $40 million for road building within four years of its request. Not quite satisfied, Chief McArdle returned to the Senate in 1956 to reiterate that proper forest management was impossible without an adequate transportation system.[80]

Before long some of the fruits of these lobbying efforts had ripened and could finally be polished and presented back to Congress. In 1957, the assistant chief of the Forest Service testified to a congressional committee that his agency was building approximately 2,800 miles of new roads each year in order to access the nation's valuable timber reserves.[81] The Forest Service's road building boom was in full swing.

BLM Roads: Commodities and Cows

Outside the national forests and national parks, American public lands lacked clear management directives for much of the early twentieth century. As overgrazing of sheep and cattle on many of these "vacant" federal lands caused widespread damage to streams, vegetation, and finally, the forage needed for ranchers' livelihoods, Congress stepped in to pass the Taylor Grazing Act of 1934.[82] Though modest by some conservationists' standards, the Taylor Grazing Act brought an end to wide-open grazing and for the first time imposed a system of fees and permits for ranchers to use public range. The act also created a Division of Grazing—later to become the U.S. Grazing Service—which proved to be a forebear to today's BLM.

When the BLM finally formed in 1946, following a merger of the U.S. Grazing Service and the General Land Office, it inherited a massive quantity of land: more than 450 million acres.[83] Though subsequent legislation pared the BLM's landbase down significantly, the agency still manages the largest acreage of any federal agency.[84] BLM lands are characteristically dry and remote from large population centers and include a history of grazing, mining, and other extractive uses.

Although increasingly recognized today for their beauty, wildness, and other nonconsumptive values, the BLM lands are generally the lands left over—the unclaimed—after two centuries of westward expansion. Many of the 83,000 miles of road managed by the BLM hearken back to the early days of an open range, where if you wanted to get to your stock, you simply rode or drove until you found them.[85]

For the first three decades of its existence, the BLM lacked any clear direction or legal authority for road management. In 1971, historian Marion Clawson summarized the agency's road policy: "[T]he Bureau has sought only to make roads across its land available to buyers of its timber and those interested in recreation. It has never sought to make the roads public thoroughfares."[86]

Unlike the National Park Service, which from the outset recognized that roads played a restricted but critical role in successful park promotion and management, the BLM lacked a prescription for developing tourism on its lands. Similarly, most BLM lands are remote or arid enough to be a low priority for the farming, recreation, and forestry that spurred road building on national forests.[87]

With the enactment of the Federal Land Policy Management Act in 1976, the BLM gained a clearer mandate to manage its lands for multiple uses. Though the 1976 act largely served to codify some of what the agency had already been doing for years, it provided the very real service of consolidating more than 2,500 laws that had influenced the BLM to that point. It also set timelines and a specific charter for the agency. The new law instructed the BLM to plan for and balance the long-term management of resources, including recreation, range, timber, minerals, water, fish and wildlife, and "natural scenic, scientific and historical values."[88] The law also required the BLM to conduct inventories of its unroaded lands and make recommendations for wilderness designations.

With the exception of heavily forested acreage in western Oregon, BLM lands' nature and uses have never led to any systematic program of road development. Most roads are scattered and related to specific purposes: to access and manage grazing leases or mining claims, to provide collector roads to connect to other public road systems, and for water or recreational developments. Recreation, or more specifically, off-road motorized recreation, has recently caused far more controversy on BLM lands than most types of road-related use.[89] Notably, at least with respect to motorized recreation discussed in Chapter 5 and later, the Federal Land Policy and Management Act also established that resources should be managed "without permanent impairment of the land and environment," rather than for the greatest economic return.[90] Though in places such a directive still sounds like a distant wish, the BLM now at least has language to point to when it chooses to make decisions that restrict roads or motorized access.

National Wildlife Refuge Roads

The BLM was not the only latecomer to the public land management arena. Even though Pelican Island was designated the first national wildlife refuge in 1903, the U.S. Fish and Wildlife Service was not created until 1940 with a merger of the Bureau of Biological Survey and the Bureau of Fisheries. The new agency did not hatch completely out of the shell of the Department of the Interior until 1956 when Congress confirmed its status and passed the Fish and Wildlife Act.[91] Ten years later, with the passage of the National Wildlife Refuge System Administration Act, the U.S. Fish and Wildlife Service finally fledged and received management of a consolidated "National Wildlife Refuge System."[92] In 1996, President Clinton further defined the mission of this system in order to "preserve a national network of lands and waters for the conservation and management of fish, wildlife and plant resources of the United States for the benefit of present and future generations."[93]

Given its late debut as a public land management agency and its reputation as a "dominant use" agency for the protection of fish and wildlife (in contrast to the multiple use programs of the Forest Service and BLM), the Fish and Wildlife Service inherited more than its share of managerial tangles, including thousands of road miles.[94] Many of these roads came not as planned routes built into refuges, but already existed by the time lands were pieced together to form a designated reserve.

Even though each refuge is created explicitly to protect a particular species or habitat, the management of which is then considered its dominant use, a host of secondary uses such as grazing, hunting, motorized recreation, aerial bombing, and road building are permitted on many refuges. In 1989, the General Accounting Office reported that of more than 400 refuges nationwide, grazing occurred on 151 refuges, powerboating took place on 262, off-road vehicles roamed on 37, mining and logging occurred on 26 and 79, respectively, and military overflights darkened the skies of 55 national wildlife refuges.[95] According to the agency's own count, there are 9,000 miles of public and administrative roads managed by the Fish and Wildlife Service on refuge lands; another 34,000 miles of trails, dikes, or other linear features have been loosely categorized as "roads" in agency inventories.[96] Some of the roads crossing refuges carry major volumes of traffic and pose a significant threat to the integrity of the wildlife and its habitat. For example, New York's Montezuma National Wildlife Refuge—home to nesting populations of bald eagles, green herons, great horned owls, turtles, deer, and dozens of other species, as well as tens of thousands of migratory geese and ducks—was established in 1938, then bisected in the mid-1950s by Interstate 90, the New York Thruway. In the mid-1990s an estimated 26,000 cars motored through the refuge on I-90 every day.[97]

A chronic lack of funds and numerous private inholdings also continue to plague national wildlife refuges and thwart management goals, such as placing limits on motorized vehicle access. Roads—past, present, and future—affect and threaten wildlife refuges across the country, whether in the form of roadkilled moose and pronghorn from an existing road on Montana's Red Rock Lakes National Wildlife Refuge or proposals to build a 20-mile road into the remote Izembek National Wildlife Refuge in Alaska.[98]

National Forest Roads, 1960 to Present

Of all the road miles on public lands in the United States today, four-fifths exist in the national forests. The U.S. Forest Service is, far and away, the top road building agency in American history. Increasingly since the 1970s, the public and Congress have questioned the agency's management of the nation's forests. As the Forest Service's road building and timber programs surged during the 1950s, the timber industry and a growing environmental movement began to clamor for very different types of agency response: the former for increased access and harvest, the latter for more preservation and protection.[99]

In the 1960s, with laws such as the Multiple-Use Sustained-Yield Act and the Wilderness Act, Congress clarified the range of uses that the Forest Service needed to consider, namely: recreation, grazing, wildlife, timber, water, and wilderness.[100] In 1969, with passage of the National Environmental Policy Act, Congress also provided an explicit process for public involvement in land management decisions.

With timber sales, roads, and clear-cuts still increasing through the 1960s in the national forests, Congress acted again and in 1976 passed the National Forest Management Act.[101] In addition to refining the agency's local planning process and setting limitations on timber harvest, the law included important language regarding forest roads. Among these, the Forest Service was required to document roads in a forest transportation plan, keep an accurate inventory of roads, and reestablish vegetative cover on any temporary road within ten years.[102] As these and other prescriptions made their way into forest planning documents in the years ahead, road-fighting conservationists would turn to them to limit road densities in wildlife habitat areas, demand road closure and obliteration programs, and monitor agency compliance with federal law.

Despite increased public concern for conservation and a stronger legislative hand in directing Forest Service activities, the 1970s and '80s witnessed a doubling time for national forest road miles nearly on par with that of the previous two decades. By 1985, the national forests had more than 340,000 miles of roads, and new construction approached a rate of 10,000 miles per year.[103]

By the 1980s, the Forest Service began to openly recognize that public sentiment was no longer solidly behind aggressive logging and road building programs. Though agency publications still touted forest roads as essential for uses that ranged from driving for pleasure to logging to outdoor recreation, they also acknowledged road-related problems including soil erosion, aquatic disturbances, cost, and impacts to sensitive wildlife species and habitats.[104] The Forest Service and timber purchasers continued to build thousands of miles of new road each year, but the agency also began road obliteration programs and watershed restoration projects in an effort to reduce some of the past damage.

In certain regions, such as the northern Rockies and Pacific Northwest, threatened or endangered species management led to specific restrictions on the number and location of roads in critical habitat areas. Since certain species, including grizzly bear and elk, are known to avoid roads or suffer population declines when roads exceed a particular density (usually measured as the linear miles of road per square mile of land area), many forests adopted standards that allow roads only up to a certain threshhold.

With the arrival of Michael Dombeck as chief of the Forest Service in 1997, agency rhetoric against road building strengthened into a moratorium against new road building in most roadless areas. In addition, Dombeck acknowledged that thousands of miles of road existed on national forest lands that his agency had not previously identified.[105] While these measures were broadly perceived as a show of greater agency concern over the proliferation of roads, road construction and reconstruction continued in most national forests.[106]

Transportation Management in a New Millennium

What we now confront in the United States is a variety of public land designations—national forests, national parks, wildlife refuges, areas under the direction of the BLM, and others—all of which are riddled with roads. Some roads have been built specifically to bring visitors to areas that have been deemed scenic wonders. We have built other roads to move raw materials out of the landscape. Still others are not so much built as they are etched into the land, year after year, from periodic motorized use—perhaps to tend a grazing allotment on a wildlife refuge, or from off-road vehicles running up dunes or ridgelines. If all these roads were actively enjoyed or needed by the public *and* caused no harm to the land, Americans might well leave them alone.

Unfortunately, most public land roads do not rest passively on the landscape. As we will see in the next chapter, many roads, even without any use, bleed steady doses of sediment into rivers and lakes, erode and destabilize mountainsides, block stream crossings, and impair fish breeding and migrations. Other roads fragment habitat into small blocks and disrupt terrestrial animal movements and mating, provide access to human hunters and poachers, and offer corridors for exotic plant and animal invasions.

Compounding the potential for road systems to cause damage, most public land agencies have a rich history of struggling to keep abreast of their road miles and maintenance. Through the 1930s, '40s, and '50s, Forest Service reports reflected an inability to keep track of either road miles or their condition. The 1935 *Report of the Chief,* for example, listed a total of 120,948 miles of road, but also noted that 31,796 miles were, "nonexisting," and 35,774 miles more were considered of "unsatisfactory standard."[107] As recently as 1999, the Federal Highway Administration rated 70 to 80 percent of public land roads in "fair" or "poor" condition.[108] National park roads have required almost continuous maintenance and reconstruction from the time of the first wagon tracks into Yellowstone.

With the abundance of roads traversing our nation's public lands, we have gradually developed a collective expectation not of careful stewardship, but of easy and immediate access. A similar attitude of entitlement has carried over to motorized recreationists with the advent of powerful off-road vehicles. Four-wheeled ATVs ride legally (and illegally) on and off trails in areas formerly open solely to horse and foot travel. Snow-machines are now so closely linked to power and speed that manufacturers advertise them as "bullets on skis." Snowmobilers actively seek "play areas" today that even a decade ago were too remote or too steep to negotiate.[109]

At the close of the twentieth century, America's public lands are so strewn with roads and motorized access that "transportation management" now sits at the top of many agencies' list of priorities. Whether built to carry tourists to scenic attractions, to access and extract natural resources, to decrease travel times or distances, or to accommodate recreational or management activities, roads permeate the American landscape in a metastasis of motorized access. There is no longer a single place in the continental United States more than 20 miles from a road.[110]

In less than a century we have converted a continent with relatively few roads into a continent characterized by them. What remains to be seen is the permanence of the conversion. Will the century to come be further marked by roads and motorized recreation or will it be noted for road removal and restoration? With many federal lands long prized as reserves spared from the rapid development of private lands, we must now contend with the realization that even our sanctuaries have become splintered. How will this affect the plants and animals, the waters and the soils of these lands we call our own? As federal land agencies struggle to manage their sprawling networks of roads, the future lies largely in the hands and values of the people who are in so many ways behind the wheel: the American public.

Roads are daggers thrust into
the heart of nature.

—Michael Soulé, 2000

3 | The Ecological Effects of Roads

For much of history, science and roads met only in the context of how we could apply knowledge of engineering, chemistry, and geology toward building better, longer-lasting, smoother, cheaper, and safer roads. In many places, road construction continues to be the primary focus of science upon roads. In recent decades, however, ecologists, conservation biologists, and others have come to roads posing new types of questions. How do roads affect long-term natural processes in landscapes or watersheds? What impacts do roads have upon plant and animal species, populations, communities, or ecosystems? How do roads combine with various uses of roads—such as logging, hunting, or driving a motor vehicle—in ways that lead to new and different consequences?

By working to answer these questions and examining the ecological effects of roads, we can better determine our priorities for future road management. Using effective outreach and education, land managers may find it increasingly feasible to remove or limit roads where they present significant ecological hazards and provide comparatively little access or public benefit. Even where the decisions are more difficult, for example when a popular road carries major ecological liabilities, a thorough understanding of road impacts will help us evaluate long-term management priorities. This knowledge—the *scientia* of roads—provides a critical link in evaluating and determining the future of roads and motorized access on public lands.

The ecological effects of roads can be lumped broadly into two categories: use effects and presence effects. Use effects, or impacts caused by human activities on roads, include some of the more commonly noticed effects from roads such as animals killed by collisions with vehicles (road-kill), road-based logging or mining operations, increased access for hunting and fishing, and the transport and dispersal of exotic plants. Presence effects, those impacts triggered simply by the existence of the road on the landscape, can be both subtle and long lasting. On land they generate erosion, habitat fragmentation and loss, soil compaction, and increased edge habitat. Aquatic impacts range from increasing sedimentation to changing the way water moves through the landscape.

These two categories—use effects and presence effects—prove helpful for a broad conceptual framework, even if they do not offer a perfect fit for every ecological consequence of roads. On occasion, the categories overlap. For example, erosion occurs both from the use of a road and from its mere presence on the land. Similarly, invasive weeds enter roaded areas both from active human transport and by wind, water, or wildlife dispersal in the road corridor. Ecological effects might also be classified usefully into categories such as aquatic and terrestrial, intentional and inadvertent, or direct and indirect. But for our purposes here, classifying road impacts by use effects and presence effects is the most appropriate because that division links the ecological consequences of roads most clearly to their causes. This can, in turn, help guide managers and citizens to address road-related problems.

Like most forms of technology, roads come with both negative and positive effects. Historically, we have emphasized the socially or economically beneficial aspects of roads, while some of the negative ecological effects have gained recognition largely in the final decades of the twentieth century. Tens of thousands of road miles built on national forest lands in the Pacific Northwest gave access to timber harvests initially, but more recently we have recognized the roads' role causing widespread erosion and damage to trout and salmon fisheries. Similarly, millions of visitors enjoy driving the paved routes through national parks, but with escalating use these roads also generate pollution and disturbance problems.

To differing perspectives, the same road can be either boon or bane. Backcountry enthusiasts might lament a road popular with weekend drivers. Other roads have simply not been maintained adequately and in their neglect cause problems ranging from inconvenient "washboard" ruts to blocked drainage culverts and massive landslides. Vehicle collisions kill hundreds of millions of animals every year, but roadkill also provides a ready food source for scavengers.

Through it all one fact remains evident and clear: roads wield a tremendous influence on the plants, animals, waters, lands, people, and natural systems of the United States (and much of the rest of the planet). A significant majority of these effects prove detrimental to biodiversity and ecosystem integrity.

Research on the ecological effects of roads comes from (and applies) beyond public lands or the boundaries of the United States. In fact, road studies include data from several continents and many types of roads. This chapter, then, addresses the ecological effects of roads generally, but with an emphasis on impacts that apply to roads most common to public lands.

Use Effects of Roads

At some point in its history, every road receives use of some kind. Activities range from the road construction work itself to a limited period of logging or resource extraction to casual recreational driving or intensive tourism. Every use of a road brings with it a different array of effects. Depending upon soils, slope, construction methods and road quality, climate, and other factors, even the same uses will lead to different effects at different times or in different places. In some areas, such as national forests or national parks, road construction can turn a formerly peaceful, remote landscape into a rolling zone of heavy industrial activity.

Of course, most roads are not only constructed, they are also driven upon. With vehicular use, new effects of roads quickly emerge. The sight of roadkilled animals has grown so commonplace to most Americans, the term now sometimes lends itself freely to recipe books, armadillo jokes, and gag food items such as prepackaged "Roadkill Helper." The amount of roadkill carnage, however, is no laughing matter: researchers estimate that 1 million vertebrates die every day on roads in the United States.[1]

Not all road use effects are as inadvertent as vehicle collisions. Hunting and fishing both lead to stress, disturbance, and mortality in wildlife and fish populations.[2] Some major hunting organizations now advocate for road closures and road removal on public lands in an effort to increase big game habitat security and improve the quality of hunting experiences.[3] Increasingly, hunters concerned with ethics and fair chase have recognized that roads and road-based hunting diminish the habitat for the animals as well as the reputations and experiences of the hunters.

On a broader scale, the human use of roads contributes to dramatic landscape conversions that can change the ecological processes, community structure, population size, and species composition of a place for the long term. From the Appalachian Mountains to the Cascades, if you see a logged forest, chances are good that you will also see a logging road. The mining industry is similarly dependent upon roads. The ranching industry also accounts for its share of road miles and use on public lands, while recreation, considered a "nonconsumptive" use of public lands by many commentators in the past, shows an increasing ability to create lasting impacts.[4]

Roads on public lands are also closely linked to developments for administrators and visitors. Human developments and use create impacts of disturbance and noise, air pollution and dust. Though chemical pollution from road use is not often as obvious as dust billowing from a passing vehicle, it is nevertheless a significant environmental effect. Road use can also exacerbate surface erosion, particularly on unpaved road surfaces. Human activity on roads provides a vector for biological invasion in many forms.

Road Construction Impacts

Even a relatively simple constructed road, such as an access route across flat Bureau of Land Management (BLM) land in the desert, requires a bulldozer to peel back the vegetation and surface soil layers to create a drivable roadbed. Few studies exist of actual plant and animal deaths caused by road construction directly, but for immobile plants and slow-moving animals on or beneath the construction route, destruction is virtually certain. With more than 8 million miles of road lanes in the lower forty-eight states (on all types of land, private and public), the land area directly covered by road surface is approximately 18,700 square miles—space enough to grade Massachusetts, Connecticut, Rhode Island, and Delaware in their entirety, and still offer 2,000 square miles of roadbed for parking.[5]

Shaving these numbers down to apply more strictly to federal lands, public land roads would still more than cover Rhode Island.[6] For a significant area of land, then, road construction has scoured natural habitat.

Vehicle Collisions and Roadkill

More than 100 people die each year as a result of vehicle–deer collisions, tens of thousands more are injured, and property damage costs range into the tens of millions of dollars.[7] Vehicle collisions kill species across the spectrum, from owls to frogs and grizzly bears to rattlesnakes.[8] In Alaska's Kenai National Wildlife Refuge, roadkill is the leading cause of death for moose.[9] On average in Pennsylvania, vehicles kill more than one black bear per week and more than 115 deer each day.[10] A Federal Highway Administration survey of selected roads in the Carolinas, Illinois, Oregon, and California counted 15,000 roadkilled reptiles and amphibians, 24,000 small mammals, and 24,000 large mammals—in a single month.[11]

Despite their ability to fly, birds also die in great numbers from vehicle collisions. The Federal Highway Administration count that sampled less than 0.3 percent of the entire interstate system still tallied more than 77,000 dead birds.[12] Although some species, such as red-winged and Brewer's blackbirds are attracted to roadside habitats and therefore comprise a large percentage of avian roadkill, the dead birds represented dozens of species with a wide range of ecological needs and habitats. The interstate highway mortality counts included, among others, mallards, mourning doves, yellow-billed cuckoos, eastern kingbirds, goldfinches, orioles, swallows, nighthawks, meadowlarks, cardinals, jays, rufous-sided towhees, dickcissels, warblers, sparrows, and grosbeaks.[13] Other studies have documented significant roadkill deaths for raptors including kestrels, northern saw-whet owls, and eastern screech owls.[14]

While high-speed vehicle collisions present a widespread threat for many large or highly mobile species, for small or slow-moving organisms even moderate road traffic on a typical public lands road can be devastating. Amphibians' small size, slow speed, and restrictive habitat and breeding requirements make them particularly vulnerable to major losses from roadkill, even on low-volume roads with relatively slow vehicle speeds.[15] Although higher traffic volumes typically lead to greater roadkill, one study estimated that a modest flow of 26 cars per hour could reduce road-crossing toads' survival rate to zero.[16] Elsewhere, 50 percent of migrating toads were killed while trying to cross a road with traffic of 24 to 40 cars per hour.[17] Vehicle-caused amphibian deaths are so widespread and numerous, some scientists now contend roadkill is a contributing factor in the global decline of frog and salamander populations.[18]

Reptiles such as snakes fare poorly on roads as well; they are attracted to warm road surfaces, move relatively slowly, and offer a large target as they crawl or stretch across roadways.[19] Regionally and federally endangered snake populations can be seriously affected by roadkill mortality, and scientists estimate that hundreds of millions of snakes may have been killed on U.S. roads in recent decades.[20]

Although roadkill obviously impacts a great number of individuals in dramatic fashion, its importance ecologically remains a matter of some debate. For common, highly adaptable species such as raccoons, blackbirds, or white-tailed deer, vehicle collisions destroy thousands of individuals every month. This may lead to important changes at the local or community level—and is certainly an issue for animal rights advocates—but overall species viability is probably not impaired by roadkill. On the other hand, populations of endemic, infecund, or rare species can be significantly impacted by vehicle collisions. The ocelot, Florida Key deer, and American crocodile are each federally designated Endangered Species. Though broader habitat protection and restoration will be crucial to the long-term survival of these species, vehicle collisions are currently their leading source of mortality.[21] In the future, as vehicle numbers or speeds increase, the impacts of roadkill on wildlife are likely to grow, not diminish.

Access for Hunting, Fishing, and Poaching

In general, with greater road access, the greater the hunting or fishing pressure becomes. Although grizzly bears are protected as a Threatened Species in Montana, Idaho, Wyoming, and Washington, each year grizzlies still die at muzzlepoint due to cases of mistaken identity during legal black bear hunts. During the spring black bear season of 2000, hunters in Montana and Wyoming mistakenly killed at least five grizzly bears.[22] Illegal poaching also contributes to bear mortality, as does the occasional self-defense killing when hunters or other armed recreationists find themselves threatened or charged. Studies have shown that the majority of grizzly bear deaths in Montana occur within 1 mile of motorized access—a result of poaching, mistaken identity hunting, vehicle collisions, and other human–bear encounters.[23] Throughout the grizzly's remaining range in the Rocky Mountains, proximity to roads and human activities has proven lethal: in northwestern Montana, 189 grizzlies have died at human hands since 1985, while in the Yellowstone ecosystem 46 grizzlies died from agency control actions, self-defense, or "other legal ways" between 1992 and 1997.[24] In 1993, the U.S. Fish and Wildlife Service identified roads as a primary factor in bear survival, stating, "Roads probably pose the most imminent threat to grizzly bear habitat today."[25]

In Yellowstone Lake, home to the world's largest population of Yellowstone cutthroat trout, illegally introduced lake trout now threaten the cutthroats' long-term prospects. Unlike cutthroats, lake trout are deepwater fish that spawn in the fall. They also eat cutthroat trout and may jeopardize the future of the area's grizzly bears, river otters, bald eagles, and ospreys who currently rely upon the cutthroat as a source of protein and calories in the spring. Yellowstone Lake is rimmed on two sides by paved roads, and without this easy road access it would have been extremely difficult to transport live lake trout into Yellowstone Lake.

Extending the Reach of Extractive Industry

As the majority of national forest road miles attest, the logging industry relies heavily upon road access. Roads enable crews to scout timber for its commercial potential, cut and clear forests, transport logs for milling and sale, and return to cutover lands for burning, post-commercial thinning, or revegetation work. While road-free helicopter or water-based logging operations are possible, these methods are seldom cost-effective or practical to implement.

Even prospectors in the gold rush days of the 1800s required roads (or railroads) to remove their ore for processing and sale; in many remote reaches of the Rocky Mountains, Sierras, Cascades, and Alaska Range, rotting roadbeds still linger from these century-old efforts. The modern mining industry often relies upon huge land-moving machines to create the open pits favored by copper and gold mining operations. Roads leading in and out of such mines must be able to handle trucks bearing hundreds of tons of ore carried on tires the size of a small house.

In southern Utah's canyon country, one of the country's most rugged and remote regions, the post–World War II uranium boom led to the development of prospecting roads on a number of lands managed by the BLM. To this day, areas featuring the uranium-rich mossback and chinle layers bear scars from the experience. Similar, even shorter-lived booms for oil shale and tar sands development sparked to life in Colorado and Utah. Long after Exxon, Chevron and other corporations pulled out of the area, the remnants of their mining dreams remain in the form of roads and drill pads in otherwise remote places.

Many ranchers and land managers drive trucks on BLM or national forest grazing allotments to work on fences, maintain water tanks, or round up livestock. The characteristic two-track roads that parallel fence-lines create less soil compaction or habitat fragmentation than their heavily constructed counterparts, but such user-developed tracks are prone to erosion and gullying, play a role in plant invasions, and can facilitate secondary impacts to the area due to increased recreation or herbicides sprayed for weed control.

In addition to the long list of environmental effects caused by motorized recreation (see Chapter 5), mountain bicyclists, equestrians, cross-country skiers, and hikers each create impacts, including noxious weed dispersal, soil compaction, erosion, wildlife disturbance, and damage to vegetation.[26] More to the point, roads increase the reach and distribution of these uses by enabling recreationists to travel farther afield before launching into their activity of choice. The average wilderness hiker, for example, ventures just a handful of miles from a road-accessible trailhead, while the majority of national park visitors keep to within a few hundred yards of paved roads. Clearly, the more sprawling the road system, the more extensively recreational use will penetrate backcountry areas.

Recreational Developments and Tourism

Particularly in national parks, employee and visitor facilities have earned a reputation for their environmental impacts. Raw sewage spills in Glacier and Yellowstone National Parks made headlines in 1999 and 2000.[27] In national parks from Acadia in Maine to Big Bend in Texas, park roads and their subsequent human developments cause habituation problems for wildlife as varied as moose, marmots, mountain goats, skunks, collared peccary, and bear. In national forests, the Term Permit Act of 1915 promoted recreational developments that included thousands of lodges, cabins, developed camps, and ski areas, many of which still exist today.[28] All of these developments depended upon existing roads or their eventual construction to assure easy access.

Noise Pollution and Disturbance Impacts

Different animals respond differently to noise and disturbance. Bald eagle reproduction is known to diminish with proximity to roads, while both bald and golden eagles preferentially nest away from roads and human disturbance.[29] Sandhill cranes avoid nesting near paved and graveled roads but seem to tolerate private roads—a possible indication that the birds will adjust to low levels of consistent use.[30]

In the northern Rockies, researchers have found grizzly bears living disproportionately in the least-roaded areas of study sites. Black bears, common to public lands from Pennsylvania to California, suffer higher mortality in areas with more roads.[31] Elk and deer have been shown to avoid areas within 200 yards of heavily used roads, and in Idaho, when road densities increased beyond 2 miles of road per square mile of land, elk habitat effectiveness dropped below 50 percent.[32]

Other animals apparently choose to live in landscapes characterized by disturbance. Despite suffering high levels of juvenile mortality to roadkill, swift fox in the midwestern United States show a strong preference for road verges and typically choose den sites within 230 meters of them.[33] A study of mallards in North Dakota also found a preference for nesting near roads, though nest success in road right-of-ways was only 3 percent.[34] Other small mammal and bird species are also known to live preferentially along roadways.[35] Researchers suspect that mallards, swift fox, and other species choose nest sites and roadside habitat not from an actual affinity for roads as much as from an ability to tolerate disturbance more successfully than predators or competing species. If the advantage gained by decreased predation or competition exceeds the negative impacts of roadkill mortality or disturbance, then species might survive well in roadside habitat.

Still other species can actually thrive in disturbed landscapes. Brown-headed cowbirds, raccoons, starlings, skunks, and various rodents are well-known for their ability to handle loud, busy, and even heavily developed urban environments. Opportunistic predators such as foxes and coyotes can increase their hunting success with the long sight distances along road corridors, but these same animals may suffer from high mortality if they linger near roads. Particularly for animals dispersing from expanding populations, some individuals also manage to survive long enough to pass through heavily roaded zones between one secure habitat and the next. Studies in Minnesota have found that wolves can survive in areas with relatively high road densities as long as they are contiguous to areas with few roads.[36] Avoidance, after all, can mean many things, from using areas of habitat less than expected to altering seasonal migration patterns.[37]

Air Pollution and Dust

For residents of virtually any modern metropolitan area, automobiles and the dense network of roads are easily linked as sources of air pollution. Yet even broadly dispersed roads on public lands contribute to localized problems of air quality. Studies have found that heavy metals such as lead, aluminum, cadmium, copper, and zinc can occur in elevated levels up to 200 meters from roads.[38] Airborne lead particles, for example, are also small enough to pass through open stomata of leaves and may also be taken in by roots.[39] With the conversion to unleaded gasoline in the United States, lead contamination is less prevalent from emissions than it once was. Lead oxide in tires still poses an active source, however, and lead persists in soils and the food web for extended periods of time.[40]

Road use, especially of dirt, gravel, or other soft-surfaced roads, generates and disperses dust in levels that vary depending upon soil moisture content, particle size, and traffic volume. Road dust on plants can lead to a number of problems, including reductions in photosynthesis, respiration, and transpiration, as well as physical injury.[41]

Road Surface Treatments and Chemical Pollution

Road surface treatments—to control dust, ice, or weeds—present some of the most common and widespread forms of chemical pollution. To suppress dust on dirt roads, in the 1970s more than 100 million gallons of used crankcase oil were sprayed on roads in the United States each year.[42] With less than 20 percent of this oil binding to the road surface, some 80 million gallons were free to wash into nearby soils and streams.[43] By comparison, 1989's Exxon *Valdez* disaster dumped 11 million gallons of oil into the waters of Prince William Sound.

Road salts used for deicing also contribute a tremendous quantity of contaminants to nearby lands and waters. Deicing salts typically consist of sodium chloride, but calcium chloride, potassium chloride, and magnesium chloride are also common ingredients.[44] These salts alter soil and water pH and chemical composition, which in turn can affect plant productivity, aquatic biota, and the ecological dynamics of streams and lakes.[45] Sodium concentrations in soil can also displace nutrients critical to physiological function in plants.[46] Though deicing salts are primarily used on paved routes, with the heaviest concentrations in urban areas and highways, they are also used on many roads on federal land and can be transported easily in solution, in snowpack, as airborne particles, and on vehicles.[47] In the 1970s, highway deicing programs used 10 million tons of sodium chloride, 11 million tons of abrasives (such as sand), and 30,000 tons of calcium chloride.[48] Deicing salts can also create a dangerous roadside attraction for wildlife.

Application of herbicides along roads for weed control is standard practice even on closed road systems for many land managers, though the overall quantity of chemicals applied and their ecological impacts have not been well-studied. Common chemicals such as picloram and clopyralid are known to persist in soil for a year or longer, be highly mobile in water, and be lethal to many nontarget plants and some aquatic organisms.[49] A single national forest in western Montana reports an annual roadside application of approximately 100 gallons of herbicide to control exotic weeds such as spotted knapweed, dalmation toadflax, and leafy spurge, though this amount is only adequate to treat 0.3 percent of the weed-infested acres in the forest.[50]

Surface Erosion and Soil Loss

Although erosion increases in roaded lands with or without vehicular traffic, road use in wet conditions can create ruts that increase channelization, downcutting, and the velocity of surface flow down roadbeds. In dry conditions, road use and tire spin can scrape surface soil layers, cause uneven wear of road surfaces, generate dust, and lead to soil loss both through the air and down slopes.

Illegal, user-created roads lack the planning, grading, and maintenance of many constructed routes and are particularly susceptible to erosion from use. These "ghost" roads (eerily absent from most agency maps) often run up ridgelines, across streams, through wetlands, or on steep slopes where vehicular use even at low levels can displace soil or damage natural landscapes. The Forest Service now estimates there are more than 60,000 miles of ghost roads on its lands and anticipates "that future inventories will verify the existence of substantially more miles of unclassified roads."[51]

Vehicles and Vectors for Invasion

Roads create many of the optimal conditions for biological invasions: a linear habitat disturbance that can extend for miles and connect with other linear disturbances, a light gap, the absence of competing vegetation (at least initially), and a route for easy dispersal—by wind, wildlife, water, or human activity.

Weeds and seeds can enter from the initial activity of road construction or from repeated uses by motor vehicles, bicyclists, livestock, pets, or pedestrians. People also introduce exotic species intentionally along roads to accelerate revegetation and decrease erosion, for aesthetics or from ignorance (including feral fruit trees started by fruit tossed from passing vehicles[52]).

Of the road-based dispersers, motor vehicles are able to travel the greatest distance in the shortest time. This makes them exceedingly effective at spreading invasions of certain types of plant seeds. In Montana, the invasion of the noxious Eurasian weed, tansy ragwort (*Senecio jacobaea*), is directly attributable to its arrival on logging equipment.[53] In Oregon and California, spores of an exotic root disease lethal to the endemic Port Orford cedar are primarily transported in soil carried by vehicles and roadway drainages.[54] A 1988 study noted that the spread of at least three other pest species in the Northwest—gypsy moth, black stain root disease, and spotted knapweed—has been facilitated by logging roads and their traffic.[55] Other types of seeds, such as the invasive hound's-tongue, form burs that cling to clothing or animal fur, which can then disperse as people or other animals travel along road corridors.

On public lands in Utah and Nevada, research determined that roadsides are substantially more invaded and contained fewer native species and more exotics than adjacent interior habitat. Improved or wider roads led to a greater percentage and abundance of nonnative species, and roads acted as conduits for invasions, especially when they passed through areas of multiple use common to BLM lands and national forests.[56]

Presence Effects of Roads

Even without human activity, roads create a number of significant ecological effects simply by their presence. These presence effects are often far-reaching, both spatially and temporally, and can combine with other presence or use effects to create dramatic impacts on landscapes and watersheds. It is important to recognize that roads have impacts even when they are closed to driving or receiving no use, since many land managers treat closed roads as if they were ecologically benign. (As discussed in Chapter 7, many road closures are also not effective at preventing all motorized use.) In fact, presence effects likely cause as many or more impacts than use effects, and often they are more difficult to mitigate or remove. Gravel and unsurfaced roads, in particular, are sources of long-term soil loss and erosion, even in the absence of vehicular use. Presence effects come in two broad classes: terrestrial and aquatic.

Terrestrial Impacts of Roads

Since the day that the first wheel mired in mud or loose soil, the presence of a compacted surface has been one of the critical and foremost features of a road. The compacted roadbed has proven itself a great asset to travel for creatures on foot, in buggies, and in motor vehicles. As a general rule, if you live or travel above ground, the more compacted the road, the swifter and easier the journey. For organisms who live or root inside the soil, however, compaction can pose a prohibitive obstacle.

Roads slice up forests and other lands to create fragments of habitat that can no longer support the number or diversity of species found in large, unroaded areas. One common way of trying to assess the degree of fragmentation caused by roads is to calculate the road density. Typically expressed as miles of road per square mile of land or kilometer of road per square kilometer of land, road density has become an increasingly useful tool for scientists and land managers to estimate the condition of the land and habitat.

While roads and their subsequent habitat changes create a competitive advantage or disadvantage for some species, for small-bodied organisms roads can create nearly impenetrable barriers to travel. With more than 1,200 square miles of public lands actually covered by roads—and an even larger amount of land subsequently affected by soil compaction, biological invasions, or light gaps—direct habitat and landscape changes from roads are substantial. Including both use and presence effects, scientists consider more than 20 percent of the contiguous United States "ecologically altered" by roads.[57]

Soil Compaction

Soil is composed of minerals, air spaces, water, and living organisms. The air spaces in soil are important for soil stability, permeability, and water absorption; as microenvironments for the living organisms in soil; and to insulate lower layers from surface heating and freezing.[58] These spaces also allow plants to establish roots and create microenvironments for the living organisms in soil. Air and water also insulate deeper layers from extreme temperature fluctuations at the soil surface. Compaction from road construction eliminates air spaces and expels water molecules, often creating a matrix that is lethal to subsoil organisms and too dense to allow plants to take root and grow.[59] In fact, road construction can increase soil density more than 200 times above that of undisturbed sites.[60]

Soil compaction can persist for decades and has been found to increase over time, even after roads are no longer used.[61] The hard surface of a road—particularly blacktopping—also increases the surface temperature. This creates abnormally warm habitat areas at night, which may in turn attract birds or reptiles and expose them to heightened risk of roadkill.[62]

Leaf litter, a key soil-building component, has also been shown to decline with proximity to roads. Soil macroinvertebrates such as insects and worms are significantly less abundant and diverse near unpaved forest roads. These impacts can then affect salamanders, birds, and other organisms reliant upon the food or shelter normally provided by these plants, soil nutrients, and invertebrates.[63]

Soil Loss

With compacted soils of unpaved roadbeds discouraging revegetation, the exposed dirt surface that remains is less stable and more prone to erosion than vegetated, undisturbed sites. Even where grasses, shrubs, or trees manage to recolonize, roads built into hillsides feature cutslopes and fill materials that are difficult to stabilize over the long term (see figure 3-1).

On open road systems, even with little to no use, roads and their verges continue to erode at a higher rate than undisturbed sites with similar char-

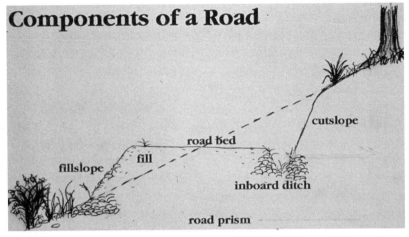

Figure 3-1: Components of a road. (Courtesy of Wildlands Center for Preventing Roads.)

acteristics. Paved roadbeds tend to hold soils in place, but cutslopes and fill material can still be highly unstable and lead to accelerated soil loss.

Habitat Fragmentation

As roads increase in number and length, the size of unroaded watersheds or habitat blocks steadily decreases. This fragmentation commonly reduces wildlife populations and creates a loss of biological diversity. For organisms adapted to conditions in a forest's shaded interior, such as the northern goshawk, spotted owl, marbeled murrelet, fisher, or woodland caribou, the diminished amount of available forage and shelter may prove insurmountable. A growing number of interior-dependent species such as these are now extirpated, endangered, or threatened in the continental United States.

Though logging practices have received well-deserved scrutiny in recent decades, roads actually create more enduring and expansive landscape fragmentation than clear-cuts.[64] Roads open forested lands to increased light, temperature extremes, and wind. With each of these changed conditions, new animal and plant species can move in and colonize areas formerly inaccessible to them. In part, this explains population and range increases for species such as raccoons, skunks, starlings, white-tailed deer, and coyotes who are able to thrive in "edge habitats" characterized by openings in the forest canopy.

Increases in edge habitat can similarly explain the historic decline of some songbirds who are unable to survive predation or edge-adapted birds. Although songbirds such as scarlet tanagers, red-eyed vireos, great crested flycatchers, or prothonotary warblers may not actively avoid thin corridor openings such as those created by roads, road gaps are wide enough to attract predatory or parasitic species such as oppossum, raccoon, and brown-headed cowbirds.[65] The parasitic cowbird is particularly effective at displacing interior songbirds, as it lays eggs in other birds' nests then leaves all rearing duties to the surrogate parents. The quick-growing cowbird young can then outcompete their more diminutive nestmates, further accelerating the cowbirds' colonization of edge habitats from one generation to the next.

A number of studies have also determined upper ranges of tolerance for species and road density. Such studies rarely distinguish whether use effects or presence effects are the key to species' survival, but for many large animals 1 to 2 miles per square mile of road density is where habitat effectiveness drops to the point of species loss or population declines. Mountain lion, elk, and wolves, for example, each show population declines as road densities rise above 1 mile per square mile.[66]

Wildlife Barriers and Corridors

Roads and other linear structures such as levees and dikes obstruct amphibians, ground-dwelling mammals, and other small, slow creatures such as snails and insects. Research has shown that roads act as barriers to salamanders and frogs trying to cross from forested areas to other habitats, but it is not clear whether the effect is due to simple avoidance or from increases in mortality[67]

Other studies have found that redback voles, dusky woodrats, white-tailed antelope squirrels, and other small mammals rarely cross onto road surfaces, even with distances as narrow as 10 feet and traffic rates of only ten to twenty cars per day.[68] Animals such as spiders and beetles have been found to cross roads—even those closed to traffic—rarely or never.[69] Roads present an obstacle even for larger animals, such as mountain lion, pronghorn, or black bear (bear crossings vary dramatically depending upon human traffic).[70]

After many generations, the isolation created by road barriers may subject small populations to increased risks from limited genetic diversity. A diminished, localized population may not be resilient enough to survive events such as floods, drought, or fire that posed only a limited threat to a large, diverse population. Similarly, with a reduced gene pool small populations can be lethally susceptible over time to the emergence of unhealthy traits or defects caused by inbreeding.

Under some conditions, roads may facilitate animal movements, reduce energy expenditures, and attract wildlife. Bison herds in Yellowstone National Park have expanded in recent years, due in large part to higher winter survival and ease of movement on roadways compacted by snowmachine use.[71] Similarly, roads cleared of snow in Alaska attract caribou, despite a subsequent increase in mortality from vehicle collisions.[72] Even grizzly bears and wolves, who generally avoid roads, will travel on closed or low-use road systems in certain conditions and seasons.

The impacts of roads on wildlife corridors are of critical importance, since in many parts of the country the most common landscape matrix is one of roads and areas strongly influenced by roads. More than 80 percent of the land in the Cherokee National Forest in Tennessee, for instance, is within a 10-minute walk from a road.[73]

Aquatic Impacts and Fisheries

Studies on deer, elk, and other prominent terrestrial wildlife species sometimes elicit the most public concern, but ecologists are increasingly pointing to roads as a factor in the decline of trout, salmon, and other aquatic populations. Sediment generated by exposed road surfaces, road-triggered landslides, and slumping slopes have contributed significantly to clogged spawning beds and diminished productivity in the waters of the Pacific Northwest and elsewhere. Endangered species listings for bull trout and Pacific salmon runs have helped to focus managers' attention on roads and the role of increased sediment in spawning redds. Some of the most significant aquatic effects of roads come from altered hydrology, or changes in the way water flows through soil and across the land.

While researchers of terrestrial species such as wolves, bear, and elk have found strong patterns of adverse effects when road densities exceed 1 mile per square mile, it is very difficult to isolate road density or any other single factor and determine how it contributes to the conditions in a specific river or stream. Many factors affect how roads impact streams, rivers, and their associated plants and animals. The distance of roads from

Photo 3-1: If they are not properly maintained, culverts can clog with debris and cause serious road damage, such as this collapse in the Boise National Forest. (Courtesy of Predator Conservation Alliance.)

waterways, the proportion of sand or clay in soils, the slope on which roads are built, climate, stream crossings and culvert designs, construction methods, road use, vegetation, and other qualities all relate to the way roads actually impact aquatic systems. Despite these complicating factors, there is substantial evidence that high road densities in a watershed will consistently correspond to degraded water quality and impaired fisheries.

Roads establish barriers to aquatic systems primarily where they cross streams. Although it is possible to construct bridge and culvert crossings in a manner that causes little disruption to water flow or the passage of biota, improper maintenance or construction decisions often lead to stream crossings that create aquatic barriers. Intermittent stream channels can sometimes fill in completely, blocking reliable surface water flow and promoting large-scale "blowouts" when seasonal runoff washes away the impeding roadfill. Culverts, the large pipes used to channel water beneath road surfaces, may not be big enough to clear debris so they become clogged with organic matter, sediments, or trash, which then increases the likelihood of a road blowout (see photo 3-1). Wood or metal pipe culverts can rot or rust and fail to transport water, causing serious cross-road erosion (photo 3-2). And not least, poorly placed pipes often become

Photo 3-2: Undersized or clogged culverts may fail to drain properly, causing water to flow across roads and cause damage. (Courtesy of Redwood National Park.)

hanging or "shotgun" culverts that poke several feet out from the road prism or streambed, making upstream migrations impossible and carving deep erosion pits where the water plunges against the slope below.

Sedimentation and Erosion

In areas with high road densities, steep slopes, and unstable soils—which occur with some frequency in trout and salmon habitat in Idaho, the Cascades, and Sierra Nevada—roads combine with dams, overfishing, and impacts from logging as an important cause of population declines. A Montana study of watersheds in threatened bull trout habitat found that healthy trout populations correlated most strongly with an absence of roads.[74] Many scientists now recognize that the healthiest remaining bull trout populations exist in the least-disrupted watersheds.[75]

Studies of more than 1,400 landslides in the Boise and Clearwater national forests in Idaho found that 88 percent were road related. Elsewhere, on Idaho's South Fork of the Salmon River, 80 of 89 slides were associated with roads.[76] Research on the nearby Payette National Forest also linked levels of fine sediments in streams to road densities.[77]

Researchers have established that "roads are the primary cause of accelerated erosion and sedimentation"[78] in watersheds and that average surface erosion rates increased 220 times on lands with timber roads compared to undisturbed forest slopes.[79]

Since many freshwater species—from aquatic invertebrates such as
stonefly and mayfly larvae to the trout and salmon who feed on them—
depend upon clear, cobbled substrates for some stage of their life cycles,
a sediment-clogged stretch of river can lead to severe declines in species'
vigor and abundance.

Barriers to Fish Migration

Problems caused by poorly maintained stream crossings and road culverts
are far from hypothetical. The Forest Service has identified a massive maintenance and reconstruction backlog on national forest roads.[80] Poorly maintained culverts and their accompanying impacts on water quality and stream
connectivity are consistently one of the largest items of concern for poorly
maintained roads. A study in Idaho determined that nearly 20 percent of
the significant road-related erosion problems involved malfunctioning or
poorly maintained culverts.[81] Another study asserted that *all* culverts that
are abandoned and not properly maintained will eventually fail.[82]

Paradoxically, unmaintained or hanging culverts have been implicated
in both species imperilment and species protection. Whereas the broken
connectivity of a stream channel can sever headwater areas from trout or
salmon populations attempting to migrate to historic spawning redds, on
occasion such isolation has also protected localized populations from
genetic dilution or competition from introduced species downstream.
Headwaters populations of westslope cutthroat trout in southwestern
Montana, for instance, include some of the few genetically pure strains
found anywhere. With introduced rainbow or Yellowstone cutthroat trout
living downstream, land managers attribute the headwater populations'
purity to hanging culverts and poorly maintained road crossings that have
prevented migration and interbreeding between the populations.[83]

Hydrologic Changes from Roads

On a naturally unroaded slope, water from rain or snowmelt percolates
into soil and gradually flows downhill. Moving through the air spaces in

Photo 3-3: Road surface erosion caused, in part, by the conversion of water from subsurface to surface flow.

uncompacted soil, this "sheet flow" of water causes little erosion and takes place steadily and slowly throughout the year. Springs and hillside wetlands often exist where subsurface water intersects a natural depression or shelf of bedrock and flows to the surface.

Road construction triggers multiple changes in the hydrology of a slope and converts gentle, subsurface flow into more rapid and concentrated runoff at the surface. The cutslope at the uphill edge of a road interrupts subsurface water and redirects it to roadside ditches, cross-road culverts or the road surface (photo 3-3). With roads converting the diffused sheet flow beneath the surface to a more concentrated pulse of surface water, roaded areas experience peak flows (i.e., seasonal runoff) characterized by higher volumes that crest more quickly.[84]

When combined with clear-cuts, roads produce significant long-term increases in both the magnitude and the duration of peak flows, essentially creating conditions more prone to flooding.[85] Higher peak flows also increase soil erosion and sediment loads carried into streams, rivers, and lakes.

In fitting testimony to the complexity of natural systems, roads not only contribute to the disruption of aquatic systems, but also unnaturally mix the flow of formerly distinct watersheds. By cutting across slopes and converting subsurface flow to surface runoff, some roads carry water originally destined for one watershed and channel it into neighboring drainages. Such road-generated transbasin diversions pale in comparison to intentional diversion projects in the Tennessee Valley, Colorado Front Range, or desert Southwest, but for small drainages high in a watershed or for spring-fed systems, even these minor shifts in runoff can seriously alter the local landscape and its residents. If a spring dries up because a road upslope diverts subsurface flow out of the drainage basin, then the community of animals and plants that once depended upon that oasis may be displaced or perish.

Implications of the Ecological Effects of Roads

An abundance of roads can carry obvious benefits to transportation and commerce, but the long-term ecological consequences may be slower to unfold. "Hyperfragmentation," which includes the combined effects of habitat loss and fragmentation on both terrestrial and aquatic ecosystems, may lead to ever more serious problems of water quality, diminished wildlife habitat, species imperilment, and biological impoverishment in the years ahead.[86] Furthermore, the effects of a road may extend for more than a mile from the road itself and the full impacts may not emerge for dozens of years.[87] In other words, our assessment of ecological conditions today may better reflect the activities and road densities from several decades ago than the true impacts of today's roads and landscape changes.[88]

Although a number of the effects of roads have likely not yet even emerged, we can apply what we know now to try to anticipate our future needs and values. For public lands with specific management directives, what we know about roads and their ecological effects ought to play an important role in agency decisions. The National Wildlife Refuge System, for example, is dedicated primarily to the conservation of fish, wildlife, and plants. Information about the ecological effects of roads should be relatively easy to incorporate into refuge plans to help managers meet their conservation objectives. Unfortunately, even on our public lands with the clearest mandates, the relevant science of roads can become subverted to local or political pressures.

Such pressures highlight the need for well-informed citizens to participate in public land decisions, many of which involve questions of roads and access. Whether to protect and restore salmon runs in the Pacific

Northwest or endangered crocodiles and panthers in Florida, how we manage road systems makes a dramatic difference. By engaging in the public decision-making process, citizens and conservationists can play an important role in determining how public lands will be managed and that we apply science appropriately.

Our understanding of the ecological effects of roads can also help shape specific management decisions. When presence effects of roads are the dominant problem, managers should work on road surface treatments, stream crossings, soil decompaction, or other habitat restoration measures. When use effects are the overriding problem, then simple road closures might suffice, as long as closures can be made effective over time. Where both use and presence effects cause problems—and often they do—then we can turn to full road removal projects such as those described in Chapter 7. In many cases what benefits the land, water, or wildlife most will also prove to be most economical in the long term.

Although we know enough already to make many ecologically informed and responsible decisions, our management of public lands will surely benefit from a deeper understanding of road impacts on aquatic systems in particular. Scientists may struggle to identify a specific road density, for example, that correlates to specific losses in salmon or trout habitat, but conscientious management policies would have us err on the side of caution in the presence of uncertainty. Ongoing research to identify the range of historic conditions can also help us determine how dramatic or acceptable road impacts may be in different areas.

You do not need to be a roads activist or a land manager struggling with access issues to care about public land roads. In time, it may take nothing more than a desire for clean drinking water from the tap to discover that these roads can affect us all.

Although we will turn more fully to values and identifying the public good in the chapters ahead, much of the debate over public land roads and motorized access also centers upon money and politics. From the halls of power in Washington, D.C., to rural county seats across the West, funding programs and political battles profoundly influence where bulldozers or wheels can turn open spaces into roaded places. Whether we are facing rebellious counties in Utah or pork-barrel politics in Congress, in order to engage road and motorized access issues effectively we will need to understand the existing political and financial structures.

Considering the many benefits and uses of a trans-
portation network across the National Forests, it is
difficult to understand why roads have been under
siege in recent years.

—U.S. Representative Larry Combest
(R-TX), May 1997

4 | The Cutting Edge: Money, Politics, and Access

A map on my wall shows the roads of the Roman Empire. For many years I was intrigued by these roads that radiated from Italy to reach lands as far away as England, Romania, Syria, and northern Africa. The Appian Way and other names echoed with history and set me thinking of worn cobblestones, red tiled roofs, and freshly baked pizza. More recently, I noticed a background of other names on the map—lead, iron, grain, timber—and I began to think about the motives for those ancient routes, and of the labor and expense of building and maintaining miles of cobblestone.

In many ways, I have come to public land roads over a similar path. National forest and park roads that once sounded scenic and free now ring with costs that I never imagined. Even relatively modest dirt or gravel roads through wildlife refuges and Bureau of Land Management (BLM) lands, I have learned, cost tens of thousands of dollars per construction mile. Simply to provide proper maintenance of the sprawling public lands road system would cost more than $10 billion.

For more than eight decades, the U.S. Congress and federal agencies have made it a priority to fund roadbuilding across national forests, into the heart of national parks, through wildlife refuges, and on BLM resource areas. The money flowed and we have the roads to show for it.

As a nation, we have made laws and empowered agencies for a road-building agenda that far surpasses that of any other culture known for such works, from the Romans and the Chaco to the Chinese and the Inca. In this one thing, to be sure, modern America reigns supreme.

From sweeping appropriations and transportation bills passed by Congress to programs that traded public forests for logging roads, the financing and politics of roads have often dictated the condition of our public domain lands. Determining whether these programs are well advised or misguided, profligate or frugal will help us shape road policy—and the condition of our public lands—as we roll into the decades ahead.

Federal Funding for Public Land Roads

For most government agencies, appropriations come as an annual challenge to win congressional funding for the coming year's projects and personnel. Agencies covet multiyear appropriations, since they can move ahead with large programs and not worry about an unreliable stream of funding. With the 1998 passage of the Transportation Equity Act for the Twenty-first Century (TEA-21), Congress established a regular schedule of appropriations for public land roads through 2003. TEA-21 is but the most recent and most comprehensive of a number of road-funding bills passed by Congress since 1916.

The Federal Lands Highway Program

Under the terms of TEA-21, Congress dedicated a total of $4.1 billion for road projects in the Federal Lands Highway Program.[1] Initiated in 1982, the Federal Lands Highway Program is designed to "serve recreational travel and tourism, protect and enhance natural resources, [and] provide sustained economic development in rural areas."[2] The program is a component of the Federal Highway Administration (FHWA), which coordinates with land management agencies to survey, plan, and construct roads on public lands.[3] For each year from 1999 to 2003, this program funds some 90,000 miles of "public lands highways" at $246 million per year.[4] Roads in national parks, public roads in wildlife refuges, 29,000 miles of national forest "highways," and roads on Indian reservations are all included as part of the program. National park roads and national parkways receive $165 million annually. Roads in national wildlife refuges—

long left out of large appropriation bills—receive $20 million per year starting in 1999.[5] With the exception of refuge roads (discussed later), funding priorities for the highway program include road planning, rehabilitation, and construction.

The Federal Lands Highway Program is designed to enable agencies to use the expertise of highway engineers and construction professionals in the FHWA, rather than filling land management agency rosters with the same. By contracting out major road projects, the National Park Service and Fish and Wildlife Service, especially, rely upon the FHWA to collect data, generate reports, and consult with land managers to plan construction, road standards, and other technical aspects of the road work. The program focuses primarily on paved routes, which represent a majority of the road miles only in the national parks. Consequently, the other agencies—and the Forest Service in particular, with some 400,000 miles of unpaved roads— still need to dedicate staff to road design and engineering.

Following construction, land management agencies can choose to pass authority for roads to the state or county. This creates a "public" road instead of an "administrative" road, and leads to higher maintenance standards and federal appropriations for public access.[6] This transference of ownership also explains, in part, why there are thousands of miles of road crossing federal lands that agencies do not calculate in their mileage totals (see Table 1-1).

National Park Roads

The total appropriation in TEA-21 for national park roads and national parkways adds up to $1 billion over the six years of the act's term. Though a massive sum, when it comes to actual roadwork in the parks, tens of millions of dollars pass quickly. In some cases, these national park roads are truly extraordinary monuments to highway engineering. National Park routes such as Glacier's Going-to-the-Sun, Appalachia's Blue Ridge and Skyline Parkways, Yosemite's Tioga Pass, or Rocky Mountain's Trail Ridge Road dazzle drivers with both scenic and engineering wonders. They can also be fabulously expensive. Officials expect a long-planned reconstruction of the cliff-hanging Going-to-the-Sun road in Montana's Glacier National Park to take up to ten years and cost from $70 million to $210 million for just 30 miles of pavement.

The Going-to-the-Sun project has already attracted its share of controversy. Starting in the mid-1990s, Glacier National Park studied a series of options for the road. Proposed choices ranged from replacing private auto traffic with a mass transit system to a piecemeal upgrade and repair. Ultimately, the stated alternatives pleased few. The original preferred alternative, the cheapest and fastest option, would close one half of the road, east or west of the Continental Divide, for two to three years of intensive construction, while maintaining access from the opposite side to the road's apex at Logan Pass. Local business leaders were piqued enough by the park's ideas that Montana's lone congressman organized a subcommittee hearing to scrutinize the Park Service's decision.[7] Subsequently, in 2000, Congress approved a $1 million appropriation for an advisory committee to reassess reconstruction options for the Going-to-the-Sun road. The advisory committee plans to make new recommendations to Glacier National Park, presumably for roadwork options that are more sensitive to the $1 million per day that Going-to-the-Sun–soaked tourists bring to the local chambers of commerce each summer.[8]

Alternative reconstruction options now under consideration include closing and working on just one lane at a time, working at night to keep the road open during the day, or working for brief periods that would close the road for just a few days at a time. With each of these choices, the road repair would stretch over the better part of a decade, nudging costs ever higher, and pinching park traffic for many years. With the final outcome still in doubt, what first appeared to be primarily an engineering challenge and financial commitment to reconstruct a historic road, now looms ever larger as a contentious political issue. In the meantime, the Going-to-the-Sun road continues to age.

National Wildlife Refuge Roads

With the passage of TEA-21, congressional attention and funding turned, for the first time, to roads on national wildlife refuges. Refuge roads in many places are characterized by their simplicity. Whereas the National Park Service from its inception has used a sizable cadre of road engineers and landscape architects to design and build technically or aesthetically impressive routes, the U.S. Fish and Wildlife Service still sends its staff to remote refuge headquarters that, in some cases, can require a long drive on dusty, rutted roads. To reach southwest Montana's Red Rock Lakes National Wildlife Refuge, staff and visitors need to cover some 40 miles of gravel road. In winter, the road to the refuge headquarters at Lakeview is only sporadically plowed and may be most easily traveled by snowmobile. For many of the refuges in Alaska, summer access is by air or water only.

Though such isolation and seeming neglect could have an effect on the morale of Fish and Wildlife Service employees, many refuge staff consider it in tune with their agency's mission: to conserve fish and wildlife species and their habitat. At the Izembek National Wildlife Refuge in Alaska, the Fish and Wildlife Service actively opposed a plan to build a road to the refuge, fearing it would degrade conditions for wildlife and habitat.[9] While some refuge personnel do clamor for better roads and services to attract visitors or improve management, a number of Fish and Wildlife Service employees have come to the agency specifically because they can focus on management tasks such as habitat protection and restoration, rather than constantly tending to tourists and the "visitor interface."

With the adverse ecological effects of roads well established, some might also question the propriety of funding millions of dollars worth of road work on refuge lands dedicated, essentially, to the conservation of biodiversity. Congress, in fact, might have found itself with something of a quandary in allocating money for refuge roads. How could it show support for an agency, its infrastructure and services, without undermining its very purpose by allocating money for more roads? The answer as it came in TEA-21 was twofold: offer a comparatively meager sum of money to refuge roads—the National Park Service received nearly ten times as much money for a road system of similar mileage—and stipulate that funds for refuge roads be used only for maintenance and improvement, not new construction.[10] (In defense of the appropriations to park roads, we should recall that national parks have ten times more paved road mileage than national wildlife refuges, handle far heavier visitor loads, and, in general, are more elaborately constructed.)

It remains to be seen how much the bureaucratic landscape will change due to programs such as the Fee Demonstration Project, discussed in the next chapter, that offer financial incentives when land managers attract more recreational tourists. To date, the national wildlife refuges continue to be the least visited, least funded, and, in most cases, the least well equipped with visitor services of the four main categories of public lands.[11]

Emergency Relief for Federally Owned Roads Program

Another funding stream that in recent years has proven to bear directly on the presence and condition of public land roads is the Emergency Relief for Federally Owned Roads (ERFO) program. Controlled, as well, by the FHWA, the ERFO program pays 100 percent of the repair costs for federally owned roads that are damaged by natural disasters or catastrophic failures (this does not include major highways and the interstate system, which are funded under separate appropriations). Under the terms of TEA-21, these emergency relief funds now have a permanent annual funding authority of $100 million; supplemental appropriations from Congress can add to this.[12]

One underutilized feature of ERFO money, pointed out by some conservationists, land managers, and restoration groups, is that emergency relief funds can be used for road removal and obliteration as well as for reconstruction.[13] By using ERFO funds for road obliteration and restoration work, some national forests and parks have turned toward progressive policies that might help avoid the mistakes of the past (see Chapter 7). As natural hazards experts like to point out, natural *hazards* don't become natural *disasters* until people—or in this case, their roads—get in the way. Using ERFO program funds judiciously to close roads and restore road-damaged landscapes can serve as a sound complement to the reconstruction of damaged roads in places where they remain essential.

Bureau of Land Management Roads

Roads and management of many BLM lands come with relatively low public interest, uncoordinated planning, and a certain degree of congressional disregard. The appropriated road construction budget for the BLM through its first fifty years never exceeded $15 million annually, and only since 1998 has it included a line item for "road maintenance."[14] With the largest landbase of any federal agency and a landscape that is caricatured, at least, as barren, the resource areas of the BLM have a problem of both reputation and geography. A good number of BLM areas feature landscapes of sagebrush or alkali flats, which can lead officials to question why they should devote federal dollars to improve roads that may never attract the interest of tourists and may only benefit a handful of locals who are adequately served by existing roads. To be sure, the choice between funding road projects in scenic parks, forests, or wildlife refuges, versus funding projects on little-known arid BLM lands consistently leads to a funding bias away from the latter.

This does not mean that there are not enough roads on BLM lands. As we have already seen, there are, in fact, more than 80,000 miles of road currently in place. But a poorly planned and disorganized road network, some of which predates the existence of the BLM, has helped to create a road system on which it is very difficult to control motorized access.

Until public or political pressures come to bear more pointedly at the BLM's overall road system—as they have in recent years for national forest roads—it will remain difficult to know for certain how many roads cross BLM lands, let alone their condition, impacts, and future needs.

National Forest Road Programs

Southeast Alaska's Etolin Island was one of the last places I expected to learn about agency road programs, but it was there, while visiting an active timber sale, that I first saw the effect of swapping standing forests for a forest road system. The fresh cut of a road on Etolin Island made the connection between money and roads very real and clear.

Although the Tongass National Forest is known for both prodigious timber sales and vast wildlands, Etolin Island seemed more prone toward the latter. Gouged by recent glaciers and whittled further by tidal currents, Etolin Island's coastline is deeply incised by fjords. Tendrils of land barely bind the island together north and south. From the Zimovia Strait to the east, Etolin rises steeply into forested slopes and alpine peaks to form an unlikely classroom to discover the significance of timber road financing programs.

In fact, the Zimovia Strait seems picture perfect for a journey by sea kayak. Deep emerald waters wend their way between sheltering islands capped with western hemlock, Sitka spruce, and Alaska cedar. If you time your passage just right, the current can nudge you along at three or four knots—doubling your paddling speed. It's a place where you can travel for days without seeing, hearing, or thinking about a car or a road, turning instead to notice the peering eyes of a harbor seal, the grateful rush of air from a porpoise, or the soothing drizzle of rainforest afternoons.

Etolin Island lies just across the Zimovia Strait from Wrangell, a place frequented by John Muir in his *Travels in Alaska,* and in the past half-century, one of Southeast Alaska's most devout timber towns. While the south half of Etolin is designated wilderness, the rest of the island has paid for its proximity to Wrangell with a number of timber sales. With these sales, more often than not, came roads.

I first paddled across the Zimovia Strait to Etolin Island in 1994, while teaching a field-based college course, Resource Issues of Southeast Alaska. Many of the roads we came upon then were freshly built, with the loggers and roadbuilders still on-site. For the first time in several weeks, we saw pickup trucks, log haulers, bulldozers, and cars, all roaming the graded roads of the island. Miles from the mainland and with no bridge connecting to a road system, the vehicles on Etolin Island seemed incongruous and isolated. It was impossible not to wonder, "What are they doing here?"

The answer, it turned out, had a lot to do with the way the Forest Service packaged and financed road construction with timber sales, a system known as purchaser road credits. While logging methods, transportation costs and other factors have each played a part in linking the timber industry with thousands of miles of road on national forests, purchaser road credits were unique in giving logging operations a crisp financial incentive to build more roads.

Forests for Roads: Purchaser Road Credits

Though purchaser road credits are officially defunct, due to a brief terminating clause in a 1999 appropriations bill, they continue to play a key role in the expansive forest road system. For thirty-five years, timber companies built tens of thousands of road miles on national forests using purchaser credits. Some observers believe the system continues, changed primarily in name.

Purchaser credits effectively minimized the cash transacted for logging public forests, added a profit margin for any road construction, then left the roads behind—along with maintenance or upkeep requirements—on the cutover lands. In places where timber was of marginal value or difficult to access, purchaser road credits may have been a prevailing reason national forest timber was sold and cut at all.

The concept for purchaser road credits was relatively simple. Before offering a timber sale for public bid, the Forest Service estimated the cost of any road construction planned for the project. The agency contracted the road construction out to the timber purchaser, then gave the purchaser a discount off the timber sale price for building the roads. The purchaser then built the roads and deducted the costs, as estimated in advance by the Forest Service, from the sale price and cash transacted for the timber.[15]

The Forest Service liked the purchaser road credit system for a number of reasons. First, road construction projects were completed by the company purchasing the timber, thereby reducing demands on agency personnel and resources. Roads and timber sales could be lumped together for environmental analysis and processed for a unified public review.

Next, the purchaser credit system gave the Forest Service a supervisory role over road construction, requiring that timber purchasers gain "acceptance" for the roads they had constructed before they would receive their credit. In practice, this meant that the agency would verify that road work met the terms of the sale contract, both upon completion of the road construction itself and at the conclusion of all harvest activities ("post-haul acceptance"). If the timber purchaser failed this road assessment and refused to come into compliance, then the Forest Service could keep a 10 percent performance bond that was posted at the beginning of the sale.[16]

The purchaser credit system also gave the agency a clear accounting system: upon completion of a timber sale, the Forest Service recorded the amount of the purchaser credit. In this manner, it could track the amount of road construction allocated for each timber sale, though notably, the agency did not tally actual construction costs incurred by the purchaser.

Finally, when the sale was completed the roads remained behind, making it easy for the Forest Service to reenter an area later for subsequent management or timber harvest. The Forest Service considered most of these leftover logging roads as assets—for recreation, fire fighting, further logging, or other access—so the purchaser road credit system seemed like a good deal. The agency essentially traded national forest trees for a forest transportation system.

Timber corporations benefited from purchaser road credits too. For timber sales that included road construction or reconstruction, the Forest Service factored in a 10 percent profit margin for companies and a 12 percent margin for overhead costs as part of the purchaser road credit. Roads were often cheaper for the purchaser to build than the Forest Service estimated, because of the agency's high overhead and administrative cost requirements.[17] With a profit margin already worked into the road construction calculus, each mile of road built for a timber sale could bring with it thousands of dollars of revenue beyond the value of the wood. The incentive to construct roads grew further if a contracted timber company managed to build roads more efficiently than the Forest Service had estimated, since the company would pocket the difference and the agency did not keep track of the outcome.

Road credits could also be shifted from one timber sale to another on the same forest, so timber purchasers could partially finance a marginal sale with another's largesse, allowing companies to cut and sell more timber and create economies of scale with multiple timber sales.

Finally, in difficult or remote terrain such as that of Etolin Island, road construction costs are so high—a million dollars or more per mile—that timber purchaser road credits could reduce the sale price of the timber to a bare minimum, while the standard 10 percent profit margin could climb to millions of dollars in its own right. As we were told by the timber foreman there at the time, "the money is in the roads, not the timber. If it weren't for the purchaser credits, we wouldn't be here."[18]

A few years ago, the last time I visited Etolin Island, the dozen or so miles of road remained in place from the 1994 timber sale, but there was not a car in sight. Determined motorists would need to haul their vehicles by boat from Wrangell to use any of Etolin's roads.

Even in their prime, purchaser credits were not the only way to finance roads on national forests (road miles built by purchaser credit averaged about 80 percent in the 1990s).[19] Small timber purchasers, for example, typically lacked the expertise or capital necessary to build roads and opted instead for a program that kept road construction responsibilities with the Forest Service, who then assessed costs back to the purchaser. Small companies, in this way, had few incentives beyond the value of the timber itself. Since most timber sales go to large corporations, this "Purchaser Election Program" has rarely represented more than 5 percent of the road-building docket.[20] The final portion of forest road development funds, roughly 15 percent, came from annual appropriations from Congress for general recreational roads and other nontimber road construction.

Purchaser Road Credits—Reconstructed

Since 1999, the Forest Service has factored logging road construction costs slightly differently, using a formula long ago adopted by the BLM. Although BLM lands are stereotypically arid and treeless, the agency does manage more than 2 million acres of valuable forestlands in southern Oregon. The O & C Lands, named after a previous owner—the Oregon and California Railroad Company—who forfeited them in 1915, not only generate millions of dollars in revenue each year for the BLM, they also include more than 18,000 miles of logging roads.[21]

The Forest Service, like the BLM, now requires timber purchasers to recover the cost of road construction as part of the price they pay for the timber sale. Prior to a sale, planners will project how much road construction will cost, based either on the Forest Service's cost book ("residual value appraisal") or on the past costs of similar construction in nearby areas ("evidence appraisal").[22] The agency then subtracts this amount from its value estimates for the timber and sets the remainder as the opening bid price for the sale. This results in reduced timber sale prices, since the expected cost of the road construction is deducted in advance from the timber's value.

However real or imagined their differences, the old purchaser road credit system on national forests drew far more criticism as an industrial subsidy than its counterpart formula used by the BLM. In 1997, fiscal conservatives in Washington, D.C., joined environmentalists to form the Green Scissors Coalition, a group dedicated to reducing government waste and enhancing environmental protection. Moved in part by this bipartisan push, the Congressional Subcommittee on Forestry, Resource Conservation, and Research that year held a hearing on "Financing of Roads in the National Forests."[23] The vast majority of the hearing focused upon a study conducted by the Federal Budget Consulting Group and Price Waterhouse LLP—a study commissioned and paid for by the American Forest and Paper Association—that concluded that purchaser road credits did not represent a subsidy to timber corporations. Despite the study's findings, one disgruntled congressman testified, "The bottom line is road construction in our National Forest System is a burden to the U.S. taxpayer."[24]

Although Congress chopped the purchaser road credit program largely due to public criticism of its generosity to corporate timber buyers, whatever bonuses existed with the original still remain with the newly adopted BLM system. Road cost estimates are still provided by the Forest Service in the exact same manner. The profit margin and allowances for overhead and cheaper, more efficient construction by private companies still exist, but now timber buyers get the road costs discounted up front, before companies expend time or money for construction. One agency timber planner told me, "If I were a timber purchaser, I would love the new system."[25]

Payments in Lieu of Taxes to Counties

Well-loved it may be, but the new road financing plan also outraged county and local officials across the West. For years, these local governments received a 25 percent cut of timber sale and other revenues made from federal lands located within a county's borders. These "payments-in-lieu-of-taxes," or PILTs, were intended to help compensate local governments for the missing tax base created by large chunks of federal land that dominate many Western counties.

With the revamped policy for roads and timber sales in national forests, county governments suddenly had their PILTs decreased significantly. Under the old purchaser road credit system, if timber sold for $1 million, the county recieved 25 percent of that million, even if the cash transaction from the timber buyer to the Forest Service was reduced by $300,000 worth of road-building credits. With the new system and the cost of the road construction deducted first, the counties were to recieve just 25 percent of the $700,000 that actually changed hands.

Counties across the West clamored angrily against the abrupt loss of PILT money due to purchaser road credit reform. In fiscal year 2000 under the original system, PILTs brought in more than $194 million to local governments. Counties were not at all eager to see the money fade away. As a result, less than a year after the change in purchaser road credits, Congress passed the Secure Rural Schools and Community Self-Determination Act of 2000 to grant relief. Consequently, counties can choose to receive federal funds each year at the traditional rate of 25 percent of timber receipts, or receive the average amount from the three highest 25 percent payments they received between 1986 and 1999.[26] Thus Congress and the Clinton administration appeared to decouple PILT money from resource extraction—a step long advocated by conservationists who viewed PILTs as an incentive for locals to support extractive industry—and counties won a steady flow of federal cash. Counties, too, might now join the chorus of those who "love the new system."

Miners' Legacy: Revised Statute 2477

Capitol Reef National Park protects a dazzling wedge of land centered around the bulging monocline of the Waterpocket Fold. This petrified wave of sandstone runs for 100 miles across southern Utah, from the heights of Thousand Lake Mountain to the Colorado River. On my first trip to Capitol Reef, my brother and I hiked for two days along a dry riverbed. Wingate sandstone cliffs framed the sky into a narrow sliver of blue. We scarcely noticed the heat or lack of water. What we noticed was silence. Once, taking a break on a rock, we heard a whoosh of air and looked up to find a raven breaking the quiet with its wingbeats, hundreds of feet above us.

On the morning of February 13, 1996, a Garfield County road crew rolled into Capitol Reef, edged off the road, and carved out a piece of hillside. Citing the right to conduct road maintenance on a historic right-of-way, Garfield County officials rumbled their way into a controversy that continues to stir southern Utah and beyond. In response to the road "improvements," or what other observers termed an act of county-sponsored vandalism, Capitol Reef officials chose not to contest the county's right to conduct road work in the national park, but rather focused their case on the legal processes that the county failed to follow.[27] Far from an unwitting procedural oversight, however, the conflict between Garfield County and the National Park Service flashed as one of many sparks that still shower public lands in several western states.

Even before the road grader sputtered to life and gouged the hillside in Capitol Reef, officials in Garfield County and elsewhere justified such roadwork by citing a single sentence in a 130-year-old mining law. That clause, known as Revised Statute 2477 (RS 2477) from the Lode Mining Act of 1866 states simply, "The right of way for the construction of highways over public lands, not reserved for public uses, is hereby granted."[28] Although the law dates back to homesteading years when the federal government gave land away to induce settlers to move west, and despite its repeal in 1976, RS 2477 continues to generate contentious "grandfathered" assertions of historic roads on many public lands.[29] Even after Clinton administration efforts to redefine the rule, and court rulings that clarified its scope, RS 2477 remains one of the most contentious and potentially far-reaching weapons wielded by proponents of wide-open motorized access.[30] In areas where RS 2477 rights-of-way prove valid, wilderness designations or administrative actions that restrict motorized use may be broadly curtailed.

Utah, along with Alaska and other western states such as Idaho, Montana, and Nevada, has seen a surge of activity for RS 2477. In southern Utah alone, counties have made more than 5,000 right-of-way assertions using RS 2477.[31] Alaskan claims number more than 1,700, including routes in Denali, Gates of the Arctic, and Wrangell–St. Elias National Parks and Preserve.[32]

A good deal of the controversy centers upon a 1988 Bush administration policy that triggered RS 2477 assertions on routes that had never
before posed as highways. President Bush's interior secretary Donald
Hodel gave a generous definition of what could qualify as a preexisting
right-of-way. Hodel declared that routes could pass RS 2477 muster
without any evidence of their historic use beyond a statement by "an
appropriate public body that the highway was and still is considered a
public highway."[33] Hodel further established that even "the passage of
vehicles by users over time may equal actual construction."[34] County
officials across the West have proceeded to assert highway rights to
places that received a handful of passes by dirtbike or Jeep prior to
1976. If historic "highway" use predated the designation of a national
park, refuge, or wilderness area, promoters of motorized access could
make RS 2477 assertions even in these protected lands, as long as the
"highway" existed on public lands not otherwise reserved at the time
and had some form of construction, maintenance, or use.[35] Hodel's policy also implied that foot or animal trails could qualify as RS 2477
"highways."[36]

The political tug-of-war over RS 2477 has waxed and waned in the
years since the Hodel policy. In August 1994, the *Federal Register* described
the whole mess with the clarity of an arid Utah afternoon: "This controversy stems in large part from the lack of specificity in the statutory language, which has helped create unrealistic expectations in interested local
and State governments, environmental and wilderness protection groups,
and other Federal land users."[37]

The Clinton administration prepared a rule for the *Federal Register* that
might have settled the question and changed key terms such as the standard to be used for "highway construction," but the Republican-led 104th
Congress tacked a rider on a bill that prohibited final rulemaking on RS
2477 until further congressional action.[38]

Although the moratorium on rule making continues at the time of this
writing, in 1997 both the Department of the Interior and the Department
of Agriculture halted further RS 2477 activity and Interior Secretary Babbitt revoked the Hodel policy.[39] Such administrative actions are only as
durable as the administrations themselves, so with a new Bush administration many observers expect new directives. Many legislators acknowledge, meanwhile, that most RS 2477 assertions do not come out of a sin-
cere (or historic) need for access, but the law remains a potential tool to

undermine wilderness designations and promote local property rights in rural counties in the West.

Evaluating Roads

Although the debate over public land roads often centers around money or the environment, we rarely bear down to ask the fundamental question of what it actually costs us, as a nation, to maintain and perpetuate our current system of public land roads. Is it even possible to determine a monetary figure that accurately represents the true cost of hundreds of thousands of miles of road? To evaluate roads realistically, we need to weigh the benefits of the road system—as it expands or contracts—with its liabilities.

Replacement Cost

One way to estimate the value of the road system is by gauging its replacement cost. According to the agencies' best estimates, cited earlier, the combined total for road mileage on public lands is about 550,000 miles. Of these, construction cost per mile varies widely. Many of the 60,000 miles of unclassified roads in national forests were never constructed and were simply created by repeated use. These roads cost the public nothing to build, but there are environmental and eventual treatment costs. Most of the road miles in national parks, on the other hand, are paved, highly engineered routes built both to accommodate heavy use and to appeal to visitors' aesthetic sensibilities. The relatively modest graded dirt or gravel roads on national forest, BLM, and national wildlife refuge lands vary considerably in cost—from $20,000 per constructed mile to $1 million or more. Extraordinary national park roads, such as Glacier's Going-to-the-Sun discussed earlier, might cost $7 million per mile.[40] At a reasonable average construction cost of $85,000 per road mile for all public land roads, the total replacement value would come in at approximately $50 billion.[41]

If the worth of the road system is measured by its replacement cost, the road system on our public lands is as valuable as its proponents have been saying all along. While a certain number of the roads we have built do serve us well and provide a valuable asset to society, the picture is not as simple as some might wish.

The first weakness in the economic argument for the value of our road system is that by most anyone's reckoning we now have far more roads than we can use. The replacement value may be $50 billion, but many of these roads we would never *want* to replace. Like an unwanted gift, just because something might be costly to replace does not mean that it has value for us. The large ceramic cow-shaped cookie jar that once stood on our kitchen counter must have cost someone $50, but we gladly gave it away simply to restore some open space to the kitchen. It is hard to know how many public land roads are ceramic cows, but a detailed inventory in almost any logged-over watershed in national forests will reveal roads stacked upon roads, many of them deteriorating, partially overgrown, and no longer serving any public or commercial benefit. In fact, the Forest Service estimates that 80 percent of the use of its system roads occurs on just 20 percent of the road miles.[42] Far from being useful or even neutral to our lives, many of the remaining roads lie inaccessible and neglected, and actually cause steady harm to the water quality, fisheries, and wildlife habitat that many of us depend upon and cherish.

Furthermore, with roads on many developed national forest lands already essentially ubiquitous, we can scarcely consider a new logging road a valuable addition to the accessibility of these lands. Motorized and nonmotorized forest users both show a recreational preference for areas with low road densities. A 1996 Forest Service report identified nonmotorized recreational opportunities as the category where demand would most exceed supply in the future.[43]

Maintenance Costs

Even where forest roads are identified for maintenance or management, they present a major underattended drain on agency finances. In recent years, the Forest Service has estimated a maintenance and reconstruction backlog from $8 to $10 billion on its road system.[44] In a 1997 planning document, the Forest Service noted, "[T]he backlog on arterial and collector roads alone is estimated to be over $10 billion, due to their age (three-fourths are over 50 years old) and their lack of adequate regular maintenance."[45] What falls between the lines of this agency confession is the fact that arterial and collector roads comprise only 26 percent of the road mileage on national forests.[46] The hundreds of thousands of miles of "local" forest roads were built to an inferior standard initially and are typically in far worse shape than the arterial and collector roads. In other words, the agency's oft-quoted $8 to $10 billion road maintenance backlog comes from an estimate of only the finest one-fourth of national forest roads.

The National Park Service, too, has a road system that is aging rapidly and not always serving the public well. Many of these park roads were designed to handle traffic volumes far beneath current levels. In a few parks, now, planners have recognized that their road systems can no longer accommodate increasing numbers of visitors. Planners have turned instead to shuttle bus systems or converting roads to rail, pedestrian, and bicycle routes.[47] The key point in many popular parks today is that existing or expanded road networks simply will not provide the experiences or the access sought by park visitors.

At the height of the tourist season, motorists in national parks from Maine's Acadia to Arizona's Grand Canyon can find themselves in bumper-to-bumper traffic or overstuffed parking lots. While more or wider roads in these places could accommodate more visitors for a short time, these developments would deeply erode the very experiences most park visitors seek, such as discovering natural beauty, seeing wildlife, and sampling the sights, sounds, and scents of America's mountains, coasts, forests, and canyons.

On the National Wildlife Refuge System, refuge administrators expect to spend $100 million by 2003 simply to "extend the service life" of existing roads and make them safer by resurfacing, restoration, and rehabilitation.[48]

Even closed roads grow old at a price. The Forest Service estimates annual maintenance costs that range up to $16,000 per mile of aging road.[49] For new roads, the agency estimates average maintenance costs of $1,500 per year.[50] Even at that rate, maintenance costs of the constructed national forest road system would exceed $500 million annually.[51] National forest ranger districts in the northern Rockies (Montana, Idaho, and eastern Washington) report that the cost of replacing vandalized gates, earth berms, guard rails, and other road closure devices averages $1,500 to $10,000 each year.[52] Additional costs from closed road systems include noxious weed treatments—which some land managers point to as their most time-consuming duty—and law enforcement patrols, which are usually severely understaffed and sparsely funded.

Environmental and Amenity Costs

Though Chapter 3 details many of the ecological effects of roads, economists have also tried to translate these impacts into monetary terms. Road-kill, for example, obviously costs animals their lives—or in selected cases, jeopardizes the welfare of populations, species, and communities—but it also takes an economic toll. One study in Utah estimated the annual cost of vehicle–deer collisions on all roads at $7.8 million, calculating both vehicle damage and a value for each deer killed.[53] Considering that nationwide more than 538,000 deer die from vehicle collisions every year, the economic loss from roadkilled deer tops $1.3 billion annually.[54]

Though placing monetary value on animals' lives or habitat seems ethically questionable, if we devoted ourselves to such efforts we could apply similar economic assessments to roadkill and reduced viability for grizzly bears, wolves, Florida panthers, and other imperiled species on whom we have spent millions of dollars in recent years to try to stabilize or recover populations. When recovery costs add up to tens of thousands of dollars per individual of these endangered species, we squander a substantial amount of cash each time an animal dies directly or indirectly because of roads. Relocation and recovery programs might prove much more effective if we simultaneously—or first—devoted funds to improve habitat by removing roads.

Roads can translate into very real financial losses when it comes to protecting water supplies for drinking, recreation, or fisheries. The notion of setting aside land to assure a clean and reliable supply of water dates back at least as far as the first charter for the national forest reserves in 1897.[55] Safe and reliable sources of water remain critical to human health and welfare, so the commitment to protect known surface water resources is of paramount—and virtually priceless—concern to many city officials.

The City of Seattle recently dedicated $90 million to a restoration program that will focus on road removal and habitat improvements (in response to logging impacts) in one of its municipal watersheds.[56] Seattle leaders determined that the multimillion dollar Cedar River watershed restoration effort made fiscal sense because it spared the capital costs of a massive filtration system or looking for new water sources in the future. The Cedar River currently provides water to 1.3 million people in greater Seattle, and over the next fifty years work in the watershed will remove approximately 38 percent of its roads. The program was supported overwhelmingly by the area's water consumers, who rallied around the expanded restoration program and slightly higher utility bills rather than letting a watershed logging plan foot the bill.[57]

From Bennington, Vermont, to Walla Walla, Washington, other cities that rely upon surface water for municipal drinking supplies have carefully staked out unroaded watersheds to protect a lasting supply of clean water. For years, Boulder, Colorado, has hired local cross-country runners to patrol the city's source of drinking water in a roadless watershed, keeping motorized and even pedestrian trespassers—and potential contaminants—away.

Recreational values present less of a life-or-death matter than clean drinking water, but they too provide good fodder for economists. Economists look at revenues generated from relevant recreational activities to get some sense of the recreational value of clean, clear water. Swimming, fishing, and nonmotorized boating are three types of recreation that traditionally rely upon clean water. According to the U.S. Census Bureau, fishing by itself contributes more than $37.8 million to local, state, and national economies every year.[58] Not all of this recreation takes place on federal public lands, nor does the water quality depend solely upon the presence or absence of roads, but if even a small portion of the recreational dollars related to roads on public lands, then the sum would still be substantial.

For fish dependent upon cold, clear waters for reproduction, such as trout or salmon, habitat modification from roads (and the oft-accompanying logging) is one of the most-cited causes of population declines. The commercial fishery for Pacific salmon, a $612 million industry in the United States in 1990 that by 1997 had dwindled to $270 million, has suffered directly from the roading of public lands.[59] Though dams on major rivers such as the Snake and Columbia have emerged as the primary culprits for the collapse of salmon populations in the Lower 48 in recent decades, and numbers have been further diminished by heavy commercial fishing harvests, another important reason for the decline is the destruction of spawning habitat in headwater streams due to roads and logging. Of the remaining healthy stocks of Pacific salmon in the Columbia River basin, most return to unroaded or sparsely roaded headwater streams to spawn.[60]

Road Benefits

Of the thousands of road miles that land management agencies planned and constructed, some portion do in fact remain useful, valuable, and worth their impacts. People do use roads, and quite a few people enjoy roads quite a lot. In a classic statement of economics, the problem with public land roads is not that they are no longer valuable, but that the supply of roads now far exceeds the demand. We have already roaded our public lands so thoroughly, the added recreational or access value of many new roads is effectively zero—or worse.

Roads for Recreational Access

Recreational use surveys of the national forests consistently find that "driving for pleasure" ranks first, outpacing fishing, skiing, hunting, hiking, camping, and picnicking.[61] On BLM lands, "driving for pleasure" checks in a solid third place behind "trail-related activities" and "educational opportunities" (i.e., ecotourism and field-based education).[62] Whether for berry picking or bird watching, Americans use public land roads.

As motorized recreation groups are quick to point out, even backpackers and wilderness advocates typically rely upon roads to access backcountry areas where vehicles are prohibited. Whether this illuminates a fundamental hypocrisy or not, we should note that even the most strident antiroads campaigns are not trying to rid the public lands of all roads. In its most common form, activism focused upon roads seeks to identify the routes that provide the most important public benefits—and to manage and maintain these routes accordingly—while also determining which roads cause the most severe damage, with little or no public value.

In truth, many road management decisions deserve little controversy. Where roads are popular and well-maintained and cause relatively few impacts, very few people will call for their removal. Conversely, where roads cause damage and provide little or no public benefits, land managers should be able to find support to eliminate them. On national forest and BLM lands in particular, the majority of low-standard roads fit this latter category. Of course, the most pressing task is simply to examine roads case by case to evaluate their relative merits and costs. Decisions will not always come easily, especially for those roads that are both popular and destructive, but the public and our public lands will both benefit from the effort.

Roads and Fires

When it comes to roads, one of the most heated points of debate, literally, focuses upon the relationship between roads and wildfires. Even as I write, in late August in Missoula, Montana, the air around town is thick from the worst wildfire season in more than fifty years. More than 650,000 acres of western Montana have already burned, and we may have another month to go before autumn snows quench the flames. The local air is thick not just from smoke, but also from the rhetoric that spirals from the flames. The timber industry and opportunistic politicians point to the rampant fires and holler angrily that we have left our forests to ruin by limiting road access and leaving old trees to burn in the forests. If only we had been vigilant these past few years, they claim, we could have thinned the forests, milled the timber, and made a tidy profit for local enterprises. Further, we would save our citizens the anguish of fleeing homes destined to burn and spare the costs of the $1 billion war we are waging against the fires.[63]

It is no easy thing to watch a cluster of homes or a nearby mountainside seethe with flame and dwindle to charred remains. For many of us who live here, the response to fire is visceral. If land management policies or politics are to blame, we might justifiably react with anger; the cost in property and human toil and long-cherished forests is simply too great to overlook or quickly forgive.[64] But what, in fact, causes such fire? Would more roads, more open roads, or more road-based logging and forest "thinning" have prevented or reduced this year's rush of flames?

In many respects, the fire season came as no surprise. Winter snowpack across the region averaged well below normal, and the water content of that snowpack was lower still. Spring broke hot and dry. June and July were among the hottest and driest on record in many places. Mix a hot dry year into decades of fire suppression and the recipe pointed toward a big fire year. Fire experts agreed, well in advance of the blazes, that this year was likely to burn.

If roads and fires did not mix well, then we would expect most large fires to burn in roadless lands. Similarly, if roads served a critical function in stifling fires, then most fires in roaded areas would be quickly extinguished. Time and again, both of these scenarios have failed.

Despite cries for more road access and more logging in the name of fire suppression, Montana's fires this year burned more in roaded, logged-over lands than they did in roadless, relatively unmanaged forests.[65] In fact, across the western United States, 62 percent of the area burned by fires in 2000 was in roaded national forest land, or took place on other types of ownership. Fires actually burned more non-forested lands and grasslands than aging or unroaded forest areas.[66] The season's largest fire in Montana, the Mussigbrod-Valley Complex, included great swaths of clear-cut forests and logging roads in the Bitterroot National Forest that had its logging program famously critiqued in a 1971 report calling for large-scale reform of forest practices.[67] One study of the fires of 2000 even determined that the fires burned hottest where road densities were highest.[68]

Roads can and do play a major role at times in fighting fires, but so do they provide access for humans to start fires. On forest lands across the nation, most fires—approximately 85 percent—start from human cause and not lightning.[69] The vast majority of human-caused fires, in turn, start from or near roads. Many people have focused on the idea that fighting fires is more difficult in the absence of roads, but this overlooks research dating back more than fifty years that demonstrates a dramatic link between roads and fire starts. One study of three national forests in California determined that 78 percent of all fires started within 265 feet of a road.[70] An interagency study found that three-quarters of all fires in national forests in California occurred within 10 feet of a road's edge.[71]

In 1999, the U.S. Forest Service gave the following ambivalent assessment of roads and fire: "Roads provide access for fire suppression forces and equipment and for human-caused fire. Road development often increases the risk of human-caused fires by increasing exposure of fuels to human activities. Human-caused fires occur frequently in areas served by roads; however, these fires are sometimes more easily suppressed because of the road access." The report also noted that, "The use of aerially delivered fire fighters into unroaded areas of [national forest] lands is often as effective as conventional fire truck suppression in roaded areas."[72]

The Forest Service makes it clear that a lack of access is not the issue: "With an existing road system estimated at 373,000 miles [sic], a variation of a few hundred miles would not have an appreciable effect on initial fire suppression effectiveness."[73] To sum, more roads and more logging would be no guarantee of fewer or more easily extinguished fires and, more often than not, road-based activities actually cause the fires.

Local Economies' Dependence upon Roads

Small towns in the West are often surrounded by public lands, which for decades provided the bulk of the revenues for local economies. Whether from mining, timber harvest and milling, grazing, or recreation, these places became resource dependent, and thereby road dependent, to a degree that in many cases has proven debilitating and disastrous. Towns bolstered for years by one or two lucrative industries quickly fall into decline when mills mechanize and lay off workers, or when mines move abroad to capitalize on cheap labor and lax regulations. Lacking diversified economic bases, towns that once swaggered in wealth may stagger to collapse.

Although the easy, angry response to this decline in many places is to point at environmental laws and the environmentalists who use them, more often than not the change has resulted from corporations looking for ever-greater profits, or from a simple exhaustion of the resource. Closed roads represent one of the most vivid local reminders of economic change—an association that leads many residents to view road closures with fear and loathing. While sweeping economic changes have occurred in the past in the classic boom–bust cycle common to oil, timber, and mining towns, the consequences of economic and social disruptions are very real and very painful, especially at the local level. In the corporate headquarters or broader levels of society where decisions form, the anguish of a local or regional bust is largely dispersed and negligable.

The misalignment of cause and effect leads to a certain amount of conflict: locals who find themselves out of work or in a slumping economy look for someone to blame—usually the government, individual, or conservation group that gave voice to the changing view of society—while those who are more distant might regret any suffering that comes to the faltering towns, but hearken ultimately to the long-term view of improved conditions for all. It is a conflict summed up almost tenderly by author Barry Lopez:

> In the part of the country where I live, thousands of men are now asking themselves what jobs they will have—for they can see the handwriting on the wall—when they are told they cannot cut down the last trees and that what little replanting they've done—if it actually works—will not produce enough timber soon enough to ensure their jobs.
>
> The frustration of these men, who are my neighbors, is a frustration that I am not deeply sympathetic to—their employers have behaved like wastrels, and they have known for years that this was coming. But in another way I am sympathetic, for these men are trying to live out an American nightmare which our system of schools and our voices of government never told them

was ill-founded. There is not the raw material in the woods, or beyond, to make all of us rich. And in striving for it, we will only make ourselves, all of us, poor.[74]

Interestingly, many of the communities that are most vocal about keeping public land roads open and available would benefit most from a concerted road removal program.

Road Removal

We can no longer justify massive roadbuilding and logging campaigns in our nation's forests, the national parks are saturated already by development and tourism, and on the remaining public lands agencies are struggling to meet the laws and mission statements intended to guide them.

There may be relief in the roads themselves—not for the prospect of rekindling their traffic in logs or ore as some still advocate, nor by their further grading and paving for tourists, but rather in their removal. Road removal may yet emerge as the shimmering thread that stitches together this gap between local economies and a changing society.

Road removal, like road construction, costs money. But unlike the incremental negative value new roads add to most public lands, road removal can create positive values. By bringing road removal programs into the communities that have been hardest hit by the changing values of public land use, we might actually recharge these local economies. Along with the wages paid for the initial work of heavy machinery and restoration that comes with road removal, there is also the long-term prospect of recovery for surrounding lands and waters.

Economic studies of central Idaho forestlands show that a modest road removal program could contribute $69 million to the regional economy.[75] By converting the objectives of heavy equipment operators, biologists, engineers, and timber crews from road building and timber harvest to road removing and restoration, the same people who have been watching their future grow dim could be retrained and put to work in this new direction. Such a shift in just a portion of the northern Rockies would produce approximately 1,500 high-paying jobs, but would also lead to improvements in the long-term "economics of quality" that people increasingly recognize as a reason to live near public lands.[76]

Whereas for decades we have been battered into thinking that a healthy economy comes at the expense of a healthy environment, we are now finding more and more cases where the two come bound together. Road removal fits this latter notion perfectly. From improved fishing and hunting to more reliable water flows, lands relieved of their excess roads can contribute to more diverse economies and vibrant communities.

A number of economic studies also support the notion that a healthy environment can create a direct stimulus for economic growth more broadly. In the western United States, growth and perceived quality of life are consistently greatest in counties that feature amenities such as protected open spaces, public lands with low road densities, and few toxic industries.[77] Nationally, states with the strongest environmental regulations have the strongest economies, while those with the weakest environmental laws have the poorest economic conditions.[78] The take-home message: environmental qualities *do* affect economic growth, as people have long maintained, but unlike the traditional view that it's a matter of "jobs versus the environment," we find that environmental amenities and regulations actually generate jobs.[79] Some eighty years after the U.S. Forest Service and National Park Service first began to weigh in for road developments on economic grounds, the scales have tipped to indicate that too many roads can stifle economic quality and sensible growth.

What we now confront along with concerns about roads, however, is the fact that roads are no longer the only source of access-related impacts. In the past few decades we have been busy creating vehicles that can bring us swiftly and in great numbers well beyond the reach of our abundant public land roads. As we will see in the chapter ahead, off-road vehicles have become more common and more powerful than ever before. We need to consider their impacts, as well, as we work to manage roads and access on our public lands.

A society of machine owners has a tendency to
think that it has a final right to everything it runs
over, whether it is woodland, sand, or water.

—John Hay, *Bird of Light*

5 | Industrial Revolutions: The Motorized Recreation Boom

When my family visited the California desert in
the early 1970s, it seemed like a remote land filled with heat and sun and
wind. Back then, if you were fortunate or patient, you might spot a fringe-
toed lizard skittering between shrubs and across dunes, come upon the
splay-footed track of a desert tortoise, or hear sand whisking against a
Joshua tree. At night, I remember the silence broken only by the yelps of
my parents, who had inadvertently set their sleeping bags atop a large
colony of biting ants. By day, we also heard the rumbling of dune buggy
and dirtbike engines.

My family was not the first to notice the sounds of engines in the California desert. For more than three decades, Howard Wilshire noticed that
and quite a bit more. As a scientist for the U.S. Geological Survey, Wilshire
studied soils and disturbances in the desert Southwest. A good portion of
his work focused on off-road vehicles (ORVs) and their impacts. On these
topics he has been prolific: his publications include dozens of articles, government reports, and a widely cited edited volume. His meticulous documentation of the ecological impacts of ORVs in the desert has proven,
time and again, to be a thorn in the balloon tires of desert vehicles. If you
probe the literature of ORV impacts on soils or arid ecosystems, you will
invariably run into the work of Howard Wilshire.

Howard Wilshire is in his early seventies, but neither he nor the California desert he studied has mellowed much with age. He still speaks with a quiet mix of wonder and reproach of his early days of research when he drove everywhere—on and off-road—to reach study sites. One day in particular stands out, when upon entering the Tecopa Lakebeds to study soils, he encountered a swarm of motorcycles. Wilshire had been reading about lunar studies at the time, and a report that Neil Armstrong's footprint would likely remain evident on the moon for a million years flashed back to him as he looked at the motorcycles cutting up the moonlike lakebed soils. He realized then that the tracks and the impacts of the machines were not fleeting or minor.

Wilshire also recognized that even as a scientist driving off-road in his own vehicle, he was part of the problem. As a result of that revelation, Wilshire began to restrict his vehicle to roads. He learned to study the landscape on foot and sometimes made long hikes into the lands he was researching.[1] In many parts of the desert today, you will notice that not everyone has decided to walk. A network of tracks, contrails of dust, and the roar of machines clue you in: to some, this is still a land of wheels.

In ways and shapes that were undreamed of even thirty years ago, ORVs are now surging to the forefront of a land manager's headache known as "access management." True to their name, ORVs are designed specifically for motoring beyond graded and surfaced roads for automobiles. In their common forms—motorcycle, four-wheel drive car or truck, snowmobile, three- and four-wheel all-terrain vehicle (ATV), or personal watercraft—ORVs can now navigate lands and waters that were traditionally well beyond the reach of motor vehicles. With technological advances in engine design, plastics, carbon fibers, metal alloys, and other materials, ORV manufacturers create lighter and more powerful machines every year.

As a result, on public lands ranging from the arid Southwest to the Green Mountains of Vermont, more vehicles are now entering more distant places than ever before. Land managers, in turn, are scrambling and often failing to keep pace with the changing land uses, the new mix of user demands, and the more aggressive impacts to the natural environment. In short, the technological and popular boom of ORVs has created a dusty fallout that is far from settled.

Public concern about these machines is nothing new. In 1971, a Department of Interior Task Force wrote, "eventually the question will boil down to: is the use of the ORV worth losses it will cause in the environment?"[2] In 1977, Howard Wilshire and seven colleagues presented their influential report, *Impacts and Management of Off-Road Vehicles,* to the Geological Society of America and noted that all areas of ORV use suffer from damage to soils.[3] And in 1979, the President's Council on Environmental Quality (CEQ) stated in its report *Off-Road Vehicles on Public Land,* "overall the CEQ sees the ORV problem as one of the most serious public land use problems that we face."[4]

Summer and winter ORVs also wield a number of social and ecological effects. User conflicts are growing increasingly common between motorized and nonmotorized recreationists. Management agencies now devote considerable time and money to managing, encouraging, or deterring motorized recreational use. On and off road, the vehicles cause damage to plants, wildlife, water quality, soils, and air. Cultural and aesthetic consequences of ORV use are also a growing topic of concern. And despite chronically inadequate budgets or personnel to monitor impacts from motorized recreation, federal, state, and corporate programs continue to promote ORV use.

The issues are complex at times, and for land managers wedged in the middle of a bickering public, few easy options appear. However, by examining ORVs and their ecological effects, the user conflicts that emerge, applicable laws, the promoters of these machines, and what or who belongs on public lands, we may gain valuable insights for how we should direct future ORV management. And, as land managers across the country are already realizing, in order for access management decisions in the future to be meaningful they will need to address ORVs as well as roads.

Vehicles for Land, Snow, and Water

Although glossy ads in magazines from *Backpacker* to *National Geographic* promote sport utility vehicles (SUVs) bravely clinging to ridgelines, dashing through sparkling creeks, or cruising across alpine meadows, the majority of these four-wheel-drive automobiles never leave pavement, and even fewer leave roads behind. SUVs have impacts, some of them dramatic, but they are generally restricted to roads and zones of influence extending outward from these roads.[5]

Motorcycles and dirtbikes have a deeper off-road history, having roamed afield for the better part of a century, but their numbers and impacts have not changed appreciably in recent years. Motorbikes *do* contribute to

Photo 5-1: A four-wheeled, all-terrain vehicle (ATV) crosses a wash on Bureau of Land Management lands in southern Utah. (Courtesy of Southern Utah Wilderness Alliance; photo by Mike Medberry.)

increased erosion, cause noise and air pollution, disturb sensitive species, and spread invasive plants—much as other vehicles do. However, two-wheeled motorcycles require a level of skill and balance that continues to limit their popularity overall, and they are typically not comfortable or large enough for uses such as family outings or big game hunting and retrieval. So-called dual sport motorcycles are gaining popularity, but the machines are still little more than powerful dirtbikes with turn signals and headlights to make them street legal (the "dual" sports being on- and off-road use).

Motorcycles also fit on pack trails built to standard widths.[6] This allows motorcycles greater range than their four-wheeled counterparts and may increase trail erosion and the prospect of user conflicts between motor-cyclists and horse- or backpackers, but it also means that trail projects and construction typically do not change dramatically just to accommodate motorcycle use.

On lakes, reservoirs, and some rivers, personal watercraft such as Jet Skis and WaveRunners affect public lands, especially national parks and national recreation areas (the latter include many dammed reservoir sites). Many of these vehicles cause water pollution, noise, user conflicts, and safety concerns similar to those created by ATVs and snowmobiles, but the watery range and marine and aquatic impacts of these machines fall beyond the intended scope of this book.

Two types of vehicles quickly distance themselves from the pack of ORVs used on public lands: snowmobiles and four-wheeled ATVs (shown in photos 5-1 and 5-2).

Photo 5-2: Snowmobiles fill the parking lot at Old Faithful in Yellowstone National Park.

Snowmobiles first appeared in the late 1950s and for the next twenty-five years were ungainly machines used for recreation, work, or hauling winter supplies into remote places. Early snowmobiles tended to founder in deep, loose snows, and though they captured the loyalty of many users, they were also rarely practical in backcountry areas away from groomed trails or roads.

With speeds commonly ranging from 35 to 50 miles per hour, snowmobiles were also infamous for their self-induced windchill, and they developed a nasty reputation for breakdowns. In winter conditions far from help, more than a few snowmobilers died of exposure or required rescue due to mechanical failure or bogging down in deep snow.

As snowmobiles began their transformative renascence from prosaic clunkers to "bullets on skis," a new breed of ORV emerged as well: the all-terrain vehicle. ATVs debuted as caterpillar-tracked or balloon-tired rigs with bench seats and joysticks. These metamorphosed into sporty three-wheeled models with saddle seats, handlebars, and modified motorcycle chassis.[7] About the time three-wheeled ATVs were banned in 1988 because of their dangerous instability, manufacturers added a fourth weel and four-wheelers quickly surged into the ATV niche. Four-wheelers now roam public lands from the Oregon Dunes to Cape Cod.

A Boom in Popularity

In three decades, the ATV market has grown from infancy to an industry that now far surpasses sales of street-legal motorcycles. In 1994, ATV sales totaled 228,000 compared to 194,000 street motorcycles.[8] By 1999, domestic ATV sales crested 548,000 and their trajectory has yet to flatten out.[9] Snowmobiles, with their longer history and dependence upon adequate snowpack, have had years of soaring sales and some—notably during the energy shortages of the 1970s—staggering drops, but recent figures show a thriving business with sales near record numbers as well.[10] From 1990 to 1997, the value of snowmobile sales tripled from $322 million to $960 million.[11]

Of course, ORV sales didn't take off just by chance. Prodding the rush from its outset, aggressive marketing campaigns have touted the thrill, power, and strength of the newest breeds of machines. An ad for Yamaha's "Big Bear" ATV boasts for instance, "No creature in all the animal kingdom is as respected as the mighty bear. So when our engineers set out to design an ATV by which all others would be judged, they knew just where to turn for the blueprint. The result is an ATV so rugged, so instinctual, you'll swear it's alive. . . . No wonder it devoured the competition in a recent head-to-head shootout. . . . [W]hen it comes to performance, Bears rule."[12]

On a slightly different tack, ATV companies have also tried to broaden their market beyond hard-core recreationists. By pitching ATVs as essential companions around the ranch, for family outings, and for hunting or retrieving big game, manufacturers have successfully expanded well beyond the traditional motorcycle market. "Buy a New Polaris ATV, Get a Rifle or Shotgun" an ad greeted readers of *North American Hunter*, just as hunting seasons opened around the country in 1998. It continued, "Right now, when you pull the trigger on a new Polaris Sportsman 500, we'll give you a coupon for a 12 gauge Remington 8700 shotgun or Remington Model 700™ 30.06 rifle. . . . Fire up your new high-caliber 4WD or 2WD Polaris ATV or Big Boss 500 6 6 before October 31, 1998, and choose your Remington firearm. Ride the best. Shoot the best."[13]

Call up your local dealer and you will need to know if you're looking for an ATV suited to "jumps and shredding" or for hauling gear; if you're shopping for "sleds" (snowmobiles), you should first decide if you are in it for powder, ease of handling, maximum power, or "highmarking" (an avalanche-risking contest of charging as high as possible up mountainsides until the machine threatens to stall or flip over backwards). Comforts such as heated seats and handlebar grips are now standard fare. In any case, whether for an average snowmachine, a lightweight "shredder," or a moose-toting family-sized ATV, expect to pay $4,000 to $8,000.[14] Top-of-the-line models can outpace sticker prices for many standard passenger cars.

Safety Problems

The cost of ORVs, unfortunately, is not limited solely to money flowing out of consumers' pocketbooks. In fact, what led to the demise of three-wheeled ATVs was their dismal safety record. Prior to the three-wheelers' outright ban in 1988, the U.S. Consumer Product Safety Commission (CPSC) issued a product Safety Alert in May 1987 that estimated that 86,400 ATV-related injuries were treated in hospital emergency rooms in 1986 alone. At that time, the CPSC had also documented 696 ATV-related deaths, 45 percent of which involved victims under the age of sixteen. The Safety Alert warned, "Over its estimated seven-year life, the average ATV has a one-in-three chance of being involved in an accident resulting in injury."[15]

With three-wheelers off the market for more than a decade, the public may now assume that ATV injuries are a thing of the past. Sadly, this is not the case. The following newsclip appeared in a corner of the B-section of my local newspaper under the heading, "ATV Crash Kills Choteau Man":

> A 40-year-old Choteau man died after an accident on the all-terrain vehicle he was riding in the St. Anthony [ID] Sand Dunes. Fremont County sheriff's deputies say [the victim] drove his four-wheeler off a steep sand dune and into a patch of lava rocks about 7:30 p.m. Friday. The machine landed on top of him, causing severe internal injuries. [He] died at the scene.
>
> It was the third serious accident in two months at the Sand Dunes. . . . [Another driver], 21, of Ogden, Utah, was seriously injured when he drove his all-terrain vehicle over a hill in the sand dunes and landed in a pile of lava rocks.[16]

The CPSC Alert, after all, urged caution for three- *and* four-wheeled ATVs. In a more recent update, the CPSC reported 2,976 ATV deaths between 1985 and 1997.[17] Though some three-wheelers remain in use and appear in these statistics, a significant number of ATV deaths in the 1990s occurred on four-wheelers. More than one-third of the fatalities come from drivers younger than sixteen years old.[18]

Ecological Impacts of Off-Road Vehicles

For anyone who has entered the backcountry of America's public lands, vehicle tracks often herald the presence of motorized use long after the vehicles themselves have gone. Some of the impacts of ORVs are obvious to passing visitors—deep tire ruts actively channel water downslope or a motorized trail gouges a hillside. In other places or seasons, the effects of ORV use may be more subtle.

The ecological consequences of ORVs range from soil compaction and erosion to noise, air, and water pollution. In many ways approximating the impacts of roads addressed in Chapter 3, ORVs directly and indirectly damage vegetation and wildlife, fragment habitat, displace sensitive species, introduce and distribute invasive species, and provide extensive access to legal hunting and illegal poaching of wildlife. In some cases, these impacts overlap or combine to create effects more dramatic—and more damaging—than one would expect at first glance.[19]

Increased Soil Compaction and Erosion

While we build and compact roads in anticipation of wheeled traffic, soils elsewhere are generally unconsolidated and vulnerable to passing vehicles. The impact of ORVs on soils will vary depending on use and soil type, but as Wilshire and his colleagues reported, *all* areas of ORV use suffer from soil damage.[20]

Soil compaction generally increases with the number of vehicle passes and is affected by factors such as the weight of the vehicle, tire width and air pressure, depth and wetness of soil, the type of soil, slope, and vegetation. Even a single ORV pass can cause lasting damage in certain environments.[21] Soils are also compacted rapidly with the first few vehicle passes, meaning that relatively low use may create compaction levels that quickly approach those caused by heavy use.[22]

As described earlier, soil compaction triggers a cascade of negative effects ranging from impacts on water quality to a shift in plant and animal communities. After vehicle tires compact loose soil, rain or snowmelt can no longer percolate fully, and the subsequent surface runoff generates hillside erosion. A study in Utah determined that soil loss on a Wasatch National Forest trail open to ORV use was nearly three times greater than erosion on a neighboring nonmotorized trail in comparable soils.[23] Other studies have documented a shift in plant succession, increased surface runoff, increased temperatures, and reduced nutrient cycling as a result of ORV use.[24]

Particularly on steep slopes and areas with fragile soils, ORVs can generate rapid and calamitous effects. Unfortunately, these characteristics coincide frequently with the kinds of terrain sought by riders. Hillclimbs are a popular and instantly erosive phenomenon, often leading to heavily scarred hillsides, deep ruts, and the subsequent channelization of water down vehicle tracks. Meanwhile, landscapes such as deserts and alpine tundra are characterized by both delicate thin soils and the open terrain that many ORV drivers seek. The combination of vulnerable soils and widespread use often causes serious damage.

Desert and arid ecosystems, such as those found across the American Southwest and Great Basin, typically have sparse vegetation. Soil stability and productivity often depend upon surface crusts formed by a mutual growth of mosses, fungi, and lichens.[25] Intact, these cryptogamic crusts slowly develop and thrive over many dozens of years. When broken or trampled, whether by throngs of cattle or hikers or beneath the spinning wheels of ORVs, these crusts are easily destroyed. Loose soils freed by the broken crust blow away in the rush of desert winds or the brief fury of desert storms.[26] In the arid desert, soils shredded by an afternoon ATV joyride may take centuries to recover.[27]

Alpine and tundra landscapes, especially common to lands in Alaska, the Rocky Mountains, the Sierras, and the Cascades, are particularly sensitive to ORV-generated impacts such as erosion, soil compaction, and vegetative damage. In the Colorado Rockies, one study asserted that damaged areas would take hundreds or thousands of years to recover.[28] In Alaska, researchers found that ORV use can damage the permafrost layer and cause changes in arctic plant and animal communities.[29] Once again, a day of summer thrills on a four-wheeler may leave its scar on a meadow far longer than the rider's lifetime.

Disrupted Hydrologic Function

Summer and winter ORVs can dramatically affect the way water moves across and beneath soil. Just as soil compaction inhibits the healthy functioning of soils, ORV use can change the speed, timing, quantity, and quality of water moving through the landscape.

Vehicle tracks concentrate runoff, increasing the erosive power of water and triggering a process of downcutting that can continue long after ORV use has stopped. As these channels and gullies form, they may carry soils well beyond the original zone of vehicle use.

Snowmobile use compacts snow, which melts later in the year due to its increased density. Heavily compacted snow can also block or divert surface water flow and concentrates spring runoff. Vegetation that absorbs moisture and stabilizes slopes may also be stunted or unable to grow if compaction abnormally delays spring snowmelt.[30]

Noise Pollution

Long before you see an ORV, as often as not, you will hear it. While engine noise from ORVs can quickly ruin an afternoon's quiet for rural residents, backcountry hikers or cross-country skiers, for users of some machines the noise levels can cause serious hearing damage.[31] With engines that have commonly run at decibel levels from 78 to 110 dBA (for comparison, the city where I live has banned outdoor rock concerts that exceed 90 decibels), some ORVs are loud enough to remain dangerous for distances of 100 yards and more, and permanent hearing damage is common among snowmobile and motorcycle racers.[32]

The impacts of noise on many other animals can threaten their very survival. With the reverberations of the summer's first thunderstorm, spadefoot toads emerge from their burrows to mate and lay eggs during the brief wet season of late summer in the American Southwest. Thunderstorms are no longer the only reliable noisemakers, however, and spadefoot toads can be enticed fatally from their burrows by the out-of-season thunder of ORV engines.[33]

Studies have also shown that ORV noise can cause bleeding from the ears and frantic behavior in kangaroo rats, and hearing loss in lizards such as the Mojave fringe-toed and desert iguana.[34] These and other animals rely upon their senses of hearing to find prey or avoid predators, breed, establish territories, rear their young, or navigate. Even with the advent of quieter machines, ORV noise can disrupt these critical activities.[35]

Air Pollution

While national forests, national parks, wildlife refuges, and Bureau of Land Management (BLM) lands have traditionally offered Americans a respite from smog-laden cities, the current land-rush of ORVs in some places is causing this to change.

Historically most off-road motorcycles, ATVs, and snowmobiles have featured two-stroke engines, which essentially offered power and light weight with the side effects of noise and smoke. Although they are smaller and far less abundant than standard automobiles, ORVs more than hold their own when it comes to producing air pollution. According to a 1999 EPA report, snowmobiles and ATVs produce 15 percent of all hydrocarbons emitted from mobile sources, including automobiles, trucks, locomotives, airplanes, and lawnmowers. These ORVs also cough up 9 percent of the carbon monoxide, despite numbering less than 2 percent of the quantity of automobiles in this country.[36]

A study of Yellowstone National Park found that winter snowmobile use was responsible for 78 percent of all carbon monoxide and 94 percent of all hydrocarbons emitted in the park during the entire year, even though automobile use outnumbers snowmobiles by more than sixteen to one.[37] In fact, a typical snowmobile produced 225 to 1,000 times more carbon monoxide than a recent-model family car, and 3,000 times the unburned hydrocarbons.[38] At Yellowstone's west entrance, air pollution from snowmobiles caused so many employee health complaints, the Park Service had to install a special air filtration system in entrance booths and offices; even with this system in place, employees have continued to complain of headaches and nausea from the poor air. The pollution and noise of the machines is so disagreeable to some Yellowstone rangers, they have programmed computer screen savers to keep an active countdown of the days remaining in the winter snowmobile season.

Research also shows that winter visitors to Yellowstone may be routinely exposed to dangerously high levels of carbon monoxide, with on-trail air samples exceeding the National Ambient Air Quality Standard of 35 parts per million (the standard for one hour of exposure).[39] For the many snowmobilers riding for hours at a time in the park, carbon monoxide exposure is likely significantly above the national eight-hour standard of nine parts per million. Health effects of carbon monoxide exposure can range from headaches and fatigue to respiratory failure and death.[40]

Many ATVs and a handful of prototype snowmobiles are switching to cleaner, quieter four-stroke engines, but these still emit a number of known or suspected carcinogens, including benzenes, aldehydes, polycyclic aromatic hydrocarbons, and the fuel additive methyl tertiary butyl ether (MBTE).[41] Even in dilute quantities, many of these substances can cause mutations and lead to cancer or death in organisms ranging from plankton to humans.[42]

Water Pollution

ORV use in forests and on other public lands can contribute significantly to water pollution. Two-stroke engines discharge approximately 25 percent of their oil–gas fuel mixture raw and unburned directly into the environment.[43] With ORV use exceeding 80 million visitor days in national forests alone, and much of the current fleet running on two-stroke engines, tens of millions of gallons of gasoline and motor oil likely enter the soils and waters of our public lands each year as a result of inefficient combustion and emissions from ORVs.[44]

For ORV use near streams, rivers, and lakes, water pollution is a serious threat. In truth, there is no place in national forests where petrochemical pollution is completely removed from aquatic systems: unburned fuel deposited directly onto soils or snowpack can percolate into groundwater, wash downhill as surface runoff, or bind to soils to accumulate or persist for years.

A study of the Yellowstone snowpack found increased levels of sulfates and ammonium that correlated positively with snowmachine use, while other studies have documented a toxic pulse that can accompany spring snowmelt.[45] Acidity triggered by pollutants stored in snowpack can prove lethal to zooplankton, aquatic insects, amphibians, and fish.[46]

Water pollution problems are not restricted to ORVs with two-stroke engines. Soil erosion caused by vehicles fills streams and waterways, contributing to increased sedimentation and turbidity. Especially where ORVs ford streams, the vehicles stir up sediments and stimulate streambank erosion. This, in turn, can lead to increases in water temperature and decreased levels of dissolved oxygen. Changes in the physical characteristics of streams and rivers can critically affect aquatic insects, fish, and other animals who depend upon clean cold waters for habitat, spawning, or food.[47] Samples from the headwaters of the Madison River in southwestern Montana, a world-renowned trout-fishing destination, found that streams near road crossings had more sediment and lower invertebrate diversity than comparable streams in a nearby roadless area.[48]

Impacts on Vegetation

ORVs affect plants directly and indirectly. Careless ORV use can trample, crush, and break plants. Soil compaction and erosion lead to diminished seed germination, exposed roots, decreased soil moisture, and a loss of soil nutrients.[49] Air and water pollution from ORVs can damage plants, and species diversity and the composition of plant communities may also be irreparably affected by exotic invasive weeds and pathogens introduced or encouraged by ORVs.[50]

Trampling lowers species diversity and can destroy individuals and reduce plant populations in areas of heavy ORV use (see photos 5-3, 5-4, and 5-5).[51] Other documented impacts from trampling include a shift in abundance from shrub species to annual plants.[52] Since shrubs tend to provide hiding cover, shade, and woody material, a loss in shrub numbers can lead to impacts on birds, mammals, and other species using an area.

Even though they tend to drive atop snow rather than on bare soil, snowmobiles are adept at crushing and breaking plants. One study found that after just one pass, a snowmobile damaged 78 percent of the tree saplings present—more than 25 percent of them seriously enough to be considered fatal.[53] Other studies have shown that snowmobiles gouge and kill young conifers and deciduous trees even with light traffic volumes.[54] Snowmobile use also leads to decreased soil temperature, since the compacted snow loses its insulating air spaces and conducts cold air to the ground more effectively. Delayed snowmelt, mentioned earlier, may also postpone seed germination and delay plant flowering.[55]

Plant invasions are currently one of the most commonly cited threats to grassland and forest ecosystems in the United States, and ORVs often emerge as a key link in these landscape-level conversions. With their combination of soil disturbance, ready transportation of seeds, and edge habitat created by wider trails, ORVs make ideal vectors for noxious weeds and other invasive plants. One study in Montana found that spotted knap-

Photo 5-3

Photo 5-4

Photo 5-5

Vegetation destroyed over time by off-road vehicle use. (Courtesy of Southern Utah Wilderness Alliance.)

weed—a Eurasian invader that now dominates thousands of square miles of the endangered Palouse Prairie ecosystem in the interior Northwest—can hitchhike thousands of seeds on the undercarriage of ORVs (and other vehicles) for distances of ten miles and more.[56]

While roaded lands and other areas with a high percentage of edge habitat are especially vulnerable to biological invasions, large roadless areas can generally provide enough interior habitat to be relatively impervious to invasion as long as active transporters—such as ORVs—are not present. Education is an important link here, as mountain bicycles, pets, stock animals, and backpackers can also disperse weed seeds. Separating ORVs from this pack of other vectors, however, is their ability to cover long distances in little time and the propensity of vehicle undercarriages to hide hitchhiking weeds from easy inspection.

Impacts on Wildlife

With ORVs affecting soils, air, water, and vegetation, wildlife suffer from adverse impacts as well. Indeed, animal species depend upon all of these other factors—in concert, directly or indirectly—for their sustenance and shelter. The condition of soils, air, water, and plant life will ultimately determine the natural condition of animals in a region.[57]

ORVs also affect wildlife very directly. Although accidental collisions between ORVs and wildlife can and do occur, people on snowmobiles, in particular, have intentionally chased coyotes and deer until the animals are fatally exhausted or can be driven over or shot.[58]

Less dramatically but far more commonly, ORVs allow legal hunters, trappers, and illegal poachers much easier and far-ranging access to pursue or retrieve popular game animals such as deer and elk or furbearers. Hunters express mixed views about the use of ATVs for hunting. The Professional Bowhunters Society, for example, calls for limiting ORV use to roads and designated trails to preserve the rules of fair chase.[59] Meanwhile, many hunting magazines feature ORV ads prominently. A survey in Montana found that hunters generally agreed that ORVs could be useful in removing kills, but that the machines also scared away potential game and did not improve hunters' success.[60] While roads typically create a larger break in forest cover than ORV routes, motorized access into wildlife habitat creates a similar threat whether by ATVs or automobiles. Ultimately, motorized access and not just the presence of a road is what undermines habitat security.

For animals that are commonly shot out of fear or prejudice or for sport—such as bears, wolves, coyotes, rodents, and nongame "varmints"— heightened access often leads swiftly to heightened mortality. For this reason and others, many species of wildlife are known to be road-averse and will preferentially occupy habitat that has low road densities.

While the impacts of roads are well-documented, as we saw in Chapter 3, ORV use of trails can lead to disturbances and a human presence very similar to the motorized use of roads. Even for animals not actively pursued or hunted, disturbances from ORV activity can prove harmful. Research shows that wildlife ranging from birds and reptiles to large ungulates avoid areas with high disturbance levels, respond to disturbance with accelerated heartrate and metabolic function, and suffer increased levels of stress that can lead to displacement, mortality, or reproductive failure.[61] Snowmobiles displace animals ranging from white-tailed deer to wolverine to cottontail rabbits.[62] South of the snowbelt, ORVs collapse animal burrows, tunnels, and nests and decrease the availability of plant forage.[63]

Several studies have sought to compare the disturbance effects caused by motorized and nonmotorized encounters with wildlife.[64] While some results indicate that humans afoot elicit more dramatic flight responses than humans traveling by vehicle—a point often rallied around by motorized recreation groups—such findings remain controversial and highly questioned. A 1986 study that determined, "Mule deer were disturbed more by persons afoot than by snowmobiles," for example, restricted snowmobiles to relatively slow speeds (10–15 mph) and existing trails, while humans on snowshoes were allowed to approach deer freely.[65] Effects on deer and other wildlife might be vastly different with free-roaming or high-speed snowmobiles compared to trailbound snowshoers kept at a similar distance.

Snowmobile impacts on snow are comparable in many respects to the soil compaction caused by wheeled vehicles. For small mammals such as voles, mice, and shrews who remain active throughout the winter, the subnivean environment between snow and earth provides a critical zone relatively protected from predators, insulated from freezing air temperatures, and offering access to food sources.[66] Snowmobile use can compact snow enough to crush small mammals to death.[67] Compacted snow can also decrease oxygen and mobility for subnivean mammals, as well as increase exposure to winter temperature extremes.[68] A decline in small mammal populations may also lead to decreased numbers of predatory species such as lynx, hawks, owls, weasels and other mustelids.

While proponents and promoters of motorized recreation often claim that there "just isn't any good science" to demonstrate adverse environmental effects of ORVs, a foray into the scientific literature—such as that presented here—quickly shows otherwise. What remains less clear is why motorized users and nonmotorized recreationists can so rarely agree on their respective impacts or experiences.

Fueling the Cultural Divide: Conflicts in Recreation

Two photos tell a story. Page eleven of the November 8, 1999 issue of *High Country News* shows two men who essentially represent opposite sides in the debate over off-road vehicles: Clark Collins and John Gatchell.[69]

Clark Collins heads the Idaho-based "Blue Ribbon Coalition," a group that affiliates itself with a bevy of vehicle manufacturers, user groups, and extractive industry. In the photo, Collins sits astride an ORV. Gloves and helmet in his lap, he is fully decked out in protective gear: plastic shoulder and arm pads, a ventilated breastplate, motorcycle pants, and a jersey emblazoned with manufacturers' names. He stares straight out from the photo, forehead slightly creased. With an indistinct hill rising behind him and a few scrubby trees, it's not clear what kind of experience Collins has had or hopes to have, but he appears dressed to protect and insulate himself from his surroundings. Beneath his helmet and motorcycling suit, he will be at one with his machine, but buffered from the world around him.

In the second photo, John Gatchell, conservation director of the Montana Wilderness Association, leans against a large boulder in full sunlight. A canyon drops away to his side and behind it looms a mountain ridge. Gatchell sports baggy shorts and a sweatshirt rolled up to the elbows. He may be resting against the boulder during a hike or may just have found it a nice viewpoint, but he can surely feel the rock at his side, the sunlight on his face, and the air against his bare legs and arms. There is little here to blanket him from contact with the nearby mountains.

Am I reading too much into these images? Perhaps. But these photos can offer at least broadbrush clues about why the views of these two men differ so markedly when it comes to trail use: ensconced in his helmet, already surrounded by the noise of his machine, it troubles Collins little to pass a hiker on a trail—he can "share the trail" with scant effect on his own experience. Gatchell, meanwhile, is confronted with an entirely new and jarring experience—even at some remove—when the noise, smoke, and speed of an ORV intersect with his meander in the mountains.

This asymmetry of experience cuts close to the heart of the conflicts that take place between motorized and nonmotorized users. From the time off-road motorcycles first began to appear on public lands, the relationship between motorized and nonmotorized users has been troubled and lopsided. Hikers, horsepackers, cross-country skiers, backcountry hunters, and birdwatchers have typically lashed out at the noise and intrusion of ORVs. Conversely, motorized users—many of whom are sociable, law-abiding, and pursuing their own version of a quality experience—often react with surprise at the hostile reception they receive from "quiet" trail users.

User Conflicts

People come to public lands for a variety of reasons. From sight seeing and bird watching to hunting or driving ORVs, each activity is not necessarily compatible with the next. The following citizen's letter to the Medicine Bow National Forest in Wyoming illustrates some of the conflicts that can arise:

> [I]n 1997 we found the forest sounds to have changed from the sounds of animals, birds, and insects to the continual drone of ATVs and dirt bikes. Abandoned and barricaded roads were now as heavily traveled as the maintained roads. Well traveled game trails and historical mining camp roads were also being traveled frequently with motorized vehicles. During the hunting season we discovered that the game was extremely flighty and seemed to seldom rest. The old trails and previously abandoned roads are now showing some signs of soil erosion and consequential defoliation. We have also found many near-permanent structures used especially by large groups of hunters that access the camps with their ATVs. Although Game and Fish laws prohibit the pursuit of game from motorized vehicles, the wardens have no way to enforce the laws on the shear [*sic*] volume of ATVs being used great distances from maintained roads. Referring to the January and February issues of *Wyoming Wildlife* magazine many hunters and back-country travelers are seeing the same sights that we've seen.
>
> I'm confined to a wheelchair and hunt from a vehicle. I like to park on the edge of clear-cuts and watch the edges furthest from the roads. I

have seen several ATVs at a time come roaring out of the timber more often than wildlife.[70]

This letter also highlights the unpredictable nature of user conflicts. The author is not especially hostile to roads or even to motorized access. In fact, confined as he is to a wheelchair, he depends upon motorized access to reach places where he can hear "the sounds of animals, birds, and insects" and hunt during big game season. The letter writer is troubled, however, by the unrestrained and damaging use of ATVs, even in areas of clear-cut forest.

This example points again to the idea that recreational impacts are not always reversible. In other words, the wheelchair-bound hunter waiting at the edge of a clear-cut may not have any effect on the ATV drivers, but the noise and disturbance created by the ATVs can ruin the hunter's day.

This dynamic fails the philosophical standard for "minimal fairness," which states that a situation is not equitable if it allows one party to use property in a way that harms the interests of others.[71] Similarly, according to scholars of political ethics, in a society that values fairness or equity, citizens have a reasonable claim not to "be forced against [their] will to absorb . . . noxious by-products of the activity of others."[72] Applied to public lands recreation, these principles point to the impropriety of subjecting hikers to ATV fumes and noise, or to the displacement of cross-country skiers by snowmobilers. Since few motorized experiences are impaired by contact with nonmotorized activities, but nonmotorized recreationists do commonly suffer when they try to "share the trails," overlapping areas of motorized and nonmotorized use consistently lead to user conflicts and the displacement of the quiet users.

In part because motorized recreationists are surrounded by noise, smoke, and the ambience of their machines whether they number one or several dozen, they commonly travel in large groups with little or no loss of experience. Indeed, group "fun runs" are a popular motorized activity. Motorists can likewise encounter other motorized or nonmotorized groups with no disruption in their day's experience. Nonmotorized backcountry recreation, however, responds differently. A couple's weekend backpacking getaway might be ruined altogether if a pack of ORVs sets up camp nearby. Hikers or cross-country skiers often cite the negative effects of noise, smoke, on-trail encounters, or lingering tracks from ORVs.[73] As displaced quiet trail users testify, shared-use trails may be virtually impossible to develop with nonmotorized and motorized recreationists.

The difference in physical impacts of the activities also accentuates the asymmetry between different types of recreation. A trail damaged or rutted by an ORV creates a lasting and negative impression for a hiker who later encounters the tracks. Even though the hiker and ORV driver may both be pursuing what seems a legitimate recreational activity, the past pleasures of the ORVer typically leave a residual scar on the land that vastly exceeds any traces left by the hiker in similar conditions. Once again, the disparity between the two experiences often leads to hostile views—at least from the hiker.

Riders and Responsibility

User conflicts occur even when motorized recreationists are driving legally and responsibly. Unfortunately, a number of riders also flaunt the law, ignore trail etiquette, and violate rules to reduce ecological harm. According to land managers, citizen complaints, and conservation group reports, ORV users' disregard for road closures, private property, and trail restrictions is commonplace. A Freedom of Information Act request submitted to all national forests in 1998 determined that 71 percent of the responding forests recorded resource damage or motor vehicle violations including improper use of forest trails, illegal use of vehicles off-road, or violating standards for noise, smoke, safety, or state laws.[74] Even an ATV-industry poll determined that more than half of the respondents had used their machines to trespass illegally.[75]

Although motorized user groups and industry-sponsored campaigns work to promote "responsible" off-road driving, having a powerful machine at fingertip command seems to inspire boorish behavior.

From informal beginnings in the 1960s, the annual Barstow to Vegas ORV race grew until it attracted thousands of participants each year (see photo 5-6). The race was halted in 1975 because of environmental impacts caused by many of the riders veering off course, disrupting wildlife, and kicking up some 600 tons of dust (these impacts were documented in a research paper by Howard Wilshire and Ken Nakata, which also cited a 90 percent reduction in small mammal populations subsequent to the race),[76] but in 1983 the BLM gave it clearance to run again. The agency's subsequent environmental analyses—widely assailed by scientists and

Photo 5-6: The start of the Barstow to Vegas race on BLM lands in the early 1970s. (Courtesy of Howard Wilshire.)

conservationists—deemed the levels of damage acceptable, until the listing of the desert tortoise as an endangered species upped the ante.

For the 1989 race, the BLM added special restrictions to mitigate damage to tortoises and their habitat: riders would need to stay within a 15-foot corridor through identified tortoise areas, participation numbers would be capped, and the start would take place in waves rather than en masse.[77] With considerable public attention focused on the Barstow to Vegas race, the 1989 event might have been a showcase of responsible riders complying with rules to retain their privilege to use the public lands. But instead, racers ignored the corridor restrictions, overran the racecourse, and pounded a final nail into the Barstow to Vegas's coffin. According to the BLM's Outdoor Recreation Planner in Las Vegas who was on-site for the final race, "There were a lot of extremist off-road motorcyclists. [They] just trashed and bashed everything."[78]

Despite the mottled record of off-road enthusiasts in the region, the BLM now permits a large dual sport motorcycle ride, the "LA to B to V," which runs for two days and nearly 400 miles from Los Angeles to Barstow to Las Vegas. The new event is noncompetitive and intended for "self-guided motorcycle touring," but honors its predecessor event both in title and by covering segments of the earlier Barstow to Vegas race course. According to Bob Bruno, the BLM planner in Las Vegas, the new event has far eclipsed the old race and, moreover, "there are absolutely gorgeous dual sport opportunities all across the West." Bruno notes that it has been much more difficult to win approval for the dual sport route in California compared to Nevada. In California, as Bruno sees it, "there are a bunch of environmental wackos running around trying to shut down everything that's motorized. The wackos have real issues about riding anything motorized anywhere. . . . [W]e've been really fortunate [in Nevada] that the American Motorcyclist Association folks are such good people."[79]

Throttling Use: Regulations for ORVs

Public outcry and land managers' concerns about ORV use were great enough in the 1960s and 1970s to spur Presidents Nixon and Carter to sign executive orders that clarify how vehicles should be properly managed on public lands. Richard Nixon signed Executive Order 11644 in 1972 to "establish policies and provide for procedures that will ensure that the use of ORVs on public lands will be controlled and directed so as to protect the resources of those lands, to promote the safety of all users of those lands, and to minimize conflicts among the various uses of those lands."[80]

Five years later, Jimmy Carter added to these terms with Executive Order 11989. Among other stipulations, this later order prescribed that "areas and trails shall be located to minimize conflicts between ORV use and other existing or proposed recreational uses of the same or neighboring public lands, and to ensure the compatibility of such uses with existing conditions in populated areas, taking into account noise and other factors."[81] These orders created a framework for federal management, but in many places ORVs continue to drive unrestricted across public lands.

Agency Prescriptions for Off-Road Use

ORV use varies widely depending upon the land's classification, local pressures, and management priorities. Summer ORV use is prohibited on national park and national monument lands but can be allowed by special regulation in national seashores, lakeshores, recreation areas, and preserves.[82] Following a survey of officials at the various national park units, the Park Service in 2000 also declared a ban on winter snowmobile use (though the most popular national park snowmobile destinations of Yellowstone, Voyageurs, and units in Alaska were excluded from the prohibition and treated separately).[83] In announcing his agency's decision, Deputy Park Service Director Dennis Galvin explained, "Quite frankly, we were surprised and disturbed by the results of the snowmobile survey. . . . [It] graphically demonstrated that years of inattention to our own regulatory standards on snowmobiles generated the problem we have before us today."[84] Despite these findings, Republicans in Congress successfully tacked a rider onto a large appropriations bill later in 2000 that eliminated funding and stalled the snowmobile ban until at least the 2002 winter season.

National wildlife refuges, generally, have a policy of not allowing motorized use off of designated routes.[85] Though occasional exceptions exist to accommodate special hunting seasons or cooperative agreements with adjacent state lands, motorized use on wildlife refuge lands is essentially limited to roads and street-legal vehicles (which excludes ATVs in most states).

The BLM applies different management prescriptions on a state by state basis, but many areas still allow cross-country motorized use in winter or summer. In southern Utah, for example, the BLM does not limit ATV use even on many of the remaining 9 million acres of roadless lands included in recent wilderness proposals. Where the BLM continues to allow such motorized use, land managers often point to the agency's multiple-use mandates. Ironically, multiple-use statutes were originally established to press agencies to manage for a broader range of uses (that were generally less extraction-oriented) than the traditional industrial uses of logging, mining, and grazing.[86] With shifting societal values, motorized recreationists and some land managers now cling to multiple-use prescriptions as a means to perpetuate activities that damage the same resources these laws once sought better to protect.

On BLM lands elsewhere in the American Southwest, dune buggy, motorcycle, and ATV use has been allowed—and studied—extensively. Though many desert lands are still wide open to motorized use, the persistent efforts of a handful of scientists, conservationists, and land managers have led to a number of protected areas.

In some places, even where agency officials are on hand to educate motorized users or enforce regulations, difficulties can arise. A forestry technician's report from Colorado's White River National Forest in 1993 illustrates this point:

> At this time . . . the third motorcyclist . . . was heading down the
> road. . . . I stepped away from the Forest Service truck on the edge of the

road and motioned with both of my hands, one with a portable radio, for him to stop. The motorcyclist accelerated and went past me. The dune buggy was 20 seconds behind the motorcycle. I again motioned with my hands for the dune buggy to stop but this time I stepped further into the road as to be sure there was no way he could miss seeing me. The dune buggy made no attempt at slowing down along the narrow road as he was approaching me. I needed to step off the road to avoid being struck by the dune buggy.[87]

Obviously not all motorized recreationists terrorize wildlife or land managers, but as described earlier, even "responsible" use can lead to serious problems. In 1996, a recreation staff officer from the Chattahoochee National Forest in Georgia reported:

ORV use is causing unacceptable resource damage on some trails. Resource damage is also occurring off trails due to illegal use. The damage to trails is caused by lack of adequate maintenance, improper trail location, lack of mitigation measures and much increased use over anticipated use. . . . Levels of use coupled with budget constraints and capability amplifies the fact that the Forest and individual districts can no longer be all things to all people.[88]

National forests continue to wrestle with ORV management and have tried a number of tactics. Drawing the cleanest lines are two forests, the Monongahela in West Virginia and Indiana's Hoosier, where ORVs are completely banned. The Hoosier, a national forest comprising relatively small parcels in a matrix of private lands, responded to property owners' widespread complaints that ORVs were damaging resources, trespassing, and creating disturbances. The forest authorities determined that there simply was no appropriate place for ORVs to ride.

Similarly, after the Monongahela assessed its lands for designated wilderness and wildlife habitat needs, only three areas remained where ORV routes would have been feasible—and each of these was small and surrounded by private land. Simplifying the decision to ban the vehicles, local ORV dealers expressed little interest in opening the Monongahela to ORV use.[89]

Elsewhere, or in national forests where public lands are more consolidated, the arguments shift somewhat. In the Green Mountain National

Forest in Vermont, a maintained snowmobile route cuts through a road-less area that provides drinking water for the town of Bennington. Some locals there are concerned about the impacts of snowmobile exhaust on the town's water quality: recall that 25 percent of the gas–oil fuel mixture comes out of two-stroke snowmobile engines unburned, and even burned fuel creates particulates and emissions that can accumulate in snowpacks.

In the Gifford Pinchot National Forest in western Washington, conservation groups have successfully fought ORV trail projects in order to protect habitat for mountain goats. Similarly, across the West, a number of areas are closed to motorized access to maintain secure areas for elk, deer, grizzly bear, or other species known to be sensitive or vulnerable to disturbance or human access. From Ohio to Idaho, agency resource managers also point to the soil loss associated with ATV and motorcycle use.

In Idaho, federally threatened or endangered fish species, such as bull trout and sockeye and chinook salmon, rely upon clear-running water and loose gravel streambottoms for reproduction. Soils displaced by heavy ORV use can fill in these spawning grounds and smother eggs. According to some officials, ORV areas are the largest contributor to soil loss in their national forests.[90]

An official's monitoring report on the Wayne National Forest in Ohio commented, "Whether it is the Wayne or any other Forest, the concept of 'off road vehicle' is contrary to the mission of the National Forests. We cannot, regardless of dollars, maintain trails that will not erode into our streams. And we cannot control users equipped with vehicles designed to go on all types of terrain."[91]

Motorized Trails or Roads?

Although we generally think of trails as benign paths for people or animals to move through a landscape, *motorized* trails come as something of a different stripe. One critical effect of motorized recreation is the creation of trails that are wide enough to accommodate ATVs or snowmobiles. The transformation of a hiking trail into a motorized trail is a difference of both trail width and character. Forest Service standards for the width of a trail's "tread" vary according to the type of recreational use each trail will receive. Hiking trails are at the narrowest extreme, with a prescription for a 12-inch tread on "most difficult" trails, up to 24-inch tread width on "easiest" trails. Mountain biking and pack-and-saddle standards fall within a range of 18 to 24 inches. On the other extreme, ORV trails have a tread width from 48 to 60 inches; snowmobile trails come wider still, with a prescription three times that of summer ORVs.[92]

The Forest Service also prescribes the amount of clearing appropriate for each type of trail use. While hiking trails require between 3 and 4 feet of total clearing, ORV trails are cleared between 2 ½ to 3 feet on either side of the tread. This clearing size combined with the tread itself leads to a total clearing width of 9 to 11 feet for trails constructed to ORV specifications. Add motorized ORVs to this 10-foot-wide route and what was once a quiet hiking trail becomes, essentially, a road. Note that these dimensions are for *minimum* trail standards; trails may be built and cleared to wider dimensions at each forest's discretion. Many other trails used by ORVs were never constructed for motorized use—or even constructed at all—and exist due to repeated use by vehicles.

Categorical Exclusions for Motorized Trails

Beyond the social and ecological ramifications of roadlike trails sprawling across public lands, conservation groups point to procedural concerns about how agencies develop motorized trail projects. According to the National Environmental Policy Act (NEPA), any action that will cause significant impacts on federal lands must go through a detailed environmental analysis that identifies different alternatives, discusses the anticipated consequences, and provides opportunity for public comment and review. Conversely, if there will be no significant impact and there are no "extraordinary circumstances" related to the project, a proposed action may be excluded from lengthy environmental review and public comment.[93]

Using this latter clause, agencies have commonly widened trails without the usual amount of public oversight. According to federal regulations, agencies can categorically exclude trail projects from full environmental review only if the work is "repair and maintenance." Although many trail projects do fit these terms, converting a trail from nonmotorized to motorized use results in upgrading, improving, and dramatically widening the trail, which clearly facilitates new uses and impacts.

NEPA regulations deem activities that are "individually minor but collectively significant" inappropriate for the categorical exclusion of environmental review. But even if a single trail project could be determined minor or insignificant, the collective impact of multiple similar projects would be significant. Finally, the criteria for "extraordinary circumstances" includes, among other factors, projects that will affect steep slopes or highly erosive watersheds, threatened or endangered species or their critical habitat, or wilderness study areas and inventoried roadless areas. One or more of these factors is often involved in motorized trail projects.[94]

Legal and administrative challenges to motorized trail projects have a history of success, but with money spilling in from both state and federal programs—and a vocal constituency of motorized recreationists clamoring for more driving opportunities—the tide of motorized trail conversions is difficult to stem.[95] If an agency allows motorized use on trails, then it may argue that trails need to be modified to mitigate erosion and other resource damage problems. Furthermore, where cross-country motorized use (i.e., driving off of existing roads and trails) remains legal or takes place illegally, ORVs create new trails each year. Understandably, then, agencies look for trail funds to reduce existing impacts, or create planned ORV routes to placate and contain motorized users. Especially for multiple-use agencies in the large tracts of public lands in the West, the politically and socially appealing route has consistently been one recently widened to accommodate motorized use rather than one restricted to hiking or traditional activities.

Laws to Rein in Use

In addition to the two executive orders, a number of laws affect where ORVs may be used and how they are managed by agencies. Each agency has its own "Organic Act," or legislation that provides guidance for its purpose and mission. For the National Park Service and U.S. Fish and Wildlife Service, these prescriptions are weighted toward specific directions: for the conservation of scenic treasures for future generations, and to protect wildlife. While ORVs are allowed in a handful of national park units and national wildlife refuges, these agencies can generally ban activities they deem detrimental to their conservation goals.[96]

In some cases the social or political climate may not make such actions popular or practicable, but the law stands pretty squarely behind the agencies. A federal district court in 1998 sided with the Southern Utah Wilderness Alliance that Salt Creek in Canyonlands National Park should no longer be open to vehicular use. Based on language from the agency's

Organic Act, the judge ruled that vehicles should be prohibited from driving in Salt Creek's riparian corridor.[97] The court determined that preservation overrides visitor enjoyment and that there is, in fact, a preferential mandate for preservation in the 1916 Park Service Organic Act. Upon appeal in October 2000, the Salt Creek case was sent back to the lower court for review and its status remains in question. However, recent court and agency statements have further established that the Park Service's primary duty is preservation (see Chapter 7).

Bureau of Land Management and U.S. Forest Service managers need to deal not only with the vagaries of local or congressional sentiments, but also with agency multiple-use philosophies that consider a number of uses appropriate. As a result, these agencies often find themselves barraged by a crossfire of competing interests, each pointing to a particular use and insisting that it be accommodated.

Compounding the management challenge is the fact that ORV use often begins incrementally, with a handful of users coming into large areas of open land and dispersing broadly. Enforcement and monitoring in such conditions is extremely difficult, particularly with agency budgets stretched thin. Many land managers do not consider enforcement and monitoring high priority programs. Even when land managers try to limit ORV activity, once use is established proper management or eliminating use can prove a daunting challenge.

The increasing popularity of ORVs has also produced local or regional constituencies for areas that were never properly developed, assessed, or analyzed for motorized use by land managers. Both intentionally and not, managing agencies have sanctioned motorized use in some cases not because it made sense to allow it in a particular setting, but because people had actively begun to use those places. When renegade activities drive the planning process, it obviously can lead to administrative confusion, ecological damage, and a loss of citizen respect for agency methods and authority.

All four of the major land management agencies must also abide by other federal laws that affect the way ORVs may or may not run across the land. The Endangered Species Act, National Environmental Policy Act, Clean Water Act, and National Forest Management Act (which applies only to national forests), in particular, have influenced access management decisions in recent decades.

Provisions in the Endangered Species Act, for instance, have led to ORV restrictions to protect the desert tortoise and other reptiles in the desert Southwest, the grizzly bear in the northern Rockies, and shorebirds on the Atlantic coastal dunes. After the Chincoteague National Wildlife Refuge in Virginia banned ORVs from 2.5 miles of beach in 1988, piping plover fledgling numbers increased ninefold from one breeding season to the next. A ban on ORVs from parts of the Cape Cod National Seashore resulted in a similar resurrection for the endangered bird.[98]

The Money Trail: Funding and Promoting Off-Road Vehicles

Working against environmental laws that protect areas from ORV damage, other laws and government programs actively promote ORV access and use. In fact, ORV funding programs operate at the national, state, and municipal levels to develop ORV routes. Some land management agencies actively court motorized recreation as a promising source of revenue. Meanwhile, ORV user groups, manufacturers, and other corporations have banded together to form potent motorized constituencies.

Federal Recreational Trails Funding

In 1991, as part of its massive national transportation bill, Congress created the National Recreational Trails Fund.[99] From 1991 to 1997, this law allocated $37.5 million to states to develop recreational trails, including ATV and snowmobile trails.[100] When Congress passed a new national transportation bill in 1998, the National Recreational Trails Fund became the Recreational Trails Program.[101]

The Recreational Trails Program is a bigger and bolder edition of the earlier Trails Fund. Whereas the 1991 version could offer states up to $30 million each year for trail projects, it managed to fund just 20 percent of that amount. The sequel promises to contribute a total of $270 million by 2003.[102] Unlike its progenitor, the Recreational Trails Program also comes with "contract authority," which guarantees stable funding over the program's six-year life.

Under the terms of this law, for which motor vehicle boosters lobbied vigorously, individual states receive federal funds for trail projects as long as the state reserves a portion of its fuel taxes for nonhighway uses. For example, California directs 1 percent of its gasoline taxes to recreational trail developments and related projects. While this portion of the annual state tax revenues generates an average of $25 million in itself, the state program also qualifies California to receive federal funds from the Recreational Trails Program.[103]

Funds disbursed through the federal Trails Program are designed to contribute to a balanced mix of trail projects: 30 percent for nonmotorized trails, 30 percent for motorized trails, and 40 percent for "diversified" multiple-use trails. While these funds do boost trail budgets for an array of projects, the approach fails to translate into balanced trail use on the ground.

Diversified trails present the main point of contention. This 40 percent block of multiple-use trails needs simply to embrace more than one activity. Mountain biking and hiking, or hiking and riding horseback, for instance, would qualify as diversified. However, the money allocated to diversified use often funds trails that include some motorized activity such as snowmobiling or driving ATVs. Because of the disparate expectations (or tolerance levels) of motorized and nonmotorized recreationists, once motorized use is allowed and becomes common on a trail, nonmotorized recreationists often stop visiting the trail.[104] A "diversified" trail built for ATVs and hikers quickly loses the hikers. As a result, many critics of the Recreational Trails Program contend that allocations break closer to 70/30 in favor of motorized trails. Since nonmotorized trail use vastly outnumbers motorized use nationwide, motorized trails would be excessively favored even if trail funding split closer to the 50/50 mix presented by the program's supporters.

State ORV Programs and Gas Taxes

The 1991 National Recreation Trails Fund stipulated that states would only be eligible for federal trail dollars if they collected gas taxes and applied them to nonhighway vehicle projects, but many states already had active programs in place to do just that. In a number of cases, state-funded programs contribute more money to ORV trails and promotions than federal funds. Washington State began its Nonhighway and Off-Road Vehicle Activities Program (NOVA) in 1974, and by the late 1980s most western states had similar programs in place. Over the years, Washington's NOVA program has contributed $40 million to motorized recreation projects compared to just $5 million for nonmotorized projects. Supporters of the program contend that NOVA works as it was intended, but with

Washington State hikers outnumbering motorized trail users by almost 32 to 1, the funding disparity raises many critics' hackles.[105]

In Montana, most motorized trail projects are funded by one of two different grant programs, both administered by the State Department of Fish, Wildlife and Parks. One, the Off-Highway Vehicle Program, is funded by an annual $5 per ORV decal fee and a $1/8$ of 1 percent state gas tax, an approximation by the State Legislature of the percent of fuel ORV recreationists consume.[106] The second program, established through the National Recreational Trails Fund, is supported by federal gas taxes but administered by the state. From these two programs, Montana applied more than $300,000 to trail projects in 1997. Montana awards most of the grants to an ORV club or association, or a chamber of commerce or government agency working cooperatively with an ORV club.[107]

In many states, gas tax funds have promoted trail construction or snowmobile grooming programs that have increased motorized access dramatically. In 1980 there were approximately 90,000 miles of snowmobile trails in North America. By 2000, these trails eclipsed 220,000 miles.[108]

Local Pressures and Gateway Communities

Small towns and "gateway communities" that border national parks or other public lands are often particularly vocal against limiting visitor opportunities that might generate revenue. As a result, where motorized recreation can represent a lucrative tourist draw land managers are often subject to local pressures. Just outside Yellowstone National Park, the town of West Yellowstone, Montana, proclaims itself the "Snowmobile Capital of the World." The local chamber of commerce aggressively promotes and subsidizes a groomed system of snowmobile trails on nearby Gallatin National Forest lands, and has also been a major voice opposing the proposed limits on snowmobile access to the interior of Yellowstone Park. Many West Yellowstone businesses point to the advent of snowmobiling as the time their town became "three-season" and not just reliant upon a hearty summer flow of tourists and a smattering of autumn big game hunters. If a National Park Service ban on snowmobile use in Yellowstone ever occurs, West Yellowstone boosters will undoubtedly try to turn to the nearby Gallatin and Targhee National Forests to support a continued industry of snowmobiling tourists.

From the desert race courses of Barstow, California, to snowmobiles in West Yellowstone, boosters of motorized recreation assert that local economies would crash without the attraction of ORVs thundering across desert sands or snowmobiles punching through powder. Moab, Utah, and many other towns that just a few decades ago relied upon heavy industry, have turned now to a recreation bonanza. Though each year Moab attracts more river runners and mountain bikers than ATV drivers, events like the annual Easter Jeep Jamboree bring thousands of motorists in a single, high-profile, lucrative weekend.

Corporate Power Driving the Market

In the market-driven U.S. economy, it may come as little surprise that vehicle manufacturers and other industrial interests actively promote their products through advertising and other direct means. Suzuki, Honda, Kawasaki, Yamaha, Polaris, and Bombardier are some of the dominant manufacturers of summer and winter ORVs, and they pour millions of dollars each year into promotions. Every bit as far-reaching, however, is the companies' financial support of motorized user groups and behind-the-scenes advocacy to open public lands up for motorized recreation. In this effort, there are some remarkable partnerships.

The Blue Ribbon Coalition formed in 1987 and now claims to represent 650,000 members (many from within other member groups such as the American Motorcyclist Association—individual members actually number just 7,000). According to its own publications, the Blue Ribbon Coalition has formed "a potent team. Snowmobilers in Illinois get involved in issues affecting motorcyclists in the California desert, 4 x 4 enthusiasts from Georgia, help protect snowmobiling in and around Yellowstone Park, OHV interests in Utah, and work with rock hounds (who use off highway vehicles in their activities) to block inappropriate wilderness designation in their state [sic]."[109]

Although the Blue Ribbon Coalition often rebukes environmentalists for trying to mobilize national support for "local issues," the Coalition obviously works this angle too as it seeks to connect Illinois snowmobilers with Utah rock hounds. For that matter, the Blue Ribbon Coalition is scarcely a grassroots organization: funding for the Blue Ribbon Coalition comes from some of the nation's largest corporations and has included Louisiana-Pacific Corporation, Marathon Oil, Noranda Montanore, Crown Butte Mines, Potlatch Corporation, J.R. Simplot, Boise Cascade, and the Rocky Mountain Oil and Gas Association, in addition to a host of vehicle manufacturers such as Honda, Polaris, Yamaha, and Kawasaki.[110]

The link between ORV users and extractive industrial development is not always readily apparent, but it presents a critical wedge against efforts to preserve public lands. Where motorized use becomes established, if even for a decade or less, agencies are unlikely to recommend wilderness designations and politicians are reluctant to alienate a vocal constituency. As a result, groups such as the Blue Ribbon Coalition are heavily funded by timber, mining, and other industrial interests to keep areas available for more lenient management prescriptions.

In Colorado, the Rio Grande National Forest's recent Forest Plan Revision recommended none of the forest's 525,000 acres of inventoried roadless land for wilderness designation.[111] According to forest planning documents, 30 of the Rio Grande's 47 inventoried roadless lands had motorized vehicle use in them at the time of analysis (these 30 areas comprised 400,000 of the overall roadless acreage).[112] Some areas were rated low for their lack of "remoteness and seclusion" due to motorized use.[113]

In Vermont, the White Rocks National Recreation Area was created as a compromise between wilderness advocates and snowmobile and mountain bicycling enthusiasts (bicycles and other "mechanized vehicles" are prohibited in wilderness areas).[114] Similarly, the Lee Metcalf Wilderness in Montana was reduced from its originally proposed size and split into multiple units in order to keep established snowmobile routes available. At congressional hearings for the Lee Metcalf Wilderness, House Interior Committee Chairman John Seiberling (D-OH) commented, "Just for the record I would note that the way this resolved the question of snowmobiling was to drop the snowmobiling areas out of wilderness. So there are no snowmobile areas in the wilderness areas in this bill."[115] More broadly, the Alaska National Interest Lands Conservation Act created an entirely new category for public lands—the National Preserve—which is managed by the National Park Service but allows activities, such as oil and gas drilling or driving ORVs, that are typically banned in national parks.[116]

Public–Private Partnerships

Although the United States enjoyed its longest economic expansion in history from 1992 to 2001, shrinking budgets consistently trimmed federal land management agencies.[117] Appropriations and personnel decreased, despite increasing visitation and recreational use. Land managers continually cite a lack of funds and personnel for their inability to monitor impacts, enforce regulations, or adequately manage increasing recreational demands. ORV use poses particular problems, since the impacts are wide-ranging, the vehicles are difficult to contain, and motorized users are often well organized and prepared to oppose closures or increased regulations.

For cash-strapped land managers, motorized recreation has also proved to be something of a boon in recent years. Despite the damage they can inflict upon the land and other users, motorized recreationists are often generous with their time or money. A number of snowmobile and ORV clubs contribute to trail construction and rehabilitation, erosion control, and route maps. More importantly, vehicle manufacturers and user groups have also emerged as high-stakes sponsors of agency recreation programs. These contributions of cash and labor, depending on your perspective, come as either potential salvation for overburdened managers or as yet another sign that agencies will pander to whatever special interest has deep pockets. And Faustian bargain or not, tapping into recreation dollars gives some agency officials hope for the future.

In all likelihood, if motorized users had not been willing to "pay to play," few public lands would be open for them to ride on today. With serious environmental degradation by ORVs already well documented, the 1971 Department of the Interior Task Force suggested that each agency require ORV groups to deposit money to "cover the costs of restoration and rehabilitation of the trails and areas used, including restoration by reseeding or replanting when necessary."[118] This was further encouraged by the 1979 President's CEQ report, which recommended that ORV owners should pay for the maintenance and rehabilitation of special ORV facilities. The CEQ wrote, "[B]ecause the federal government has allowed ORVers to consume public resources free of charge, the general public has in a sense subsidized the ORV phenomenon."[119]

More recently, in 1996 Department of Agriculture undersecretary Jim Lyons proclaimed of the Forest Service, "Recreation is going to be our business in the future. By the year 2000, recreation will account for $97.8 billion of the $130.7 billion generated by activities on national forests."[120] While this would seem to promise more protection for lands as extractive timber and mining fade, a recreation boom could be every bit as devastating—and perhaps even more difficult to regulate or control—as traditional industries.

Photo 5-7: At facilities such as this off-road vehicle area in Oregon, the Forest Service provides loading ramps, trail guides, and dozens of miles of designated routes.

In some places, such as the Umatilla National Forest site shown in photo 5-7, timber sale areas have been retrofitted specifically to accommodate motorized recreational use. Legal scholars who note the overall decline of logging, grazing, oil and gas, and mining industries on public lands suggest that public land battles of the future will come from conflicts between motorized and nonmotorized recreationists.[121] In recent years federal agencies have begun to look to the private sector, not just for role models of corporate efficiency but also to create "win–win" arrangements that provide corporate funding or administrative help in exchange for concessionaire contracts, favorable publicity, or a share of recreation profits. These public–private partnerships now feature prominently in every agency's recreation future.

One group that has played a key role in such public–private unions is the American Recreation Coalition (ARC). Formed in 1979, ARC seeks to "catalyze public/private partnerships to enhance and protect outdoor recreational opportunities and the resources upon which such experiences are based."[122] This translates to two distinct policy positions: (1) free market incentives should apply to public land management, and (2) in order to do this succesfully, the private sector will play an important role. The National Recreational Trails Fund, discussed earlier, and Recreation Fee Demonstration Project are both major initiatives recommended by ARC.

Though public–private partnerships may sound attractive to many land managers and other Americans, ARC's agenda raises a number of troubling questions. As we have seen, ORVs currently cause significant ecological and social impacts on public lands. Just as conservationists have railed for years against below-cost timber sales in national forests, so have they raised concerns against spending federal funds to accommodate the noise, smoke, and dangers of ORVs on public lands. But what if the federal government actually made a hefty profit by allowing such uses? Would the amount of destruction caused by ORVs be justifiable if the profit margin were handsome?

The prospect of transferring land management decisions from unwieldy government agencies to crisply run private corporations has certain allure to some policy-makers, but granting private industry control of the commonly held lands of the nation simply for the sake of efficiency promises to undermine public interests for private gain. American Recreation Coalition members such as the National Rifle Association, American Petroleum Institute, American Suzuki Motor Corporation, National Hot Rod Association, Exxon, International Association for Amusement Parks and Attractions, and Walt Disney Corporation surely have commercial interests in mind, but their contributions to the public good may be less clear.[123] While philosophers, legal scholars, and policy analysts claim that the Sagebrush Rebellion of the 1980s was a notable failure in its attempt to shift public lands to private control, fundamentally this same effort may be alive and well today, simply dressed up as public–private partnerships.

On the San Bernardino National Forest in southern California, the forest's budget for recreation and wilderness management dropped from $2.7 million to $1.9 million from 1994 to 1998.[124] As government funding dropped, the San Bernardino turned to making partnerships with private corporations. By routing funds through a nonprofit organization, the San Bernardino Forest Association, the San Bernardino National Forest raised more than $1.3 million. Contributions have come from sources ranging from the U.S. Environmental Protection Agency to a local elementary school, but a sizable portion of the funding comes from companies with distinct economic interests: Snow Valley Ski Resort, Southern California Edison, and Honda, which alone donated $250,000. Honda and other vehicle manufacturers have also equipped the San Bernardino with a squadron of cars and ORVs.[125]

Adding to suspicions that more than philanthropy may be involved, the San Bernardino Forest Association's board has included Paul Slavik, an off-highway vehicle coordinator for American Honda. Honda helped design a 204-mile ORV route in the San Bernardino National Forest and has contributed to an annual motorcycle "enduro" event held there. Quoted in a 1998 *Los Angeles Times* article, Slavik described the Forest Association's role as one of prototype, "We wanted to develop a business plan for the forest that would make it self-sustaining and be a model that could be exported to the rest of the country."[126]

Such a plan should sit well with advocates who seek to apply free market policies to government agencies, but for others who decry the "commercialization, privatization, and motorization" of America's public lands, this template sounds disastrous.[127] Scott Silver, director of the Oregon-based group Wild Wilderness, is one of the nation's most outspoken critics of public–private partnerships. Silver points to industry-backed coalitions, whether Forest-specific organizations such as the San Bernardino Forest Association or national groups like the Blue Ribbon Coalition and American Recreation Coalition, as the vanguard of an attempted commercial takeover of nature in America.[128]

The Fee Demonstration Project

The leading edge of the commercialization of public lands may have emerged in 1996 when Congress granted the National Park Service, U.S. Forest Service, U.S. Fish and Wildlife Service, and BLM special authority to collect user fees "based upon cost recovery or fair market value" at a limited number of sites around the country. The Recreation Fee Demonstration Project, commonly known as "Fee Demo," has turned into a quietly heated debate that runs most sharply between those who view public lands as a freely available public good—like clean air or clean water—and those who think lands should be managed for a profit. Originally scheduled to expire in 1998, the Fee Demo program later received a congressional blessing to run experimentally until September 30, 2004. It remains to be seen if Congress and the agencies will turn to user fees on a permanent basis in order to ride the surging wave of outdoor recreation, but current numbers make this an enticing prospect.[129]

People are flocking to the public domain in nothing short of land-rush numbers. More than 35 million people visit our nation's wildlife refuges each year, a 46 percent gain since 1985.[130] BLM lands received 73 million recreational visitor days in 1995, an increase of 176 percent from 1982 and 600 percent since 1964.[131] The National Park System has seen patronage increase by more than 700 percent since 1950, to reach 287 million visits by 2000.[132] In national forests the boom is louder still: a 1,161 percent increase from 1950 to 1995 to reach more than 340 million annual recreational visitor days.[133] At the close of the twentieth century, outdoor recreation was a $350 billion industry, and approximately $140 billion of this was attributable to public lands.[134]

Adding luster to this apparent pot of gold for federal land managers, the Fee Demo program directs revenues back to the sites and agencies from which they were collected. This comes as a marked departure from former revenue streams. In the past, national parks and national forests charged fees at entrances or campgrounds, but whatever funds they raised flowed to the U.S. Treasury. The agencies then sought appropriations from Congress and disbursed funding as determined in broad planning documents. With Fee Demo, money returns directly to the agency and at least 80 percent is retained for the sites at which it was collected.[135]

Not surprisingly, an interagency report issued to Congress in January 2000 gave glowing reviews of the Fee Demonstration Project.[136] In the first three years of Fee Demo, the BLM, National Park Service, U.S. Forest Service, and Fish and Wildlife Service doubled their annual recreation fee revenues— and nearly all of it returned directly back to the agencies. In North Carolina's Uwharrie National Forest, for example, an ORV Fee Demo area raised $24,300 in gross revenues in fiscal year 2000 by charging $5 per vehicle per day or $30 for a season pass.[137] From these collections, the Uwharrie spent $18,500 on activities ranging from labor and supplies to the maintenance and administration of distinct ORV, horse, mountain bicycle, and hiking trails. The fee collection itself consumed $2,900 of the gross revenues.[138]

By the end of fiscal year 1999, the four agencies brought in $614 million from Fee Demo and expressed enthusiasm for expanding it to a permanent, nationwide program.[139] Both inside and outside the agencies, however, the Fee Demonstration Project has some critics. Land managers point to their lack of training (or interest) in running public lands as a business, as well as the difficulties of creating payment systems that are efficient or effective. Particularly for sprawling BLM, wildlife refuge, or national forest lands where there is often no single attraction or entrance gate, the logistics of fee collection can be overwhelming.[140]

Others note with alarm that the Fee Demo system creates an incentive for activities and developments that can bring in revenue, regardless of their appropriateness on public lands. If, for instance, ATVers are willing to pay $20 per day to drive through mountain streams, but anglers insist that they have a right to fish the streams for free, the market-driven Fee Demo system would favor ATV use. Fee Demo also essentially privatizes some public lands by encouraging public–private partnerships similar to those discussed earlier. As the Forest Service notes, "an important strategy to keep facilities open has been to permit concessionaires to run campgrounds and other facilities."[141] As agencies grant concessions to private enterprises for campgrounds or interpretive centers (or increasingly elaborate resorts, as some envision), the public good may be siphoned into the corporate good. For anyone who believes that these are not necessarily one and the same, the result is—at best—cause for concern. Finally, Congress has shown a tendency to reduce agency appropriations as Fee Demo revenues increase. This can create the appearance of steady budgets for agency programs, but in fact strictly limits the types of activities that receive funding. Restoration and monitoring work, for example, do not typically bring in Fee Demo receipts. As appropriations drop, these types of programs feel the fiercest cuts.

Rights of Passage: The Motorized versus Nonmotorized Debate

"What are they going to tell the guy who just went down and bought himself a brand new 4-wheeler for five thousand bucks? You can't ride that thing anymore? You think he bought it just to keep it shiny sitting home in his garage? No way! They can't keep us out."

I'm at an Interagency open house in Missoula, Montana, to learn about the BLM and Forest Service's newest proposal to manage ORVs on trails and roads. Though the atmosphere inside is relaxed and cozy, aided by the first real snowfall of the year and the twinkling of holiday lights across the Clark Fork River, not everyone is feeling warmed by the prospect of being restricted from areas currently open to all types of motorized use.

The man chatting next to me in a denim "Big Sky 4-Wheelers" jacket is in his mid- to late thirties, wears a trimmed mustache, and speaks the motorized recreation party line: "It doesn't make any sense. You tell us we can't go into places where we've been going for years and you expect us to just walk away? It's not going to happen. What they're saying is you can hike anywhere you want, but if you want to ride your ATV you're out of luck. What's the matter with these people? They're elitists! Do they need to go back to kindergarten or something so they can learn how to share?"

Regardless of how lengthy a list you can put together about the adverse impacts of ORVs or their economic benefits to local coffers, your ultimate views on these machines will depend upon values and ethics, not numbers on the page.

What difference does it make, after all, if ORVs are harmful to elk if you don't care about elk? If the highest imaginable value of a given piece of land is for you to drive there easily and swiftly, then allowing motorized use might be the obvious choice. Each of us will choose to manage land very differently depending upon whether we are interested in preserving scenic vistas or native biodiversity, for example, or in maximizing revenues or annual visitation. As a result, the most daunting questions that face agencies trying to manage ORV use are those that tap into our societal values of who or what belongs on our public lands.

Though ORV boosters try to embrace middle-class values when they portray themselves and their sport, the purchase of even a mid-range machine would require an average American to spend 20 percent of his or her annual salary. Indeed, a survey of backcountry users in Idaho found that ORV users averaged higher incomes and were younger than nonmotorized recreationists.[142] Other research found that vehicle-based campers and backcountry campers had no significant differences in income levels, though both were above average.[143] These findings run contrary to the stereotype portrayed by many motorized use groups of youthful, elitist backpackers trying to close off public lands to all the "regular folk."

A survey in the early 1970s of cross-country skiers and snowmobilers in Minnesota did find that the skiers were more urban and more wealthy than the snowmobilers.[144] But the only point common to each of these studies was the finding that nonmotorized users were better educated than their motoring counterparts. If education is the yardstick by which we measure elitism, then motorized recreationists may have a valid gripe; otherwise, it remains very much in question whether hikers or horsepackers are much different socioeconomically (i.e., more wealthy, youthful, or urban) than ORV users.

At the most polarized edges of the debate over motorized recreation on public lands, arguments tend to break in several directions. To motorized users, their opponents are selfish elitists who thoughtlessly elevate their own "special uses," such as hiking, cross-country skiing, or riding horseback, above the equally valid activities of driving ATVs or snowmobiling. Conversely, to "quiet trails" advocates, motorized users are consumptive motorjunkies who believe in a version of "might makes right": if their machine *might* be able to drive somewhere, then they ought to have the *right* to give it a try. Generally more allied with the quiet trails side, conservation biologists and others argue that access of all kinds may need to be controlled to protect biodiversity and sensitive species.

Of course, the middle ground between these clashing views is cluttered with philosophical debris. Nonmotorized horsepackers and mountain bicyclists sometimes side with the "mechanicals" and sometimes with the quiet trails advocates; some people are both hikers *and* ORV riders; consumer safety advocates consider ATVs an unconscionable hazard to young riders, whereas other groups point to the "family values" gained by children and parents banding together for a day trip on their machines; some hunters use ATVs, whereas others loathe them. A number of ORV boosters identify themselves as conservationists and choose to drive through the wilds in order to "experience nature." And though their organizations tend to present the appearance of a unified, monolithic agenda, motorized recreationists individually differ in their opinions about what kinds of activities should be allowed in certain places.

Protecting The Public Good

Throughout America's history, societal needs and preferences have largely dictated the nation's policies. Through much of this time, land use has focused on the elusive concept of the public good. As our society changes, it makes sense that the ideals of the public good change as well.[145] When motorcycles first puttered onto public lands in the early 1900s, for example, people were captivated more by the novelty of the new machines than by concern over their impacts. Today, the opposite is largely true.

Social values, like laws and land use regulations, change over time. If, for instance, we didn't realize that ORVs adversely impacted the landscape, wildlife, or other visitors, why would we worry about trying to limit them? What we know and understand as a society rightfully plays a role in the degree to which we modify our policies and apply restraint.

What we are facing to varying degrees on our federal lands is a failed policy to manage motorized recreation as one of several uses. In fact, as just described, motorized recreation almost invariably becomes a dominant use of the land, violates principles of minimal fairness, degrades nonmotorized experiences, damages wildlife habitat, harms water quality, and diminishes other public goods.

If we as a nation seek to maximize short-term profits by charging user fees, privatizing public lands, or commercializing public goods, then we might well encourage the proliferation of ATVs or snowmobiles. If, however, we seek a different vision that retains public land as a shared, common good for the long term, then even the current level of motorized recreational use appears to be excessive. Statistics and studies play an important role, but ultimately the choice we face is a subjective one of values and public benefit. As a society, we will need to find the political and administrative will to make and implement decisions that provide for suitable types of recreation in suitable places. Even in the third-largest country in the world, there is not enough space for everyone to do everything everywhere.

Assessing Recreational Values

Acknowledging an ethic of restraint and being able to stir this element into access management policies are not always synonymous. We continue to struggle to appreciate or quantify nonconsumptive land use values. It is relatively easy to chop down a tree, mill it into two-by-fours, and determine its value at the lumberyard. But numbers fail us when it comes to evaluating the worth of a peaceful day's hike in the forest. Or, for that matter, how much it is worth for a forest simply to exist.

Economists have tried several methods to characterize nonmarket values, but these efforts typically suffer from the contortions of stuffing abstract aesthetic or spiritual values into the crisply defined boxes of a financial ledger. One method quantifies how much a person spends to participate in a particular activity, and transfers that value to the activity itself. If the forest-bound hiker pays five dollars in gas to drive to a trailhead, that activity might be "worth" five dollars. Similarly, if the hiker pays five hundred dollars to fly to the Olympic Peninsula for a stroll amid the ancient rainforest, that hike would be worth five hundred dollars.[146] One problem with this method comes from the variability of costs to the hiker. If you climb on your bicycle, ride to a trailhead, and go for a hike in the nearest national forest without ever paying a cent, what is the travel cost value of that experience?

A related method for identifying nonmarket values is to ask people what they would pay to create or prevent a hypothetical change in the resource. If you are accustomed to hiking through the stubble of overgrazed fields of weeds, how much cash would you hand over to walk through a healthy tall grass prairie on the same site? Or back to the walk in the forest, how much is it worth to you to hike among the trees without any clear-cuts? The responses here would likely differ if your annual income was $10,000 versus $500,000. Turn it again and we can also try to estimate how much it is worth to retain a forest for some potential extractive or medicinal use.[147]

Using some of these methods, analysts pegged 1995 "recreation benefits" on national forest and BLM lands at $9.8 billion.[148] Going beyond recreation, another study tried to compute the value of "ecosystem services" contributed by wetlands, forests, grasslands, and other natural systems. Using an imputed market value, these ecosystem services totaled to a formidable $294 billion on national forest and BLM lands.[149] Measured by receipts to the federal government during this same year, extractive industries such as timber, grazing, and mining generated a relatively modest $11.4 billion.[150] Nonmarket economics can illustrate shades of value for recreational or environmental amenities, but this doesn't necessarily lead to money flowing into bank accounts—a measure that many people trust more thoroughly.

Although some economists distinguish between cash flow and value to society, it is generally easier to measure and reap the commercial value of motorized recreation on public lands than it is to quantify the value of nonmotorized activities that require little or no specialized equipment.[151] If a day's snowmobile rental in West Yellowstone, Montana, is worth $160 to the outfitter renting the sled, is the same day's outing on snowshoes only worth the $15 snowshoe rental price? By these terms, a day spent on cross-country skis that cost $100 would pale in comparison with a day on a brand new $8,000 Polaris snowmobile. Land managers or retailers interested in taking a cut of the profits may be inclined to make these types of judgments, since recreationists may be willing (and able) to pay more to use a pricey snowmobile than a relatively cheap pair of skis.

Private Lands or Public Goods?

At least one effort to assess the propriety of civic actions dates back more than 2,000 years. Greek philosophers sought to evaluate the relative merits of individual gain versus the collective good. In *Ethics,* Aristotle argued that the good of a nation "has a higher, diviner, quality" than the good of the individual.[152] Extending this rationale to the recreational use of public lands, federal management would emphasize collective national benefits rather than individual thrills or profits.

The ethical prospects for motorized recreation pale even further under the friendly gaze of political and legal philosophy, realms inhabited by founding fathers of American property rights such as John Locke and Thomas Jefferson. Locke's tenet of land ownership focused on human labor—a foundation upon which the Homestead Act and General Mining Law were based—and is often cited by advocates for private property rights. Locke qualified his views, however, with the assertion that land acquisition is appropriate because of its benefit to others.

In a similar manner, Thomas Jefferson supported the property right of usufruct, which literally means "use and enjoyment." While this view supports recreation as an appropriate land use, it does not countenance destructive recreation. Stemming from Locke, Jefferson, and others, Americans came into a tradition that emphasized use without destroying, damaging, or diminishing the land.[153] Any claim to ownership or personal gain remained limited to the service of the common good.[154]

For much of the nineteenth and twentieth centuries as a nation we lapsed from this tradition, but by the 1960s and '70s we had returned more strongly to the fundamental premise of using land—private or public—without degrading it. President Richard Nixon noted this view in 1970:

> We have treated our land as if it were a limitless resource. Traditionally Americans have felt that what they do with their own land is their own business. This attitude has been a natural outgrowth of the pioneer spirit. . . . The time has come when we must accept the idea that none of us has a right to abuse the land, and that on the contrary society as a whole has a legitimate interest in proper land use.[155]

To many environmentally minded citizens today, there is an ecological and moral imperative that people will not survive long or well in a severely degraded world. Along with this view comes a certain respect for the land, water, and ecosystems that sustain human and other lives.[156] With advances in science, we now have gained an increasingly clear understanding of how integrated humans are in natural processes and events, ranging from climate and the hydrologic cycle to evolution itself. Toward this end, environmental philosophers, conservation biologists, and others seek to construct new ethics that more appropriately describe a sustainable human relationship to the natural world.

In his 1980 book, *Mountains without Handrails,* Joseph Sax wrote, "The attitudes associated with an activity may be more important than either the activity itself or its setting. . . . While ORVs have sometimes caused great and long-lasting damage, the vehicle itself is not the crucial factor in the controversy its use has created."[157] Sax was writing primarily about motorcycles in a time before four-wheeled ATVs were mass produced. Although he was astute to point to attitudes—these still play a major role in the debate today—the vehicle type and its setting now also matter critically. Even the most timid and courteous of ATV drivers can cause impacts of noise, smoke, trampling, and erosion that an aggressive hiker simply cannot. As a study of the Cape Cod National Seashore concluded, dune vegetation "does not have a 'carrying capacity' for vehicles."[158] In this setting and many others, the machine is the problem.

Pursuing the Public Good

Despite our best efforts to quantify the cost of motorized recreation or roads on public lands, the equations spin differently depending upon the values considered—values not just in dollars, but also in terms of quality of life, lifestyle, tradition, and family history. Regardless of the cost–benefit analyses we may churn out, the future of recreation, roadbuilding, or road removal on public lands remains uncertain.

Looking out broadly at the landscape of our choices, we face a lingering question of economics and policy: is it appropriate to stop building roads or limit motorized access simply because of their costs? This question, like so many relating to roads and motorized recreation, ultimately points to issues of values that cannot be settled solely by a scientist's report or an accountant's books.

Access and road management on our public domain turn finally upon a painfully simple question that science and money will not answer: what is the public good? In order to approach the heart of this question, we will need to turn more fully to examine the role of government and the common struggle between local interests and federal control. We will need to look, once again, at what we think our public lands are for, what role they play in our lives and our society, and how we would like to pass them on to our children and beyond. We already know a good deal about roads and ORVs and what they cost. We have yet to figure out what our public lands are truly worth.

*If its purity and quiet are destroyed and broken by
the noise and smoke . . . then it will cease to belong to
the whole people and will be unworthy of the care
and protection of the national government.*

—1st Lt. Dan C. Kingman,
U.S. Army Corps of Engineers,
Yellowstone National Park, 1883

6 | Public Values, Public Lands

As a boy growing up in Colorado, I had a neigh-
bor who was an avid off-road motorcyclist. Nearly every Friday afternoon
in the summer, Gary would load his high-suspension trailbike into the bed
of his pickup and head for the mountains. Each Sunday he would come
home with his motorcycle, boots, and pants splattered with grit and mud.
Gary, like a number of trail riders, loved being outdoors, enjoyed using
national forest trails, and, I have little doubt, was courteous to other folks
he met. He liked to ride slowly. He had a shelf full of trophies from com-
petitions in which the winners were not the motorcyclists who finished
first, but rather those who managed to travel the course slowly without
touching their feet to the ground.

There may have been hikers or horsepackers who occasionally met
Gary on trails and cursed him, or who later came across his tire tracks and
grumbled at the ruts, but I never heard him talk about user conflicts. Colorado was not pristine in the 1970s, but forest trails were still entirely free
of three- or four-wheeled off-road vehicles (ORVs) and mountain bikes—
these machines had not yet been commercially produced—and the backcountry seemed to have trail miles to spare.

In recent decades, conditions and use on public lands in Colorado and
many other places across the country have changed. Fast-growing cities

from Colorado Springs to Fort Collins have doubled the state's population and increased the recreational pressure on nearby public lands. As discussed in Chapter 5, the proliferation of four-wheeled all-terrain vehicles (ATVs), mountain bikes, and other outdoor products has brought different uses to area trails and triggered new varieties of user conflicts. Hikers who were once tolerant of a handful of motorcyclists react negatively to ATVers, even careful ones, who drive on or off trails, or who need modified, widened trails. And, as the pool of mechanized trail users has expanded beyond the relatively skillful or dedicated few, the number of irresponsible, aggressive, or destructive riders has increased.

Despite the ubiquity of roaded lands, when federal agencies try to restrict motorized access or close or obliterate roads, it often creates a tremendous wave of resentment. In Idaho's Targhee National Forest, which abuts Yellowstone National Park to the west and is infamous for its swaths of clear-cuts and a noodling network of roads, a modest plan to strengthen travel restrictions so outraged locals that the state's congressional representatives intervened, pressed the agency to conduct a costly revision of its environmental analysis, and published a scathing critique in *Range Magazine*.[1] Even in areas where roads were built and never scheduled to be open for public access, "wise use" and motorized recreation groups have complained bitterly when agencies announced plans for road closure or obliteration.

Whereas ORV users were once restricted by virtue of their machines or skills to certain landscapes, to a great degree they no longer are. Public land managers now regularly confront a cohort of users who believe that because they are able to motor anywhere they please, legally they should be allowed to do so as well. At times, agencies have simply changed laws to accommodate new technologies without pausing to assess the environmental or social consequences.[2] The land, and people seeking peace and quiet outdoors, consequently suffer from ever increasing levels of motorized use (see Chapter 5).

Adding to the mix, scientists and land managers have grown increasingly aware of the impacts to soil, wildlife, water, or other visitors that motorized use—even responsible motorized use—causes. After the 1973 passage of the Endangered Species Act (ESA), agencies also needed to keep a closer watch to protect sensitive animal and plant populations. Other laws passed in the 1970s tightened the reins on ORV use and gave increased guidance for the management of multiple-use lands (Chapter 5).[3]

Although motorized access restrictions on public lands remain controversial in many places, these limits may simply represent a natural evolution of public values and ethics. A number of "wise use" groups assert that restrictions on motorized access are an unfair imposition of federal authority on individuals' rights, but these regulations may actually reflect changes in our society and the environment appropriately translated into public policy. If ethics determine how we ought to live, then ethical public policies will need to apply this sense of right and wrong to behavior on our public lands, even at the expense of some constituents' desires.[4]

My neighbor Gary was basically a good guy: he was friendly and quiet and had a decent sense of humor. He seemed to be happily married, had nice kids, worked hard, and, at the time, recreated responsibly. In the context of the mid-1970s, his motorcycling on national forest trails caused little concern. However, with the changes we have witnessed since that time, motorized recreation in many of these same places today might cause problems.[5] If Gary's interests did not keep pace with changing times, he would surely be disappointed, perhaps even outraged, to return one day to a trail he had motorcycled and find it open to hikers only.

This brings out an important point about ethics: we might not always like what they tell us to do. Ethics guide us to act with restraint. As philosopher Holmes Rolston III notes, "Ethics is not merely about what humans love, enjoy, find rewarding, nor about what they find wonderful, ennobling, or transforming. It is sometimes a matter of what humans *ought* to do, like it or not" (emphasis in original).[6]

Passions tend to flare over public lands. These places represent, after all, the extremes of our attitudes toward land. They are the places we deemed too precious to turn over to private ownership, the crown jewels of our nation's lands, and they are those "wastelands" we considered too barren or dreadful to possess. In either case, public lands can inspire us with feelings that range from profound spirituality to desperate greed.

As a result, for public lands—as with other public goods such as air, water, or wildlife—we have needed to recognize an ethic that supplants individual desire for the rights of people collectively. If applied successfully, this system of values for managing our public lands and the access to these lands would respond more to the whole than the parts, and cater more to the collective good than to individual gain. Environmental laws and other policies have codified some of these protective measures already, but legislation and ethics need to keep pace with society's pressures. The federal government originally managed public lands with an eye toward giving them away, but since the late 1800s the United States has strengthened its view that public lands represent an enduring public good.[7] In fact, the federal government broadly accepts a responsibility to manage public lands as a public trust.

Ethics, and more specifically, environmental ethics, can help frame the debate that results from trying to make public policy out of disparate views. There will inevitably be people who feel excluded from the process, or who chafe against the policies that emerge, but by focusing on ethics and values we can at least make decisions about roads and motorized access that come from our best effort to determine what is the right way to live with our public lands. This land management ethic will need to consider ecological, economic, social, and spiritual interests, among others.

From the earliest years of public land management, dating back to the first U.S. Army managers of Yellowstone National Park, Americans have made distinctions between the way we should treat land generally and the way we should treat it within federal land reserves. As a result, we have gradually developed several recognizable *land management ethics* for our public lands.

Similar to the land ethic described by Aldo Leopold in *A Sand County Almanac,* land management ethics encompass the policies and characteristics we consider "right" for our public lands.[8] Our land management ethic, like Leopold's, should also extend the boundaries of our ethical community "to include soils, waters, plants, and animals, or collectively: the land."[9] There are other common traits to public land management ethics. For example, we should manage these lands for the public good rather than for individual or corporate gain, and we should manage lands to protect their integrity for centuries to come. In addition to these commonalities there are also distinct ethics for the different types of federal land.

Getting There: Access and Ethics on Public Lands

Americans have consistently placed a high value on getting to public lands, whether to visit the beaches of the Atlantic seacoast, the geyser basins of Yellowstone, the South Rim of the Grand Canyon, or the towering forests of the Pacific Northwest. For more than a century, we have made it easier to get to this public domain from wherever we are.

Despite this fact, tens of millions of Americans still value these national parks, forests, wildlife refuges, and BLM lands even when they have no chance or desire ever to visit them. We treasure our public lands not only for the opportunities these places grant us for recreation, revenue, or revelation, but also for their very existence. Americans have, in effect, declared for many decades that our lives are richer simply because Yosemite National Park exists within the landscape of California's Sierra Nevada.

And yet, when it comes to roads and motorized access, we have to decide exactly how these lands ought to be managed. They come abundant with scenery, wildlife, forests, forage, oil and gas, and precious metals. And increasingly, our public lands come with roads and recreational demands that press us ever more to identify what constitutes the public good.

To clarify the public good, we can look in a number of directions. Many people recognize that customs and values necessarily change as a society's circumstances change.[10] In this fashion, cultural traditions and ethics developed in a sparsely settled continent gradually shift as people modify the land and their own lifestyles on the continent. In the United States, broad trends in land management policies have largely matched the degree of settlement and industrialization. As we touched upon earlier, in the context of mid-nineteenth-century America, laws that "disposed" of western land by giving it away in 160-acre homestead parcels, mining claims, or extensive railroad grants likely made a certain amount of sense because the nation's ideals were different. The West appeared to be a wide-open land that simply needed people to fill it, use it, and make it productive.[11]

Today, however, these same wide-open lands are vestiges of what once existed. People increasingly recognize now that relatively undisturbed landscapes are growing scarce and can have tremendous value—even, or *especially,* in an undeveloped condition. Out of a total landbase of 2.3 billion acres in the United States, in a little more than a century of highly mechanized activity modern Americans have managed to road, privatize, or industrialize 90 percent of the country.[12] Nationwide, lands that have not been roaded, logged, or otherwise heavily impacted by human activity are becoming quite rare.

Public opinion polls indicate that as a nation we place a high value on protecting the federal lands that remain free of roads.[13] Land managers increasingly share this view and the policies of most federal land management agencies now lean toward conserving roadless areas. What remains relatively unattended is how we should treat the majority of public lands already roaded or noticeably impacted by human activities. For decades, these lands have fallen beyond the watchful gaze of wilderness advocates and national conservation initiatives, primarily due to the perception that only the wildest lands are still worthy enough or possible to save. By these terms, two-thirds of our public lands would thereby be "too impaired" to merit widespread action. As a result, we have collectively dismissed some of the landscapes where we are potentially most useful. If we can apply an environmental ethic to all of our public lands, including those heavily roaded or degraded, we may still discover how we can manage them for the public good—and for their own good.

The Beginnings of a Land Management Ethic

The American frontier closed most famously in 1890, a date historian Frederick Jackson Turner pointed to as the time when Western lands were settled.[14] I have always been a little slow to receive history, but 100 years later, in 1990, the frontier finally closed a bit for me too. In mid-July of that year, my friend Bart and I hiked to the most remote location in the lower forty-eight United States and discovered it was just one long day's walk from the nearest road.

That place, near the southeast corner of Yellowstone National Park, remains roadless primarily thanks to former National Park Service director Stephen Mather. Though Mather was the Park Service's first, and in many cases most strident, champion of road building to promote tourism, in his 1920 *Report of the Director* he wrote, "It is my firm belief that a part of the Yellowstone country should be maintained as a wilderness for the ever-increasing numbers of people who prefer to walk or ride [horses] over trails in a region abounding in wild life."[15]

More to the point, Mather then headed off a proposal to construct a road through the southeast portion of the park: "I think a road around Lake Yellowstone or in the Upper Yellowstone and Thorofare country would mean the extinction of the moose. I am so sure that this view is correct that I would be glad to see an actual inhibition on new road building placed in the proposed extension [of the park boundaries] bill, this proviso to declare that without the prior authority of Congress no new road project in this region should be undertaken."[16] The road proposed for Yellowstone's southeast corner was never built, while countless roads elsewhere were, and Thorofare now remains the last place in the country more than eighteen miles from a road.[17]

It is not by coincidence that there are no roads in Thorofare country, along the east or south sides of Yellowstone Lake, or in the 105 million acres of designated wilderness in the United States. As a nation, and as individuals within this nation, we have made conscious decisions not to allow roads into every last piece of the public lands. These decisions ultimately come in response to questions of values.

In many of our scenic national parks, we still encounter beauty and nature not too distant from that found a century ago. In fact, even the policy of building key routes into national parks, but leaving large expanses free of roads, dates back more than 100 years. In 1887, U.S. Army captain Clinton Sears deemed it preferable in Yellowstone to build "thoroughly good roads and bridges . . . rather than attempt to secure a greater mileage of inferior roads."[18] Three decades later, in his 1918 Statement of Policy for the National Parks, Secretary of the Interior Franklin Lane declared, "In the construction of roads, trails, buildings, and other improvements, particular attention must be devoted always to the harmonizing of these improvements with the landscape."[19]

Despite occasional lapses in architectural judgment or today's traffic-jammed roadways, the National Park Service still provides many experiences that cater to our popular sense of aesthetics, whether we are near a road or not. We can visit Acadia National Park and still be moved by the first glint of sunrise hitting Cadillac Mountain or marvel at the rush of sea bursting from Blowhole Rock. Though some are crowded, threatened, or disturbed to a critical degree, many of these places still allow us to discover beauty and grandeur, much as the early national park supporters must have envisioned.

Road projects took shape differently and far more extensively in national forests, but these roads were also constructed with a philosophy particular to the lands' status as federal reserves. Roads and the lands within the national forests were managed largely from the utilitarian framework established by the agency's first forester, Gifford Pinchot. In 1905 Pinchot wrote, "In the administration of the forest reserves it must be clearly borne in mind that all land is to be developed to its most productive use for the permanent good of the whole people, and not for the temporary benefit of individuals or companies . . . where conflicting interests must be reconciled the question will always be decided from the standpoint of the greatest good of the greatest number in the long run."[20]

Although interpretation of this dictum has shifted at times in the ensuing decades—to build roads for tourist access, logging, or fire protection; to allow or limit motorized recreation; or even to prevent or remove roads—the Forest Service has continued to point to Pinchot's utilitarian principle. Despite the varied application of the agency philosophy, the utilitarian ethic itself remained intact.

From their inception, national parks and national forests came with clear reasons to build roads and, for the most part, the agencies have oriented to these ideologies: to provide a limited range of easy, aesthetically pleasing opportunities for park visitors, and to use the natural resources of the national forests to benefit the populace over the long term.

The Bureau of Land Management (BLM) broadly applied a utilitarian approach akin to that of the Forest Service, but never with the stentorian effect of Pinchot's vision. Lacking clear executive or legislative direction for much of the twentieth century, and working with lands that came patched together from common rangelands and the former domain of the General Land Office, the BLM often played into the hands of special interests keen to make money in the name of a financially conceived "greatest good." As a result, we have many roads on BLM lands that serve a local or industrial need, but that carry little or no public service. To this day, the BLM describes nearly all of its roads as "administrative." These routes are typically open to public use, but the classification allows the agency to manage roads more to its own terms and standards and not as part of the Federal Lands Highway Program discussed in Chapter 4.

A number of roads in the national wildlife refuges also came without the strong guidance of an agency mission or purpose. As noted earlier, the refuge system was cobbled together beginning with the designation of Pelican Island in 1903. As we brought these lands and their plants and animals into federal care, we also adopted the existing roads network as a public responsibility. Congress recognized the first part of this role more widely by passing the first ESA in 1966 (a predecessor to the more renowned 1973 act), but we continue to search for a consistent ethic to apply to roads and access.

Adding to the challenge, some refuge managers face problems more pressing than roads. The Big Oaks National Wildlife Refuge in Indiana, for example, was created in June 2000 from 50,000 acres of the Jefferson Proving Ground, a military range now cluttered with depleted uranium, unexploded ordnance, and other potential hazards to wildlife and human visitors.[21]

While the National Park Service and U.S. Fish and Wildlife Service have management prescriptions that already encourage movement away from new road construction, for the BLM and the Forest Service access and road management decisions hang more upon how we define the greatest good for the greatest number over the long term.

Each of these agencies now has some identifiable land management ethic—to manage for beauty, wildlife, and aesthetics in the national parks; to maximize utility sustainably in the national forests and BLM lands; and to fulfill our commitment to conserve biota in national wildlife refuges. Despite the fact that many animals, plants, watersheds, and landscapes receive protection as a result of the agencies' management goals, however, federal land stewardship remains focused on people.

The guiding language for national park policy, for example, states that parks "are set apart for the use, observation, health, and pleasure of the people."[22] Similar in its focus toward people, the early national forest policy statement penned by Gifford Pinchot declared, "All the resources of the Forest Reserves are for *use,* and this use must be brought about in a thoroughly prompt and businesslike manner, under such restrictions only as will insure the permanence of these resources (emphasis in original)."[23] In his 1996 executive order that gave the National Wildlife Refuge System its specific mission, President Clinton declared a policy "to preserve a national network of lands and waters for the conservation and management of fish, wildlife, and plant resources of the United States for the benefit of present and future generations."[24] The BLM makes this similarly clear: "It is the mission of the BLM to sustain the health, diversity and productivity of the public lands for the use and enjoyment of present and future generations."[25]

A focus on managing public lands for the well-being of people makes a good deal of sense. At some fundamental level, most of us will value our own lives or those of our fellow humans above those of the Douglas fir or white-tailed deer that we observe or plan to use for shelter or food. We may still regard these other living beings with respect and care, but our land management priorities point toward humans first. With this attitude largely intact, we have been willing to build roads into forests or drive ORVs across deserts to pursue goods or happiness for people.

Managing Lands for the Good of the People

Some long-held management philosophies still lead to sensible and ethical policies, but as amenity values of public lands rise—with booming industries in recreation, tourism, and others characteristic of the "New

West"—and extractive industries such as mining and logging sag into decline, land managers ought to adjust their preferred objectives.[26] Such a shift is already emerging in the Forest Service, as we saw earlier, where agency officials have begun to point to an emphasis on recreation revenues and the diminution of logging and mining activities.[27] The agency's September 2000 report, *The Recreation Agenda,* described some of its goals for a recreation focus, stating "We will encourage travel and tourism opportunities in collaboration with tourism professionals and State Tourism Offices."[28] Of course, the change to a recreation emphasis might create ethical problems of its own if agency recreational policies allow corporations to privatize public goods, or if the quality and quantity of recreational activities cause serious damage.

Considering past degradations and the changing economies of the western United States, a shift in land management priorities from mining or logging to recreation has certain appeal. This transition does not represent a fundamental change in agency philosophy—whether recreation or timber harvest is the top priority, the Forest Service still caters its management for the people—but it shows an ability to evolve with changing conditions. In other words, the agency still functions with utilitarian principles, but it may be an increasingly modern utilitarianism as officials recognize and adapt to changes in society and the environment.

Again, it remains to be seen whether a recreation emphasis on public lands will lead to reduced or increased roadbuilding and motorization. Since the majority of road miles in national forests came as timber roads, a decrease in logging activities might correspond to a reduced need for road access. However, different types of recreation generate different demands. Backpackers, horsepackers, and backcountry skiers might work to protect roadless areas and advocate for road removal, since these activities are not directly dependent upon roads and, in fact, often come as part of an effort to get away from roads. Other activities, such as fishing, wildlife photography, or hunting tend to benefit from low road densities and the improved habitat that brings, but anglers, for instance, may appreciate easy access and not associate roads with poor fishing. Meanwhile, motorized recreationists, "Sunday drivers," or berry pickers might lobby for steady or increased road access, since these activities are more obviously road dependent.

The balancing act of road costs and benefits carries to national park and national wildlife refuge management as well. Roads allow people to come to these public lands easily and swiftly. After visiting first-hand, people may then be more likely to develop an ethic of care and concern for these accessible but relatively natural places. From its early years to this day, the National Park Service has built roads, lodges, and restaurant facilities to entice tourists to visit. There is, of course, the counterpoint that roads and subsequent crowds of people can overwhelm the natural features of a place or render it inhospitable to native plants and wildlife.

Americans, and indeed many people throughout the world, tend to know and care about the national park system. Places such as the Great Smokies, Yellowstone, and Yosemite are not only famous, they are loved. People visit these parks by the millions each year, and we commonly talk or read about them; national parks have become prominent in our national psyche. Ask a ten-year-old to name a national park, and you are likely to get a smile of recognition and a list of several scenic wonders. Ask the same child to name a national wildlife refuge, and you may receive a blank look.[29] When did you or your neighbor, for that matter, last visit a national wildlife refuge?

The policy of building roads into parks and other refuges to encourage tourists to come and appreciate these public lands works well, especially if we are managing with human interests as the priority.

Even if it maintains a focus on people, equating a healthy environment with healthy long-term economies can lead toward different actions and, in time, new ethics. Although politicians continue to subvert environmental protection for presumed economic prosperity, many economists and citizens view the two as components of a whole. In the Pacific Northwest, for example, road building and logging have severely impacted the multimillion dollar salmon fishery. These activities in the tributary watersheds of rivers such as the Snake, Columbia, and Salmon have reduced the rivers' productivity for the spawning and rearing of young salmon, even though the impacts may occur far inland and removed from fishing fleets on the coast.[30]

Environmental degradations from dams, agriculture, and roads have clearly led to economic losses for the fishing industry. In this case, concern for the salmon fishing industry and concern over excessively roaded public lands align very well. Restoring national forest watersheds in the Pacific Northwest to a less roaded condition could contribute nicely to an economic boost for the fishing industry (especially if coupled with strategic dam removal). In this way, concern about the fishing industry's survival can prompt new approaches to land management and road construction, maintenance, or removal. In short, the loss of salmon can lead us to think differently about how we ought to manage heavily roaded (or still unroaded) headwater areas. In response, we might create a new land management ethic that emphasizes reducing road densities to try to enhance fisheries. This change is, in fact, already taking place in the Northwest.

The case for reducing road miles and motorization on public lands may also come out of concern for future generations. Relatively undisturbed landscapes remain prized as storehouses for scientific discoveries and genetic diversity, as well as places for communion with nature.[31] Many people believe these practical and spiritual attributes are the strongest reason of any for preserving the remaining roadless public lands, restricting motorized recreation, and removing unnecesary, obsolete roads.

These arguments for limiting or reducing roads on our nation's public lands rest upon the traditional utilitarian idea that the best policy is one that promotes the greatest happiness (or greatest good) for the greatest number of people. Although other factors such as the conservation of biological diversity may play a role, the determination of what is "right" still comes down to a determination of what is right for us. The reason to protect biodiversity, then, as we have traditionally constructed it, is to preserve some potential scientific, medical, aesthetic, or other benefit for humanity.

These human-focused (anthropocentric) arguments for removing roads or limiting motorized recreation appeal since we generally can relate to prospective benefits to other people—even if those individuals or communities exist in a different place or in the future. Utilitarian claims for road removal or other environmental actions are also relatively secure legally, as they match well with some of the existing purposes of land management agencies and laws. If we demonstrate convincingly that road removal contributes to the public good, it is but a short step to reach a Forest Service policy that ascribes to that management philosophy.

The problem with a utilitarian approach, identified effectively by philosopher Eric Katz, is that it relies entirely upon the desires and circumstances of the human society at the time.[32] The public lands, waters, or wildlife in question remain valuable only for their potential or actual usefulness to people. Thus, the land never gains rights in and of itself, but rather exists as an instrument of the people, to be consumed or conserved as the populace and its leaders at the time see fit.

Back in 1920, Francis Sumner wrote in *Scientific Monthly*, "[L]et us not justify every step that we take by appeals to economic and crassly utilitarian motives."[33] Since that time we have added the beneficial insights of scientific evidence, economics, and changing social and geographical circumstance in order to contend that it is time to reconsider what it means to manage access for the public good. In fact, we have reached a time not just to ask about the kinds of utilities we value on these public lands, but also to question the fundamental role of utilitarian approaches to land management more generally.

Practicing Restraint on Public Lands

Applied to the context of roads and motorized recreation on public lands, the search for an environmental ethic leads us to ask how we should continue to live with and access our public lands. As with most questions that hinge upon values, there are no easy answers. That is not to say that there are no right answers. It is now commonplace to hear politicians or neighbors consenting to "agree to disagree," but we are in fact well accustomed to making value judgments and abiding by them in the name of ethical decisions.

As a nation we have a wealth of laws that attempt this exactly, rendering certain opinions more or less valid than others. We have, for example, century-old laws that essentially declare that my personal desires are less valid than society's collective wishes. As a result, regardless of how fervently I might want to run a power turbine off of Old Faithful, my wishes are subverted in deference to the public good and uses permitted by federal law. Similarly, even though I might want to drive seventy miles per hour through Yellowstone or drive off-road, the laws in place dictate that I keep myself to forty-five miles per hour and stick to the roads.

In this same spirit, sightseeing from a vehicle is a rightful act on national park roads, while the same activity would lead to a heavy fine if you were caught doing it within a wilderness area (where roads and motorized vehicles are banned entirely). Even though we, as individuals, may sometimes shy away from making determinations of "right" versus "wrong" in other people's actions, as a nation we have a long record of making such distinctions. In Yellowstone National Park in 1920, recall, Stephen Mather declared that it would not be right to construct a road in the Thorofare country. As a nation, we have not so much agreed to disagree as we have agreed that certain actions and points of view are more "right" than others. This is, at least in part, what laws do.

In the United States, the distinctive qualities of particular national parks, national forests, wildlife refuges, and BLM lands have fostered certain customs and expectations about how we, collectively and individually, will treat these lands. Even as a child, for example, I quickly associated visits to Rocky Mountain National Park with a heightened sense of respect and I acted accordingly: I held off on collecting shiny stones or picking flowers, and didn't try to chase, feed, or ride the animals. The land's designation as a federal reserve encouraged me to develop a different ethic for my behavior there. My neighbor Gary, too, made a distinction between motorized access in national forests, where he liked to motorcycle on trails and considered it appropriate, and national parks where he restricted himself to driving on paved roads or hiking on trails. Gary understood that both individually and as a society we valued the integrity of the national park enough to forgo the privilege of driving wherever we pleased.

More broadly, as a society we have learned more and more to recognize our dependence upon the world around us for our long-term survival. As ethicist Paul Thompson puts it, "People have widely accepted the notion that the present generation is morally obligated to pass an ecologically whole environment on to our progeny."[34]

Spirituality and Nature

For many people, our relationship to public lands can roam from the occupational or recreational into the spiritual. John Muir, naturalist and founder of the Sierra Club, frequently referred to nature in terms rich with spiritual resonance. In a letter to Ralph Waldo Emerson, for instance, Muir wrote of "a month's worship with Nature in the high temples of the great Sierra Crown beyond our holy Yosemite."[35] When the Bureau of Reclamation proposed to dam the Colorado River and flood parts of the Grand Canyon in the 1960s, the Sierra Club ran newspaper and magazine ads that clearly linked nature with spirituality: "Should we also flood the Sistine Chapel so tourists can get nearer the ceiling?"[36] Indeed, to witness billion-year-old Vishnu schist in the depths of the Grand Canyon or to walk through ancient redwood forests can quickly move us to thoughts of creation and evolution and the wonder of life on Earth.

In fact, many religious traditions are also compatible with a strong environmental ethic. Although religion, unlike ethics, relies upon divine revelation for its basic truths, principles such as humility and restraint commonly run through both. Organizations such as the Christian Evangelical Environmental Network advocate for both religious faith and environmental protection, helping to emphasize the fundamental compatibility of spirituality and caring for the natural world.[37]

Regardless whether we make decisions out of faith-based or secular values, the resulting ethic can contribute to progressive policies for access management on public lands. A decision not to steal from our neighbors might come out of respect for the law, respect for a religious code, pragmatic interest in sustaining a healthy relationship, or something else altogether, but the result is likely positive regardless. Similarly, we might choose to restrict motorized access on public lands in keeping with a number of different values and the result can be productive. Especially in the pluralistic society of the United States that includes people of many different faiths, a land management ethic that accommodates a variety of traditions will surely prove most durable and successful.

The Relationship Between Law and Ethics

In order to last, a nation of laws must also be a nation open to change. Where we once extolled the courage of men—Lewis and Clark, for instance—for shooting and killing a plains grizzly bear, we would now fine or incarcerate them for a similarly unprovoked deed. It is not a matter of Lewis and Clark suddenly growing villainous in our eyes, for they have not; rather, the change comes from a shift in our values and ethics as a society—that is, in the way it makes sense for us to lead our lives—and for the subsequent or accompanying adjustment of law. Simply put, we (generally) no longer kill grizzly bears out of curiosity or ignorance, because few wild grizzlies remain, we value their continued existence, and we have learned to reduce conflicts with bears using nonlethal techniques such as taking care of our food and garbage.

Just as laws such as the ESA have responded to our increased recognition that plants, animals, and their habitats might be irreparably lost without a law that conveys certain restraints—and that we do not want to lose these components of our world—so have we established other environmental laws to mark and codify changes in appropriate land use, resource extraction, or recreation. In this manner, laws that established the land management agencies, as well as other environmental laws, have demonstrated shifts in the popular view of how we should manage our public lands and the common good.[38] Whether you admire it or not, this body of environmental law represents one of the clearest clues about our national environmental ethic.

The first of the Organic Acts that established direction for land management agencies came in 1897 and identified purposes for the national forest reserves. The 1897 Organic Act responded to several broad concerns in American society: the nation was losing its forest lands at an alarming rate, timber thieves were stealing millions of dollars worth of trees each year, and soil and water conditions were worsening.[39]

Leaders at the time recognized that something needed to be done or the nation as a whole would lose. As Secretary of the Interior Columbus Delano stated in his 1874 *Annual Report,* "The rapid destruction of timber in this country, and especially that which is found on the public lands, is a source of great solicitude to all persons who have given the subject any consideration. If this destruction progresses in the future as rapidly as in the past, the timbered lands of the Government will soon be denuded of everything that is valuable. Effective legislation protecting these lands from such waste is absolutely necessary, and cannot longer be neglected without serious injury to the public interest."[40] Three years later, Interior Secretary Carl Schurz noted, "How disastrously the destruction of the forests of a country affects the regularity of the water supply in its rivers necessary for navigation, increases the frequency of freshets and inundations, dries up springs, and transforms fertile agricultural districts into barren wastes, is a matter of universal experience the world over."[41] It still took all of two decades and extensive negotiations in Congress to pass legislation, but the 1897 law finally set forth to protect the public interest in forest lands.

Laws, however, are not the same as ethics. At this moment, I could *legally* drive an ATV cross-country on many roadless wildlands managed by the BLM or Forest Service. But many people—conservationists as well as some motorized recreationists—would contend that such an action would not be *ethical* if it displaced other users, harmed water quality, or disturbed plants and wildlife. In a similar fashion, if a group of citizens barricaded a national forest road in order to prevent motorized access to endangered wildlife populations, agency officials could arrest the activists for illegally closing a public road, but the blockade might be an entirely ethical response to the situation. In this manner, we have historically treated nonviolent civil disobedience as an illegal but ethical reply to certain conditions.

If we view laws more broadly as ethical landmarks, we can identify gradual trends in our cultural landscape as it has shifted from an attitude of utility and the extraction of resources to one of increased public involvement and the conservation of our nation's lands, waters, and wildlife. As we work to determine how we should manage the roads and motorized vehicles that currently course liberally across our public lands, we will need to confront these questions of values and ethics as well as those of law.

Protecting The Public Trust: Access Management and the Public Trust Doctrine

One useful convergence between law and ethics comes with our nation's obligation to protect the public trust. Just as Americans turned the care of endangered and migratory wildlife over to the federal government's trust, so have we developed the expectation of federal care for certain lands and waters. Although the public trust was originally applied to questions of navigation and public waterways, many legal scholars now point to the concept more broadly as one staunchly supportive of land and environmental protections.[42]

In 1966, five citizens took a ski corporation, American Resort Services, to court over a proposal to develop a ski area and tramway on Mount Greylock, the highest peak in Massachusetts. The plaintiffs claimed that the ski resort would essentially and inappropriately change a public good, the Mount Greylock State Reservation, into private gain. Although the Massachusetts Legislature had previously granted permission to American Resort Services to build the tramway and other facilities on the mountain, the Supreme Judicial Court of Massachusetts ruled against development. The court stated that it exceeded the authority of Massachusetts to transfer public lands into private control for "commercial venture."[43]

To justify its decision, the Massachusetts high court turned to an unlikely ally: an aged legal principle called the public trust doctrine. Passed to the American judicial system by common law dating back to the British and Roman Empires, this legal doctrine establishes that certain public goods are so important they should not be privatized or managed to the benefit of the few over the interests of the many.[44] Especially when an action threatens diverse public interests for the sake of a narrower constituency, the public trust becomes a key ally.[45] Although the Greylock ruling occurred at the state level, and some state courts have applied trust responsibilities even in the absence of a specific statute, the public trust has emerged in federal cases as well. Philosophically, and perhaps legally, this same doctrine can apply to the management and removal of roads on public lands.

Court interpretations of the public trust have now extended well beyond the traditional bounds of navigable waterways and compelled state and federal agencies, such as Redwood National Park, to take action to protect land resources.[46]

In a series of lawsuits from 1974 to 1976, the Sierra Club sued the U.S. Department of the Interior for not preventing logging activities on private lands adjacent to Redwood National Park.[47] Citing specific statutes such as the 1916 National Park Service Organic Act and Redwood Park's charter, the Northern California District Court determined that it was the secretary of the interior's responsibility to protect the park—by negotiating logging contracts and purchasing the land threatened by logging.[48] While the court depended primarily upon statutory provisions, its ruling also cited "a general trust duty" on the part of the Park Service. In this fashion, the court included trust language to help force a federal land managing agency into action.[49]

As early as 1886 the U.S. Supreme Court acknowledged and affirmed the existence of the public trust in land disputes: "All the public lands of the nation are held in trust for the people of the whole country," but left the determination of how that trust would be expressed to the Congress.[50] Thirty years later, the Ohio Supreme Court turned to the public trust in a 1916 decision: "An individual may abandon his private property, but a public trustee cannot abandon public property." The state court thereby made it clear that the public interest could not be ignored.[51]

If we view public lands under the lens of the public trust doctrine, we can consider the Forest Service and other agencies to be trustees of a sprawling network of roads. In accord with the early court rulings, the agencies should not abandon or ignore this public property. By this measure, we might wonder if agencies have upheld their public trust obligations as tens of thousands of road miles fall to poor maintenance and neglect. All these roads need not be kept open and in a usable condition—

as we have seen, we already have more access than we need—but such obsolesence needs to be planned and systematic rather than an arbitrary abandonment if we are to keep the public trust.

Law professor Joseph Sax, an expert on the judicial applications of the public trust, extends its role beyond issues such as abandonment. Sax contends that the government has a duty to prevent harm to the public interest.[52] Where federal statutes acknowledge a trust responsibility—as they do in many cases either explicitly or implicitly—federal actions should be designed to promote trust values for public benefit.[53] Under this rationale, agencies could assume a duty either to maintain roads in a condition that contributes to the public good, or to remove roads adequately to prevent further harm. Similarly, agencies would have a duty to protect public lands from harmful ORV or snowmobile use. Such a view actually emerges, though without any direct mention of trust obligations, in the two executive orders (E.O. 11644 and 11989) that restrict ORV use on public lands. The first of these serves "to protect the resources of [public] lands" from damage by ORVs.[54]

This attitude of protecting public benefits is also supported by the broad philosophical language found in the National Environmental Policy Act (NEPA). According to this law, the nation's policy toward the environment "will encourage productive and enjoyable harmony between man and his environment . . . [and] promote efforts which will prevent or eliminate damage to the environment and biosphere and stimulate the health and welfare of man."[55] In setting goals for federal agencies, NEPA states that the federal government should do everything practicable to "fulfill the responsibilities of each generation as trustee of the environment for succeeding generations."[56] The language of the law supports the government's duty to act for the lasting public good.

Professor Sax describes the public trust as a legal doctrine to protect the public from destabilizing changes in the commons.[57] Sax has established specific questions that proper administrative action should satisfy: (1) Has public property been disposed of below market value for no obvious reason? (2) Has government granted private interests the authority to make resource-use decisions that subordinate public uses? (3) Have diffuse public uses been reallocated to private uses or public uses with less breadth? (4) Is the resource being used for its natural purpose?[58]

As long as there are laws that provide relevant legal obligations to land management agencies—such as provisions in the National Forest

Management Act—we may apply these questions to agency roadbuilding. The answers consistently point to management practices that have destabilized the commons and broken the public trust. The multibillion-dollar maintenance backlog of national forest roads, for example, suggests that public property has been managed to a dramatic deficit and in many cases this neglect has effectively disposed any practical benefit of these roads.

Similarly, when motorized recreation excludes or displaces other activities on public land, broad public uses are subverted to meet the needs of a narrow constituency. As the land management agencies increasingly court private–public partnerships, we also see an increasing number of cases where private interests subordinate the public uses of the land. Privatized Fee Demonstration sites may provide a financial boon to the concessionaires operating visitor centers and other facilities, but for the public these operations can create a disincentive to visit formerly free public attractions and recreation areas.[59] Such a scenario pits a diffused public interest—free access to public lands for a variety of activities—against concessionaires who may offer experiences that appeal to a narrow but powerful interest group, such as vehicle manufacturers. This imbalanced representation of interests, and the subversion of a broad public good, is exactly what scholars contend the public trust doctrine should prevent.

The American public is justified in expecting the federal government to manage its lands in a trust condition to preclude their lasting degradation, consumption, or privatization. Considered this way, federal agencies have ethical and legal obligations to manage lands to sustain public uses consistent with the lands' "natural purpose," which according to Sax should fortify the defense of broad, poorly represented public interests.[60] In most cases, natural landscapes in a largely unaltered condition will provide for the broadest range of public benefits. Thus the Mount Greylock decision to prevent the conversion of a mountainside to a ski slope supported broad public interests over the narrower interests of the skiing public.

To manage public land roads or motorized recreation in a way that meets the terms of the public trust, agencies need to demonstrate that this narrowing of the natural condition "promotes a significant public purpose."[61] A certain number of roads for timber sales, recreation, or fire lookouts might have met this standard during the past century, but with today's vast road network the public benefit of most new roads has diminished compared to its liabilities. Applying and extending the concept more actively, we can justify the rehabilitation and restoration of many roaded, degraded lands using the public trust doctrine. In this manner, removing roads or closing certain areas to motorized recreation actually *liberates* lands—as opposed to locking them up—by allowing a broader array of public interests to thrive, including nonmotorized uses that were displaced, healthy wildlife and plant populations, clean air and water, and healthier soils.[62]

Protecting the Public Interest with Environmental Laws

To preserve a broader public good, Congress has passed a number of laws that limit the range of permissable actions by individuals, agencies, and corporations. Even 100 years ago, when Congress established the national forests, it was clear that the greater good—or ethical choice—was to favor the needs of the many over the privileges of the few. Americans at the time knew that it was possible to get rich by cutting and selling vast quantities of public timber (and, indeed, temptation has won out on numerous occasions), but the public responded by creating lasting protective measures for environmental and economic amenities. Congress did not agree to disagree on this matter, rather it affirmed that the public good must take precedence over the prospect of getting rich quickly and making future generations suffer.

Congress acted with similar reasoning early on in setting aside dramatic national parks from Yellowstone in 1872 to Rocky Mountain in 1915.[63] After the United States finally established a national park system with the passage of the 1916 National Park Service Act, the agency's most prominent policy prescription emphasized that the national parks "must be maintained in absolutely unimpaired form for the use of future generations as well as those of our own time," and that "the national interest must dictate all decisions affecting public or private enterprise in the parks."[64] Once again, the prospect of lasting public benefit looms prominent, even at the potential expense of individual or short-term gain.

As a general rule, environmental laws have steadily limited administrative authority in favor of greater protections of the public good during the past century. This trend has been most apparent with the Forest Service, which witnessed a series of increasingly prescriptive laws, from the broad Multiple-Use Sustained-Yield Act in 1960 to the Wilderness Act in 1964, the Resources Planning Act in 1974, and finally the National Forest Management Act (NFMA) in 1976.[65]

The NFMA, which applies solely to national forests, includes some of the most specific guidance for managing roads and ORVs of any law. As a result of this act, the Forest Service must document each of its system roads as part of an overall transportation plan, and must reestablish plant cover on roadways within ten years after they are no longer actively used.[66] NFMA also requires the agency to classify where ORVs are prohibited or allowed. Where ORVs are permitted, the Forest Service must manage them to minimize impacts to soils, watersheds, vegetation, wildlife, habitat, and other recreational uses.[67] Successful administrative and legal challenges from conservationists bear witness to the Forest Service's continued struggle to reliably meet the terms of the law.

After Congress passed the BLM's guiding law, the Federal Land Policy Management Act (FLPMA) in 1976, both multiple-use agencies had new prescriptions for managing their lands.[68] Although both agencies received Congressional affirmation of their multiple-use purposes, the new laws also required more systematic planning to ensure sustainable practices, protect viable populations of vertebrate species, consider land for wilderness designation, and prevent unnecessary degradation of the public lands.[69] Despite vague language and loopholes that allowed for varied implementation, the FLPMA expressed a heightened awareness of an increasingly threatened environment and gave the BLM the opportunity—though generally not the requirement—to manage lands with environmental concerns as a priority.

Agency actions have also been affected by the National Environmental Policy Act (NEPA) and the ESA, which respectively opened federal actions to a public participation process and created specific measures to protect imperiled plants, animals, and their habitats. With these laws working in concert, by the late 1970s American citizens for the first time were able to review and influence management plans for many public lands. To protect wildlife habitat for elk or bears, for example, and meet the terms of laws such as the NFMA and the ESA, the Forest Service set road density limits in portions of many national forests. Elsewhere, the BLM had to restrict some of its lands from cross-country (off-road) motorized use to protect fragile soils or populations of endangered desert tortoises. NEPA effectively opened the door for people to peer in on agency actions, and once citizens scrutinized land management decisions they could turn to other laws to press agencies to limit road building and motorized access.

The NFMA and FLPMA point toward an increasing appreciation for the dwindling number of federal lands that give refuge to native plants and animals. As we look at the question of how we should properly manage our heavily roaded and increasingly motorized public lands, these and other laws direct us in particular and important directions—with most holding to a bearing that emphasizes conservation and restoration.

Philosophically, the most dramatic environmental law passed in the United States dealt with plants, animals, and their habitats rather than any one type of public land. When President Richard Nixon signed the ESA of 1973, he sanctioned an expanded vision of how we would agree to live with our environment. In effect, the ESA expanded the traditional limits of public policy to include rights for animals and plants. Although the ESA stopped short of granting any intrinsic rights, the language of the act did recognize that animals and plants "are of esthetic, ecological, educational, historical, recreational, and scientific value to the Nation and its people."[70] For the first time, the United States agreed to restrict a broad range of human activities on a variety of land classifications to avoid extinguishing species or populations of animals and plants.[71] And significantly, Congress included nearly all types of living organisms, from invertebrates and fungi to large mammals, birds, and reptiles, for protection under the ESA.

Although by 1973 the United States already had a long history of setting aside lands such as wildlife refuges and national parks, or passing hunting and other conservation laws to protect dwindling animal populations, the ESA for the first time applied to inconspicuous species such as the snail darter in Tennessee or water howellia in Montana. In addition, the law declared stiff penalties for illegally "taking" (killing individuals or destroying essential habitat) imperiled species and extended its reach to private property owners. Philosopher Holmes Rolston III commented of the ESA, "It does not say: Save those species that are economically valuable. To the contrary, Congress says: Temper economic growth by saving species that have other kinds of values. . . . [the ESA] is a congressional resolution that the nation and its people ought to live as compatibly as they can with the fauna and flora on their continent (and abroad), and it deplores the fact that we are not now doing so."[72]

While protections for plants and animals in the ESA are generally recognized as some of the strongest ever passed into law, the legislation does not dramatically restructure land management philosophy.[73] The ESA, like other environmental laws, remains grounded in a value system that gauges right and wrong primarily in human terms.[74] This focus makes good pragmatic sense and, as discussed earlier, can lead to policy changes that would limit motorization, call for road removal programs, and benefit plants, animals, and habitat in some dramatic ways. But we need not restrict ourselves, ethically or legally, to considerations of what is in the human interest only.

Extending Ethics to a Broader Community

In the 1940s, Aldo Leopold wrote, "When we see land as a community to which we belong, we may begin to use it with love and respect. There is no other way for land to survive the impact of mechanized man."[75] In *A Sand County Almanac,* Leopold made the bold and controversial suggestion that humanity extend its concept of a moral community to include "the land." Specifically, this extended land ethic would apply to "soils, waters, plants, and animals."[76]

Other writers and thinkers have offered similar suggestions for extending our values. Albert Schweitzer advocated a "Reverence for Life" that Rachel Carson later described as "something that takes us out of ourselves, that makes us aware of other life . . . we are not being truly civilized if we concern ourselves only with the relation of man to man."[77] And in the 1970s, legal philosopher Christopher Stone published "Should Trees Have Standing?" in which he outlined the steady historical progression of rights as they extended gradually outward to include not just men of status, but children, women, wives, slaves, and even certain animals and pets.[78]

An ethic that granted rights to animals, plants, water, or soils would lead us to land management decisions that could extend beyond human expedience. Clean, clear-flowing streams and rivers, for example, would have rights to exist for their own sakes, in addition to the reasons we currently use such as supporting fisheries, preserving drinking water supplies, or offering pleasant facilities for recreation. Importantly, this would not require that we apply the rights of rivers and streams to the same level or degree as we do those of humans, but it would elevate these considerations as points of discussion.

Similarly, rather than building roads on steep slopes or poor soils, if we recognized the rights of forests and hillsides to exist intact, it would not preclude human interests from outweighing those of the forest or hillside, but it would grant these inanimate, nonhuman factors some heightened degree of consideration in land management decisions. In effect, an extended moral framework would raise the burden of proof for high-risk developments. The result would almost surely benefit people in the long run and encourage us to act more cautiously and wisely.

Some existing environmental laws already include language that leans toward a broader view of community. The 1916 National Park Service Act, for instance, established the Park Service "to conserve the scenery and the natural and historic objects and the wild life therein *and* to provide for the enjoyment of the same in such manner and by such means as will leave them unimpaired for the enjoyment of future generations"[79] (emphasis added). Though the agency has long struggled to meet a dual charge of conservation and human enjoyment, this language and recent court rulings emphasize that the first and primary obligation of the Park Service is to conserve scenery, natural and historic objects, and wildlife.[80] The guiding language of Interior Secretary Franklin Lane's 1918 letter to Park Service Director Stephen Mather also made this clear: "Every activity of the Service is subordinate to the duties imposed upon it to faithfully preserve the parks for posterity in essentially their natural state."[81]

Although it seems unlikely that the sixty-fourth Congress in 1916 was attempting to subvert human interests to that of biological conservation, such legislation gives a strong message that many types of interests should be considered and valued by society, and that in national parks it is appropriate to tip the balance toward the broadly conceived goal of conservation. The language of the law makes it clear that the conservation component stands for itself and not *in order to* provide for the enjoyment of the people. The legislators at the time apparently considered conservation goals to be compatible with humanitarian goals—a concept that remains pertinent today.[82]

The National Forest Management Act of 1976 also encourages an approach to land management that extends beyond human utility. As the bill's sponsor, Senator Hubert Humphrey, explained in a U.S. Senate hearing, "The days have ended when the forest may be viewed only as trees and trees viewed only as timber. The soil and water, the grasses and the shrubs, the fish and the wildlife, and the beauty that is the forest must become integral parts of resource managers' thinking and actions."[83]

These views emerged most clearly in the regulations for the NFMA, which requires that "[f]ish and wildlife habitat shall be managed to maintain viable populations of existing native and desired nonnative vertebrate species."[84] This provision is not contingent upon whether it fits the logging industry's wishes or even whether humans will necessarily benefit directly from the preservation of native vertebrate species. The law simply requires us to preserve biodiversity for its own sake.

The provision for viable populations in the NFMA offers a clear example of how ethics and law can apply to roads policy. In defining what constitutes a viable population, the NFMA regulations state that the population "has the estimated numbers and distribution of reproductive individuals to insure its continued existence is well distributed in the planning area."[85] This requirement for distribution and reproduction prohibits habitat isolation—such as that commonly caused by high road densities or heavy motorized use of roads and trails—if it would prevent "reproductive individuals" from interacting with prospectively critical mates elsewhere in the planning area.[86] In essence, national forest planning regulations dictate that roads and motorized recreation can exist only to the extent that they do not undermine the ability of native vertebrates (and desirable nonnatives) from mixing and reproducing successfully over the long term.

Pursuing Ethical Results

Ultimately, the results of our actions may prove more critical than their philosophical underpinnings. It may matter less that land management agencies and society fully embrace nontraditional or ecocentric ethics, as long as land management decisions protect the existence and natural integrity of the environment. In other words, whether or not we adopt an ethic that recognizes obligations to plants, soil, animals, or water to the degree that some environmental philosophers advocate, we can still act in ways that benefit these constituents.

Given our current setting of laws and ethics we can make decisions that promote the ecological good, restore roaded and degraded lands, and benefit a large array of interests including and extending beyond the human. Whether it is a matter of personal restraint or spirituality, working with our neighbors to find forms of recreation appropriate to our particular places, building citizen-based initiatives, or redirecting access management policies of our federal agencies, the choices we make and the actions we undertake may, to paraphrase Robert Frost, make all the difference. With our land management ethic honed ever further, we may soon discover a number of roads "not taken" for the simple fact that we have taken them off the land.

If Adam had known what harm the serpent was going to work he would have tried to prevent him from finding lodgement in Eden; and if you were to realize what the result of the automobile will be in that wonderful incomparable [Yosemite] valley, you will keep it out.

—James Bryce, British Ambassador
to the United States, 1913

7 | Changing Landscapes: Society, Technology, and Road Removal

Doug Edgerton sits on his bulldozer and squints down at us beneath the folded brim of his John Deere cap. It's hot and July in Montana in the Gallatin National Forest just west of Yellowstone National Park. Along with Edgerton, I'm here with the Gallatin's Susan Lamont, my wife Marion, and a half-dozen college students from around the country for a field course on "Restoration Ecology in Greater Yellowstone." Today's lesson is road removal and Doug Edgerton is our guy.

Edgerton lives in nearby West Yellowstone, Snowmobile Capital of the World, but also home to a national training center for the U.S. Biathlon Team. For nine or ten months every year, he tinkers with snowcats and modifies heavy machinery so it can run atop the snow to groom perfect tracks for the nation's best skiers and biathletes. During the rest of the year—the two or three months that in West Yellowstone seem to compress into spring, summer, and fall—Edgerton fills his time by ripping out excess logging and illegal user-created roads that plague the Gallatin National Forest.

Lamont and Edgerton have already explained to us how he customized his rig for roadripping: he's replaced the spiky concrete rippers in back with broad, spade-shaped "winged lifters"that burrow into compacted roadbeds and lift the soil, loosen it, and set it back down intact but porous and receptive to seedlings and grasses. We're almost ready now for him to demonstrate how his contraption works, but he has a few parting warnings about staying clear of the dozer and the handful of trees he'll be knocking down to clutter the doomed roadbed. In the quiet before Edgerton kicks his machine to life, a student swats and curses one of the horseflies that has been buzzing us and piercing our skin. Edgerton looks down at us and mutters, "Horseflies don't bother me." The engine starts with a roar.

The next year when we return with a different group of students, Doug Edgerton can't meet with us: he's been elected mayor of West Yellowstone and is consumed by duties of his new office. Thick-skinned, helpful, and taciturn, Edgerton's both a rare breed and something of a prototype for a new wave of workers emerging in places around the country. Regardless of whether he likes or dislikes roads, Doug Edgerton has discovered that taking them out can be as satisfying and lucrative as it once was for engineers and road planners to put them in. With the added promise of restoring habitat for elk, threatened grizzly bears, and cutthroat trout, road removal also carries a restorative yin to offset the destructive yang traditionally associated with heavy machines. And perhaps most dramatically, here in the context of West Yellowstone, Montana, with its predilection for motorized recreation, Edgerton has managed to live with his neighbors even as he challenges some of the long-held assumptions about what the town needs to survive.[1]

With more than 217,000 miles of national forest road rated by the Forest Service "at a level less than adequate for current use," the agency still counts 150,000 road miles "fully maintained"and available for public use.[2] Regardless how great a commitment we might make toward road closure and obliteration, for many decades to come there will be far more roads in our nation's forests than people likely would ever want to drive, ride, or walk. The most difficult task before the Forest Service and other agencies is not so much how to keep enough roads and motorized recreational areas open, but how to close areas effectively to prevent resource damage and illegal or unwanted use.

Even as land management agencies find themselves pulled in different directions by local pressures and administrations with conflicting agendas, the long-term trend shows a shift away from new road construction. The National Park Service is moving away from private vehicle access in a few of the most popular or congested parks. The National Wildlife

Refuge System, similarly, can point to a dominant use philosophy that emphasizes conservation over visitor convenience. Of course, national parks and wildlife refuges contain just 3 percent of the road mileage on federal public lands.

The two multiple-use agencies—the Bureau of Land Management (BLM) and Forest Service—have been slower to come to a policy of reduced road building. Until the early 1990s, the Forest Service was still constructing thousands of miles of new road each year. Under the Clinton administration, the Forest Service approved a policy to prohibit new road construction on the 58.5 million acres of remaining unprotected roadless lands it manages and devised new regulations for managing all of its roads.[3] While the new Bush administration's efforts to undermine the policy demonstrate how tenuous such administrative measures can be, the Forest Service has now clearly stated a rationale for more protective measures on a substantial portion of its lands.

The BLM has perhaps been the slowest to demonstrate a change in priorities. On all but its heavily forested Oregon and California lands, the agency has had little cause to systematically construct new roads, but motorized recreation has long been a popular use of BLM lands. In 2001 the agency published a "National Management Strategy" for off-road vehicles (ORVs).[4]

In some places we are already well on our way to meeting the challenges of appropriate public land management and access. Conservation groups and education and service organizations are working with agency officials on collaborative road removal projects, providing volunteer labor to support agency initiatives. Other nonprofit organizations have created sophisticated digital maps of road networks and habitat areas secure from motorized access. Groups have also worked to identify areas where road removal could most benefit habitat and wildlife recovery. The Federal Highway Administration uses digital video and global positioning systems (GPS) to analyze road conditions and improve the accuracy of its maps. In western Montana, national forest road engineers have developed "roll-up roads," which are designed to be temporary, easy-to-remove roads. Private businesses have also developed programs to work with federal agencies and reduce road dependence.

For example, a private consulting group, Arcata, California–based Pacific Watershed Associates, conducts training and works with public land managers, nonprofit organizations, and private landowners to assess road risks and plan and implement road removal projects.[5] Pacific Watershed Associates is currently working with the BLM to remove roads and restore habitat in northern California.

These and other initiatives play an important part in demonstrating that we can find new directions for access management on federal land, and that the role of roads on the land can be both diminished and improved. Unlike much of the initial road construction that benefited a single extractive industry and only secondarily offered a broader public benefit, road removal projects can create jobs, improve habitat, and contribute to multiple levels of society. If done properly and thoughtfully, road removal will prove to be an inspiring example of the good that can come from intelligent, innovative, and sustainable land management policies. To meet these terms, we will need to make decisions that consider human dimensions and needs, make use of new ideas and technologies, and plan for the long-term good of the public lands, fish and wildlife, and the environment. In other words, the task ahead is both challenging and worthwhile, and it is necessary.

From Cooperation to Confrontation: The Role of Conservation Groups

Although the federal land agencies are increasingly turning to new approaches to road and access management, a number of these changes have been prompted by actions and pressure from conservation and non-profit organizations. In fact, concerns about road developments and the increased motorization of public lands led to the creation of two of the groups currently leading the national charge in this field: The Wilderness Society in 1935, and much more recently, Wildlands Center for Preventing Roads (Wildlands CPR) in 1994.[6]

With a membership today of more than 200,000, The Wilderness Society has worked from its inception to protect lands from roading and motorization. Among the organization's founders, Aldo Leopold and Bob Marshall are widely recognized today as historic leaders of the American conservation and wilderness movements, and they both were spurred to action by their concern over roads' impacts on America's public lands. Both men also managed to lead distinguished careers within the Forest Service, yet worked outside the agency to develop effective citizen-based efforts to reform land management practices.

Wildlands CPR, as its abbreviated and full names suggest, emphasizes dual treatments of restoration and prevention in order to improve the integrity of wildlife habitat and watersheds. Though the group functions essentially as a small, grassroots organization, with just a half dozen employees working out of a renovated grain elevator, from the 1990s to today Wildlands CPR has established an impressive record of national outreach and collaboration with other groups and agencies. One of the few organizations that focuses its efforts fully upon motorized access and the ecological impacts of roads, Wildlands CPR has developed a bibliographic database with more than 6,000 scientific studies pertaining to roads and ORVs—a resource that is used by environmental activists and federal land managers alike.

These groups and others have successfully pushed for a national discussion about roads and ORV use on public lands. Similarly, a number of local and regional organizations continue to make a real difference on the ground.

In 1994, the Bozeman, Montana–based Predator Conservation Alliance began its "Roads Scholar Project" to assess road densities in grizzly bear habitat on national forest lands in the northern Rockies. "Roads Scholars" working on the project set out to compare Forest Service maps with aerial photographs of selected habitat areas. Where there appeared to be discrepancies between the maps and photos, teams of researchers would go into the woods by car, mountain bicycle, and foot to verify whether or not roads existed and, if they did, measure them and chronicle their condition. After covering each habitat area, Roads Scholars recorded their findings in a geographic information system (GIS) that could display digital spatial information on standard map grids. The final product—a series of maps that showed ground-truthed roads for each habitat area and graphically compared this with the agency's official records of the road system—consistently found that slightly more roads existed on the ground than the Forest Service had recognized. Of the more than 5,000 miles of road inventoried by Roads Scholars in 1994 and 1995, 6 percent had not been properly mapped or accounted for by the agency.[7]

Furthermore, Roads Scholar Project field crews documented the condition and effectiveness of road closure devices, such as steel gates or earthen barriers, in each habitat area. The GIS maps could then indicate which road systems were open to public access, which were legally or illegally used by ORVs, and how this compared to Forest Service access plans for open, restricted, and closed roads. With this closure information factored in, Roads Scholar Project maps determined that far more grizzly bear habitat was open to motorized access than the Forest Service claimed, and that some areas were violating road density standards prescribed by the agency's own land management plans. In fact, only 50 percent of the 800 closure points surveyed actually prevented motorized access as planned.[8]

In some ways what was most significant about the project was not that Roads Scholars discovered ineffective road closures and "ghost roads" that had not appeared on agency maps, but that a small, citizen-based effort managed to apply sophisticated digital mapping technology to the challenge of road management. Although the Forest Service criticized details of the Roads Scholar Project for using loose definitions of what qualified as a road, for discrediting certain road closure techniques, or other points, the agency was a half-step behind for several years before fully converting to GIS for its own roads database.

By 1998 every national forest in the northern Rockies had incorporated the same GIS technology for its own road system database as that used by the Roads Scholar Project, and nationally the chief of the Forest Service acknowledged the existence of some 60,000 miles of unclassified "ghost roads" that had been lost from agency counts or created by unplanned motorized use in national forests. The agency has now adopted the task of identifying every road's accurate location and condition as it develops a "road atlas" for each forest, though this and the challenge of determining what to do with each road will continue for many years.

Groups in other parts of the country have also led or accompanied land management agencies in applying these methods and technologies to road and access management. In southern Arizona's Coronado National Forest, agency inventories have documented illegal ghost roads and largely confirmed results from surveys conducted by citizen groups such as the Sky Island Alliance.[9] Since 1998, more than 250 volunteers for the Sky Island Alliance have inventoried nearly 1,000 miles of road. Although the citizen group and federal agency have disagreed at times on what should be done with these unplanned roads, the Coronado now plans to close 100 miles of road per year to meet its road density standards.[10]

In a curious case of one federal agency essentially creating problems for another across administrative lines, in the Canelo Hills and other isolated ranges of the Arizona–Mexico borderland, field-based road inventories have found that the greatest increase in actual road mileage (compared to previous agency records) is from routes created by U.S. border patrols trying to prevent illegal immigrations.[11] While the overlap of agency jurisdiction may be extraordinary in these borderlands, many thousands of acres of federal land elsewhere suffer from uncoordinated management goals between adjacent lands and different agencies. This is starkly visible in some places, such as the west border of Yellowstone National Park where it meets the Targhee National Forest. The Targhee clearcut its forests vigorously for several decades, leaving a swath of logging roads and stumps to contrast with the forested lands protected within Yellowstone Park. Interagency planning has grown increasingly common in recent years, however, and in most cases such efforts lead to better land management.

At times, citizens and organizations turn to administrative appeals and lawsuits to ensure that land managers abide by all existing laws. While such actions can spur public criticism and may polarize the public and its land managers, appeals and lawsuits can also prove to be the only way to keep resource industries in check or provide effective oversight of access management decisions. In some cases, what begins with litigation can lead to constructive dialogue and important reform of agency policies.

In Yellowstone National Park, for example, the Fund for Animals and several other citizens and groups sued the National Park Service in 1997 for inappropriately allowing snowmobile use to degrade the park's environment and change the habitat conditions for Yellowstone's bison. The environmental impact statement created as a result of the legal settlement identified adverse impacts to park resources that ranged from disturbances to wildlife to air and water pollution to human safety and visitor conflicts.[12] The Park Service ultimately responded with a plan to phase snowmobiles out of Yellowstone by 2004—a plan that is doomed, at least for revision, with the shift to a Bush administration. Though Park officials now publicly express support for a ban on snowmobiles, the prospect of different management may never have occurred without the initial lawsuit.[13]

A number of groups have also succeeded in creating cooperative projects with land managers to meet habitat goals or legal standards. Organizations with missions as diverse as the Rocky Mountain Elk Foundation, AmeriCorps, and high school biology classes have chipped in to help agency planners remove roads or fortify road closure devices. These cooperative efforts can bring seemingly disparate parties together for a common goal and demonstrate to land managers that citizens do care and are willing to help fix (and not just complain about) problems. They also provide volunteer labor to boost thin agency restoration budgets. Additionally, these work projects create a chance for citizens and land managers to interact in a positive way, which helps develop mutual trust by both parties.[14]

The Student Conservation Association has developed a long history of using work crews on a contractual basis with the Forest Service and other agencies to construct or repair trails using student labor. This model mutualism of land management agency and nonprofit organization could also be applied to the relatively new field of road removal or road closure treatments, thereby helping to train a new generation of students about the critical role of road and access management in proper land stewardship.

Change and the Land Management Agencies

Despite fine efforts by many individuals, the land management agencies face constant challenges to achieve goals and meet their legal standards. Many agency actions seem encumbered with bureaucracy and at odds with the mix of public desires, the law, or local sentiment. While it remains true that a number of federal actions take place only after prodding by citizens or the courts, each of the land management agencies has shown signs of change and a shift toward more cautious road and access management policies.

A New Mission for the BLM

The BLM may still earn its reputation as the agency most generous to industrial land users, but new approaches are starting to emerge. As noted in the previous chapter, the passage of the Federal Land Policy Management Act (FLPMA) in 1976 finally gave the BLM a unified set of regulations and directions, and also required the agency to inventory its lands for wilderness suitability to determine which lands were sufficiently free of roads and human impact to qualify for protection as wilderness. Though many of these wilderness inventories and the subsequent agency recommendations have generated controversies of their own, especially for being too miserly, the process has at least focused more attention on questions of roading, motorized access, and the appropriate application of land use restrictions.

In 1994, when the BLM created its mission statement, the agency pointed toward the priorities of health and diversity of the public lands, ahead of their extractive resource productivity. In this way, the agency for the first time broadly served notice that business might no longer be as usual.

Recently, on a more specific front, the BLM has revisited its management of ORVs. With an assessment of its national ORV policy released in January 2001, the agency emphasized its commitment to existing laws and executive orders and noted that, "because of the advances in OHV [off-highway vehicle] technology and an increase in their popularity, some of the BLM's land use plans need updating and budgets and staffing need to be increased."[15] The national strategy stops short of requiring managers to change access plans, but it does encourage them to make site-specific determinations and adopt stricter standards for motorized use where appropriate.

On a regional level, the BLM in Montana and the Dakotas went somewhat further and adopted a policy to prohibit ORV use off of roads and designated trails.[16] Though the new policy still falls short of conservationists requests—and essentially accepts the ongoing use of illegal, user-created routes (pending "designations" of trails)—it does add a new level of restrictiveness to a formerly wide-open ORV policy.

Improving the National Wildlife Refuges

The national wildlife refuge system, too, recently received a new mission statement and attention to its management and purpose.[17] Though the wildlife refuge system continues to be funded at just a fraction of other land management agency budgets, there are now special programs to finance and create collaborations between citizen groups and wildlife refuges for habitat restoration projects and environmental education.[18] Some refuges, such as the Cabeza Prieta in Arizona, have reworked management plans in response to concerns about motorized use.[19] This refuge and more than seventy others have also seen congressional designation of 20 million acres of wilderness within their boundaries.[20] The Cabeza Prieta is currently immersed in controversy for allowing vehicles on more than 100 miles of wilderness "trails"that lead to bighorn sheep watering sites. Depending upon such site-specific management decisions, wilderness designations can preserve the areas existing roadless and motorless characteristics.

Overall, U.S. Fish and Wildlife Service employees point to several actions that indicate a changing program for wildlife refuge management.

President Clinton's 1996 executive order and the National Wildlife Refuge System Improvement Act of 1997 both give specific directions for refuge management. One of these, a requirement that comprehensive conservation plans be completed by every refuge by 2012, emphasizes the need to monitor the status and trends of plant and animal species in each refuge. Significantly, considering the ecological impacts of roads and motorized recreation discussed in earlier chapters, the Refuge System Improvement Act also requires that the refuge system maintain its "biological integrity, diversity, and environmental health."[21] This may lead to continued and increased regulation of motorized access in sensitive portions of refuges.

In July 2000, Fish and Wildlife Service director Jamie Clark also ordered a wilderness inventory for each of the refuges, which should identify existing roadless lands and assess their suitability for permanent protection by the end of June 2001 (this deadline is expected to stretch, in some cases, for many years).[22]

Mass Transit in National Parks

America's national parks are the flagship lands of the country's public domain. As a result of their prominence, national parks attract a great deal of public attention when managers propose a change in roads or access.

Beginning in May 2000, Zion National Park in Utah closed the popular Zion Canyon Scenic Drive to most private automobiles and turned instead to a shuttle system that moved tourists at six-minute intervals to the popular scenic points at the heart of the park. Despite local concern and early predictions that tourists would avoid Zion, by the end of its first summer season of operation (the shuttles run April through October) the shuttle system drew praise from 85 percent of park visitors, and visitation to the park was up by 80,000 over the previous summer.[23] Park visitors expressed newfound appreciation for the quiet, wildlife sightings, and convenience that came with the shift from private vehicles to free shuttles.[24]

In Arizona, Grand Canyon National Park planners have clearly stated their concerns with the status quo: "[A]fter entering the park, visitors do not find the silence and solitude that one would hope for or expect from Grand Canyon. Actually, many visitors never even find a parking space. Instead their visit is accompanied by the cacophony of automobile engines and horns and the constant growl and screech and smoke of bus motors and brakes. A parking lot, even at the Grand Canyon, is still a parking lot,

with all the fumes and conflicts and fender benders."[25] Grand Canyon officials have determined that the best way to respond to overcrowding and
congestion at the West's busiest national park is to remove automobile
access from the South Rim. Instead, the park plans to convert existing roads
and parking lots to bikeways, pedestrian paths, and a light rail system.

If implemented as planned, the actions at Grand Canyon will represent
one of the most dramatic changes in public access at a national park since
cars were first permitted at Mount Rainier National Park in 1908.[26] The
multimillion-dollar light rail system, gas or electric buses, and forty-five
miles of bicycle–pedestrian trails are expected to be financed, designed,
built, operated, and maintained by a concessionaire secured by a long-
term contract. Grand Canyon hopes to have the new transit system in
place by 2004.[27]

Yosemite National Park, one of the most heavily used of the country's
large scenic parks with more than 3.6 million annual visitors, is similarly
in the process of converting to a shuttle system that should partially sup-
plant automobile use in the heart of Yosemite Valley.[28] Although the
park's management plan has called for such action for more than a decade,
social and political opposition has stalled agency implementation repeatedly. In 1997, however, the Merced River flooded many of the visitor facilities in Yosemite Valley, and park officials worked to capitalize on the
event to institute the long-recommended changes. Yosemite officials envision a threefold reduction in parking spaces within the valley, among other
efforts to reduce the presence of car-choked roads in the park.[29]

Acadia National Park in Maine was the first national park outside of
Alaska to implement a shuttle system. The "Island Explorer" began in
1999 as an optional service and, like its later shuttle counterpart in Zion,
runs frequently, carries passengers and bicycles free of charge, and pow-
ers through the park on low-emission propane. In its inaugural year, the
Island Explorer carried more than 140,000 visitors to scenic stops around
Acadia's Mount Desert Island, and in 2000 use increased by 39 percent to
nearly 200,000 passengers.[30] Acadia has encouraged use of the shuttle by
catering to "car free" travelers, who connect with existing mass transit
options and can visit Acadia from virtually anywhere in the United States
or Canada without needing a car. This opens the park admirably to the 30
percent of Americans who do not own a car. The shuttle also makes use
of a number of simple promotions to encourage use, such as offering shuttle passengers discounts at local shops.

The trend toward alternative transportation in national parks has also come with some support from the private sector. For example, Charlier Associates Inc., one of the main designers of the plan for Grand Canyon, works specifically to promote new kinds of transit systems for national parks, urban areas, and other road projects.[31]

Cars on roads are not the only type of motorized traffic coming under scrutiny and reform. A petition organized by the Bluewater Network in 1997 led to a Park Service decision to ban personal watercraft (i.e., Jet Skis and WaveRunners) on all waters administered by the agency, except for twenty-one sites that included national recreation areas such as Utah's Glen Canyon and Nevada's Lake Mead.[32] The Bluewater Network sued over these exceptions, and in August 2000 the Park Service agreed to allow personal watercraft use only in units that completed site-specific environmental analyses and a formal rulemaking process and that could meet all pollution standards.[33]

In response to a similar petition relating to snowmobiles, submitted by the Bluewater Network and more than sixty other organizations, the Park Service in 2000 announced a ban on the use of snowmobiles in all national park units except for a handful of the most popular destinations, including Yellowstone and Minnesota's Voyageurs. Even if the Bush administration or Congress succeeds in reversing the broad snowmobile ban—which has drawn ire from motorized recreation groups, industry, and other business interests—the snowmobile industry for the first time has expressed a commitment to produce quieter and cleaner machines. Further, in September 2001, the U.S. Environmental Protection Agency introduced a program, that, if implemented, will require snowmobile and other ORV manufacturers to reduce average engine emissions by 50 percent by 2010.[34]

As mentioned earlier, Yellowstone has been embroiled in its own particular snowmobile controversy, since the Fund for Animals and others sued the park for grooming roads within Yellowstone and for not planning properly for thousands of snowmobiles each winter season. The environmental impact statement and decision to stop snowmobile use at Yellowstone are distinct from the nationwide effort initiated by the Bluewater Network's petition.

The decision to ban snowmobiles from Yellowstone National Park is particularly controversial since several "gateway"communities on the periphery of the park have grown to focus upon snowmobile and winter recreation revenues during the otherwise lean winter months. As we saw earlier, West Yellowstone, Montana, has developed a winter economy that appears to rely predominantly upon snowmobile rentals and tours and related tourist spending for lodging, food, and souvenirs. The first snowmobiles entered the park in 1963, and with a snowmobile boom in the the late 1970s and 80s, Yellowstone's winter visits doubled from 70,000 per year in 1980 to 140,000 by 1993.[35] Before the winter recreation bonanza, only a handful of businesses remained open year-round in West Yellowstone. By the late 1990s, winter revenues for the town of 1,000 averaged more than $9 million, and some 61,000 winter visitors came to the park from its West Yellowstone entrance each year.[36]

Under the new Park Service plan, winter visitors would still come to Yellowstone, but they would enter the park's interior using group snowcoaches that generate less noise, pollution, and disturbance than individuals on snowmobiles. Approximately 10 percent of Yellowstone's winter visitors already make use of snowcoaches or skis to access the park, and towns such as West Yellowstone, Gardiner, and Cooke City, Montana, would continue to promote snowmobiling on the hundreds of miles of national forest trails and other lands that remain open to motorized recreation. Idaho's Fremont County, which borders Yellowstone to the southwest, estimates that it already receives 300,000 snowmobile user days per year outside of park lands.[37]

Economies in places such as West Yellowstone may also be more diverse than snowmobile boosters suggest. Other tourist facilities, ranging from the nearby Big Sky Ski Resort to the nordic ski trails maintained by Doug Edgerton's specialized groomers to an IMAX theater, will continue to bring winter visitors to West Yellowstone. In fact, the Park Service's environmental impact statement for winter use estimated that employment and revenues to the five counties surrounding Yellowstone Park would drop by less than 0.5 percent with a winter ban on snowmobiles.[38] The State of Wyoming estimated losses three to four times this amount, but assumed that snowmobilers banned from the park would not continue to use adjacent lands, and that other types of winter use would not increase as a result of a snowmobile ban. The Park Service analysis rejects both assumptions, and data from recent years show that even when winter visitation to Yellowstone has dropped, winter tax revenues from West Yellowstone businesses have increased.[39]

Economics aside, even snowmobile advocates admit that change is necessary. Opponents of the Park Service ban have pointed to cleaner, quieter snowmobiles—such as those now being built with four-stroke engines—as a way to accommodate environmental protection and motorized recreation.[40] Snowmobile manufacturers have already used Yellowstone as a high-profile testing ground for the new generation of machines.

Though emissions and noise are two of the most glaring problems with current snowmobile use in Yellowstone and elsewhere, quieter and cleaner machines would not necessarily reduce problems of physical disturbance to wildlife and habitat, human safety, or traffic management and congestion. Winter, after all, remains a time of marginal existence for many species, and this is especially so in a place like Yellowstone where snowpack lasts from November through May and winter temperatures often drop below minus twenty. The cleanest and quietest of snowmobiles will still generate pollution and noise enough to impact wildlife and water quality.

Whether or not these new machines are deemed appropriate to again roam by the thousands across our nations first national park, land managers across the country should take note of the industry's apparent willingness to promote cleaner, quieter snowmobiles and ORVs. As motorized recreation surges in popularity, such machines would surely represent a necessary prerequisite for use on public and private lands nationwide, even if they never find their way en masse back into Yellowstone.

Beyond these specific measures, on September 8, 2000, Park Service director Robert Stanton issued Director's Order 55. Hailed by some as a bold interpretation to put environmental protection at the fore of the agency's long-standing "dual mission" of preservation and providing for visitor's enjoyment, the director's order states that preservation is, in fact, the overriding obligation of the National Park Service. While visitor opportunities will continue to be a priority, when tourist services conflict with conservation practices, the latter must prevail.[41] It remains to be seen how deeply the new order will influence the practices of agency land managers and future projects, but the order comes both as an affirmation of Interior Secretary Franklin Lane's 1918 decree that these lands "be maintained in absolutely unimpaired form,"[42] and as support for court rulings that have found that preservation trumps "pleasuring" in the national parks' mandate. In fact, Stanton's Order 55 quotes a number of court rulings that have repeatedly identified the agency's "overarching goal of resource protection," and that the Park Service has "but a single purpose, namely, conservation."[43]

A New Agenda for the Forest Service

Despite these changes and affirmations by the National Park Service and other agencies, the most dramatic recent shift in agency policies may be taking place in the Forest Service. The Forest Service has a long proud history, but for the four decades following World War II its penchant for cutting trees grew to the point where many conservationists and corporate interests viewed the agency as little more than an extension of the logging industry. Congress expressed a rising distrust of the agency's forest practices beginning in the 1960s. It reflected this by passing increasingly restrictive laws to dictate logging methods and environmental considerations. In the mid-1990s, however, the character of the Forest Service showed signs of change.

In 1993, the Forest Service reported an annual timber harvest of 5.9 billion board feet and road construction or reconstruction totalling 3,441 miles.[44] By 1998, five years into the Clinton administration, the agency's log haul had dropped to 3.3 billion board feet and road construction and reconstruction had dropped slightly to 3,146 miles, but a new line item—road decommissioning—had checked in at 2,099 miles.[45] Though the terminology itself has caused confusion and debate, decommissioning represents the Forest Service's attempt to remove roads from the land (and agency inventories). The work varies from merely treating stream crossings or replanting road surfaces to fully recontouring the roadbed to restore the land's original slope, appearance, and function. Whether the work is relatively superficial or results in true road removal, the intent of decommissioning is to decrease the agency's economic and environmental liabilities caused by roads.[46]

By the mid-1990s road removal gained funding, and by 1998, Forest Service officials spoke openly of a road system in disrepair and of the environmental and economic liabilities of the sprawling road network. In 2001, the agency confirmed a moratorium on new road construction in unroaded areas and also created new guidelines for managing its entire road system.

At about the same time that these changes in road policy and timber harvest were taking place, the Forest Service began pointing to recreation—not logging—as the industry that held promise for the future. Of course, we have yet to see whether a recreation-focused agency can manage its lands more sustainably than a timber-based agency, or for that matter, whether new administrations will revert quickly to traditional extractive industries, but at the close of the Clinton administration the change in the Forest Service appeared to be genuine and determined.

More than ever before, the American public has also taken notice of the agency's actions. For the environmental impact statement that accompanied the Forest Service's initiative to stop building new roads into roadless areas, the agency received more than 1 million citizen comments—more than had ever before been recorded for any federal action.[47] Though the public overwhelmingly supported the change to protect roadless lands, thanks in part to national campaigns launched by the Sierra Club and other conservation organizations, the response was not quite unanimous. At a hearing in my hometown of Missoula, Montana, the vast majority of people who testified supported the roadless conservation plan, but beyond the hearing room's walls hundreds of logging trucks rumbled through town to protest the agency's proposed action. The loggers ensuing protest rally included fiery speeches by Montana's Governor- and Congressman-elect, and testimonials by mill owners, timber industry spokespersons, and ORV enthusiasts who forecasted the imminent demise of their "traditional" lifestyles. The rally concluded with the ceremonial death and burial—casket included—of the region's timber industry.[48]

Much of the credit, or blame, for the change in Forest Service policies has gone to Forest Service chief Michael Dombeck, who served from 1997 to 2001. Although Dombeck surely responded to the economic, environmental, social, and political conditions of the time, he also consistently pointed to the need for new approaches to management. He supported his views with scientific, legal, and ethical appeals and worked to promote and support agency personnel willing to implement the new programs. In a departure from a long line of silviculturists, Dombeck was trained as a fisheries biologist (his predecessor, Jack Ward Thomas, was the agency's first biologist chief), and his focus on roads and roadless land protection no doubt arose in part from his concern for water quality and fisheries habitat. Dombeck also came as only the second chief to be appointed from outside the agency's traditional ascension through the ranks of line officers. The Forest Service may yet pay the price for its newly politicized bureacratic ranks, as succeeding presidential administrations could yank the agency back and forth toward different objectives, but through the 1990s the change led to a relatively swift and progressive agency reform.

Road Closure Controversies

Change in access management has emerged on the ground and at the local level on multiple fronts. Throughout the Northwest and in other places, agencies have devoted regular staff time and funds in recent years to road removal programs. Road removal programs can create controversies, however, as people sometimes react strongly against the notion that they will lose access to local destinations. One of the most vigorous disputes in recent years has occurred in Elko County, Nevada.

Jarbidge River, Nevada

Heavy rains washed out a 1.5 mile stretch of road along northeastern Nevada's Jarbidge River in 1995, and set into motion a conflict that has drawn national attention, led to the resignation of one of the Forest Service's rising leaders, involved parties as disparate as Montana loggers and Idaho trout, and carried on for more than five years.[49] The Jarbidge's South Canyon road dispute highlights many of the issues that make road and access management such a challenge for agencies.

Prior to its collapse in 1995, the South Canyon road was a forest development road maintained by Elko County. South Canyon road was used primarily to access fishing and camping sites on the Jarbidge River, as it flows from Nevada into southern Idaho. The Jarbidge River is home to one of five distinct populations of the bull trout (*Salvelinus confluentus*) that received protection as a threatened species under the Endangered Species Act in 1998. Even at the time of 1995's fateful rainstorm, the U.S. Fish and Wildlife Service was considering the bull trout for protection. After the road washed out, Elko County locals recognized that an endangered species listing for bull trout could affect the reconstruction of the Jarbidge Road, since the fish are sensitive to sediments, such as those caused by roadwork. The Humboldt-Toiyabe National Forest proposed converting the road to a scaled-down trail or ORV route, and had worked out an agreement to that effect with Elko County.

However, on July 15, 1998, Elko County moved in a different direction and passed a resolution to rebuild the Jarbidge road on its own. A week later, county crews rumbled into action to reconstruct the road. During that process, roadcrews managed to dump fill material directly into the Jarbidge River and send a sediment plume more than three miles downstream—just as bull trout were moving into their seasonal spawning runs. On July 24, the State of Nevada and Army Corps of Engineers issued a cease and desist order against Elko County, fined the county $400,000, and heated up a controversy that pitted the county and its supporters against the federal government and its employees.[50]

During the course of the ensuing dispute, the recently promoted Humboldt-Toiyabe Forest supervisor Gloria Flora resigned her post citing an atmosphere of violence and intimidation, and Elko County attracted a national "Shovel Brigade," started by a Montana logging mill owner, that sent thousands of shovels and a few hundred volunteers to help locals rebuild the road by hand. In 2001, Elko County commissioners and the U.S. Forest Service finally agreed to a deal by which the county could rebuild the washed-out section of road and contribute $200,000 toward additional road and watershed improvements, while the Forest Service would pay for environmental analyses and drop trespassing charges against the Jarbridge rebels. The settlement still hinges upon approval by the U.S. Fish and Wildlife Service, Environmental Protection Agency, and a National Environmental Policy Act review.[51]

In Elko, as in other cases where federal agencies plan to close or remove roads, locals reacted more to the *idea* of losing motorized access than they did out of any deep need to use that particular road. Although the complaint often sounds bizarre from the outside, rural westerners' lingering resentment of federal intrusion into the management of federal lands remains one of the critical points land managers must deal with as they work to change road and access management on public lands.

Crashing the Gates

Particularly for the national forest and BLM lands where agencies have allowed a variety of widespread uses with comparatively little regulation, placing limits on access—whether real or perceived—causes heated debates and often draws the ire of locals. The Forest Service identifies six closure types for "access control treatments," ranging from boulders and logs to concrete barriers to steel gates to obliteration of the entire roadbed.[52] While each closure type has its features or liabilities— including cost, convenience, permanence, ecological effects, or aesthetics—some studies indicate that many existing closure devices are not effective at preventing motorized access.

Two studies of grizzly bear habitat areas in Montana found that roads closed with gates, earth berms, or other temporary devices were not consistently effective at excluding motorized use. In the Flathead National Forest, only 62 percent of the road closure devices surveyed prevented motorized access to closed roads, while in the Cabinet-Yaak grizzly bear recovery area closure effectiveness was 52 percent.[53] A more expansive inventory of road closure devices in grizzly bear and elk habitat units in Wyoming, Montana, Idaho, and Washington determined that less than half of all road closures actually worked to prevent motorized access.[54]

The illegal breaching of closure devices poses a constant and costly headache for land managers, to whom only a portion of the responsibility should actually fall. The most difficult type of access to control is ORV traffic, and clearly the motorized recreation constituencies must embrace and abide by certain codes of conduct if they are to preserve the privileges of using public land. Some ORV groups have already devoted themselves to "ethical riding"or cooperative trail maintenance agreements with agencies, but there appears to be a fundamental difficulty in restricting riders whose machines are designed to travel virtually anywhere. There also continue to be too many cases where ORV drivers act with disrespect, belligerence, or even violence when approached by law enforcement officials or other public land users.[55]

This is not to say that agencies remain powerless to improve the effectiveness of road closures. Many land managers take great care in designing closure points so that the public knows about them and expects them, thereby defusing the anger that can come from a backroads drive being abruptly halted. Closure placement and design also make a difference, both to avoid a temptingly easy gate detour and to create a convenient turnaround or trailhead so drivers can retreat in their vehicles or continue by foot, horse, or bicycle (most closures apply only to motorized access). The Forest Service also prescribes decompaction of road surfaces, even for a short initial stretch, to quickly discourage further motorized access, as well as camouflaging a closed road with rocks and logs, obliteration and recontouring, or tree plantings.[56]

New Technologies and Ideas for Improving Road Management

If necessity is the mother of invention, then controversy must at least come as a dearly loved aunt. Whether spurred by necessity or controversy, a range of new ideas and technologies have emerged in recent years to help change the way we look at roads and motorized access on our public lands.

In an effort to defray the costs and controversy associated with road construction and road removal, Lolo National Forest road engineers in western Montana have developed "roll-up roads." These timber sale roads are built with a minimum clearing width and with clear advance notice of their temporary status. All topsoil removed for the road is left on site as fill material, which can then be cheaply and easily returned to the roadcut to restore the slope's original contours after log hauling is finished.[57] Although some conservationists express concern that these temporary roads simply make it easier to justify the significant impacts of timber harvest and road construction, Lolo's engineers consider the roll-up roads as something of a "win–win": the timber industry gets wood to the mills, and the forest may quickly return to an approximation of its unroaded condition (minus a certain number of trees). Since the roads are built with their subsequent removal included in the plan, Lolo officials can also defuse the common claim that public access is somehow being lost.

Whether for a temporary road or a permanent system road, one of the most dramatic changes in the Forest Service and other agencies is their increasing ability to keep accurate inventories of road mileage, road conditions, and motorized access. A look at the annual reports of the Forest Service illustrates the fact that the agency has long struggled to keep track of its roads. In 1932, the annual report listed 84,756 miles of road, with 26,199 miles "nonexistent."[58] The 1935 report identifies 120,948 miles of forest highways and development roads, but also notes that 31,796 miles do not exist.[59] By 1966, the forest road system had expanded to 189,975 miles, but the report no longer distinguished existing roads from nonexistent roads.[60] The agency is still trying to determine the exact location and condition of all of its forest roads, both to assess the roads' maintenance needs and to gauge their utility as passable routes.

Anyone who has tried to conduct an inventory of winding, bifurcating, and interconnecting roads will testify that the challenges are many. Basic definitions, such as how to distinguish a road from a wide trail for motorized vehicles, can present unexpected difficulties. Where roads have been abandoned or become overgrown, simply following the roadbed may be a chore. Measuring the distance, marking locations accurately on maps, and making yearly updates are ever present challenges as well. With the advent of increasingly functional technologies for GIS and global positioning systems (GPS), many of these problems can now be overcome.

The Environmental Systems Research Institute, the manufacturer of popular ARC/INFO and ArcView GIS programs, has developed a real-time feed to allow researchers in the field to carry handheld GPS units that record a steady stream of inputs. As a result, it is now possible to travel along a road while recording its location and distance. By later downloading this information into the GIS software, road system managers (or citizen activists) can create precise, accurate maps. Using tabular databases that link to the maps, managers can also include detailed information about the condition of the road surface, vehicle types and use, erosion problems, closure devices, or other notes that can help describe the condition of the road and its adjacent habitat.

Some conservation groups also use GIS technologies to create maps of habitat reserves that would protect roadless or restore roaded areas for the conservation of biodiversity. By combining information about road densities and locations, land ownership, vegetation or habitat features, and the needs of species, these reserve design maps can portray where critical plant or animal populations exist, where these organisms are likely to find satisfactory habitat conditions, and where land management may be most conducive to the lasting conservation of critical populations. Although most habitat reserves center upon existing wilderness, national parks or roadless lands where ecological integrity generally remains highest, large-scale reserve plans also include many areas that are degraded, roaded, or otherwise in need of habitat restoration. Private organizations have now developed site-specific proposals for large habitat reserves for most regions of North America, from Arizona to Maine to the North Cascades, Florida, Minnesota, and the southern and northern Rockies.[61]

The Federal Highway Administration is also applying new technologies to public land roads. By using digital video to analyze road conditions and needs, the agency can plug photos of roads into a computer program to assess and rate road conditions. The Highway Administration can also feed GPS-tracked road locations onto topographic maps, or use aerial or satellite images to generate updated accurate matches between road locations and the landscape itself. Applying these techniques from 1998 to 2000, the Highway Administration inventoried more than 90 percent of the road miles in the seventy-three national parks that have more than fifteen miles of road.[62]

While these technologies tend to grab the attention of land managers and the public, some more subtle changes have also contributed to new responses to roads and access. Beginning in the late 1980s, the field of restoration ecology emerged as a credible and recognizable discipline.[63] In 1988 the Society for Ecological Restoration was created, and five years later it began to publish a peer-reviewed journal, *Restoration Ecology*.[64] Restoration ecology remains an evolving and young field, but scientists, land managers, conservationists, and others such as artists and writers now have a clearer forum in which to discuss their ideas. These, in turn, can shape the approaches we take to solving problems generated by roads or ORVs.

Aspiring restoration experts can now find training and role models to respond to habitat degradation and blighted public lands. Many colleges and universities offer courses in restoration ecology, and restoration budgets increasingly appear in agency ledgers. Thanks in part to restoration ecology and other relatively new fields such as conservation biology, public land roads are no longer the domain solely of engineers. Instead, people with backgrounds in ecology, economics, fisheries and wildlife biology, landscape architecture, soils and hydrology, as well as philosophy and anthropology, are participating in the discussion about how and where motorized access should be developed, promoted, restricted, or banned.

Even engineers, traditionally trained in the technical aspects of construction and performance, have participated in and been influenced by the emergence of restoration ecology. In 1996, the Forest Services Technology and Development Program, staffed largely by engineers, published *A Guide for Road Closure and Obliteration in the Forest Service*.[65] Though it comes with an opening disclaimer that cultural, biological, budgetary, resource, and decision-making constraints "are not within the scope of this guide," the guide provides detailed information on topics ranging from site assessment to actual treatment methods. Produced to a large degree by the agency's Road Closure and Obliteration Project, the guide also notes that restoration work presents an opportunity for "environmental healing" and that such activities are considered "a critical component of ecosystem management."[66]

Despite objections raised by the "wise use movement"and others who condemn the "locking up"of public lands caused by road obliteration projects, very few road removal projects actually affect access. As a 1997 announcement for road removal in the Clearwater National Forest explained, "Most of the roads proposed for obliteration have been inaccessible to large vehicles for several years because they have overgrown with vegetation, or have eroded to the point of being impassable. Even though the road has revegetated, it may still contain considerable mass failure hazards."[67]

Removing Roads

Of all the factors that contribute to the decision to remove a road, the most important point may be that overgrown, revegetated roads still pose a risk for massive failures. In the single decade of the 1990s, thousands of road-triggered landslides occurred on public lands in California, Oregon, and Idaho. These were but the most recent round, as road failures have been happening now for decades (landslides also occur naturally in the absence of roads). The vast majority of these slides, also described as "debris torrents," took place on roads that were not being used, were overgrown with shrubs and trees and, in some cases, had long ago been scratched from agency records or forgotten.

After a spate of slope failures and landslides hit Oregon's Siuslaw National Forest in February 1996, forest supervisor Jim Furnish became outspoken about the need to remove roads and restore habitat in the coastal forest ecosystem: "Within forty-eight hours we recognized this as a once-in-a-lifetime opportunity to evaluate how logging and road building affect forests on a landscape level during times of great change. We'd had plenty of clues, but this was the first time we could say with some certainty that bad things could happen from what we've been doing."[68] Following the 1996 storm, the Forest Service documented 1,786 landslides in the Siuslaw and found that 77 percent were caused either by roads or clearcuts.[69] Even prior to the 1996 storm, the Siuslaw was working to remove and stabilize a sizable percentage of its roads. In addition to taking out culverts and fill from 70 miles of road, the forest has also installed water bars and removed failing sidecast material from nearly 600 of the 2,600 miles of road on the lands it administers. A subsequent comparison of conditions on treated and untreated road segments found that problems existed on both, but that the most severe problems occurred on untreated roads.[70]

The Siuslaw is far from alone with its landslide problems or with its program to remove roads. In fact, there are a number of road removal and restoration efforts under way on lands across the country, ranging from the modest to the extraordinary.

Roadripping

One of the simplest, cheapest, and most common road removal treatments is to decompact or "rip"the road's surface. Roadripping works especially well in flat areas where there is very little road cut to disrupt the natural flow of water and where erosion potential is low. In these cases, a surface treatment such as ripping can be a fast and effective way to discourage motorized use and encourage plant cover to recolonize the roadbed.

As we saw in the beginning of this chapter with Doug Edgerton's dozer in the Gallatin National Forest, stock machinery can easily be fitted with concrete rippers or modified lifters that will plow the roadbed and break up its compacted surface. This gives plants a chance to work their roots into the soil and can also make it difficult for wheeled vehicles to gain traction without bogging into loose ground. On flat roads in the Gallatin, a skilled roadripper can cover about 1 mile in an hour at an equipment cost from $100 to $500 per mile.[71] Add in some brushpiles or a few knocked-down trees to obscure the road entrance and roadripping can effectively close a number of roads. As photos 7-1, 7-2, and 7-3 illustrate, a handful of volunteers and one piece of heavy equipment can make a significant difference in the condition of an old logging road.

When I have returned to the Gallatin roads in the years since we worked with Doug Edgerton and Susan Lamont, most of the ripped roads were scarcely evident and many of the lodgepole pine seedlings we planted that year have grown waist high. Even though the roads we treated were small and the mile or two we removed represent just a fraction of the 1,300 miles that exist on the Gallatin, our work helped nudge a piece of the fragmented forest back into a more functional natural condition. And, whether for fisheries or grizzly bear habitat improvement, Lamont and Edgerton chip away at a couple more roads each summer season.

Photo 7-1

Photo 7-2

Photo 7-3

Ripping a road in the Gallatin National Forest in Montana. Felled trees on the roadbed are intended to discourage use and offer shelter for planted seedlings.

Roadripping also has its limitations. On roads that cut across slopes, simple surface treatments may do little to restore the area's natural hydrology. Water can still seep and flow across road cuts to create gullies and channel erosion, so cross-road drainage bars need to be installed to dissipate the energy of surface runoff. Roadripping usually leaves the road prism intact, which does little to reduce the failure potential of road cuts or fill material. On the Boise National Forest in Idaho where I visited several ripped road segments, the arid granitic soils had hardened into an impenetrable crust that shed water and supported the weight of vehicles much like the original, compacted roadbed. In conditions such as these, roadripping needs to be planned for the appropriate season or combined with other measures such as replanting or mulching if it is to improve, even superficially, the condition of the road. Both literally and figuratively, roadripping scratches the surface of road removal techniques, but if applied knowledgeably it can be a cost-effective way to restore a degree of hydrologic and ecological function.

Road Obliteration

Just one hour's drive west from my home in Missoula lie some of the most heavily roaded public lands in the country. Here, in the Clearwater National Forest in Idaho, historic trails used by the Nez Perce and Lewis and Clark now blend into a maze of logging roads constructed to access the region's forests of cedar, hemlock, pine, fir, and spruce. In some places these roads, called "jammer roads"after the logging method they served, pile atop each other at densities in excess of forty miles per square mile (see figure 7-1). At densities this high, one Forest Service official estimates that more than one-fourth of the lands surface is road template (which includes roadbed, cutslopes, and fill).[72]

In an effort to maintain water quality and threatened or endangered fisheries that include chinook salmon, steelhead, and bull trout, the Clearwater National Forest has set a road removal goal of 80 to 100 miles per year.[73] Actual miles obliterated have ranged from a low of 1.4 in 1993 to a peak of 134 in 1998.[74] The Clearwater has already identified an additional 600 miles for obliteration.[75] In most cases, with a combination of aggressive outreach, education, and field trips to show locals what the work involves, Clearwater officials can obliterate these low-use, high-risk roads and still enjoy the support of the public.

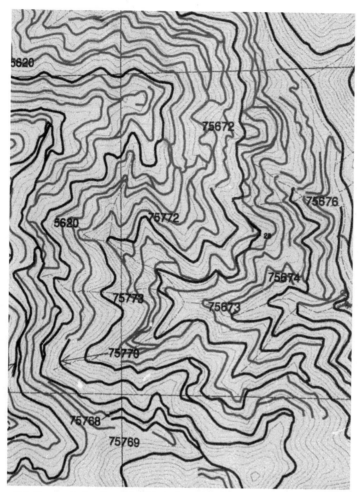

Figure 7-1: Computerized geographic information system maps can portray and measure road density in areas such as this heavily roaded square mile of the Clearwater National Forest in Idaho. Thick black and gray lines are roads; thin lines show contours.

The jammer roads of the Clearwater highlight two important facts that need to emerge in discussions of public land roads: a majority of the roads on the land do not provide public access, and with or without access these roads can cause problems. The Clearwater National Forest's Anne Connor, who directs road removal efforts in the forest, describes her program as one that "focuses on retaining access where we have access, but fixes watershed problems. Road obliteration becomes a lot more contentious when you remove access from the forest."[76] Brooks Beegle, a hydrologist working with Connor in the Clearwater, adds, "There's a broad misconception that roads that have been there for twenty years are stable and in place. People tend to think, 'If it didnt fail in 1974, why would it fail now?' This is one of the most important myths we need to dispel."[77]

During the winter of 1995 and 1996, the Clearwater National Forest suffered more than 900 landslides after heavy rains saturated the snowpack. Researchers in the forest determined that 58 percent of the slides were related to roads.[78] The landslides dumped some 200,000 cubic yards of soil and debris into the Clearwater's streams and rivers—enough to fill 20,000 large dump trucks—raising concerns over some of the interior Northwest's best remaining salmon spawning waters. In response, the Clearwater spent approximately $8 million for emergency repairs and began a concerted effort to remove unnecessary and high-risk roads.[79]

The rains of 1995 and 1996 helped focus attention on the risks roads posed to the Clearwater, but even before that, agency officials knew they had more roads on the ground than they wanted. In fact, dating back to 1992, the Clearwater had already obliterated more than twenty miles of road. None of these treated roads failed during the floods, nor has one failed since.[80]

Anne Connor has worked in the Clearwater National Forest for fourteen years, holds a bachelor's degree in forestry and a master's degree in civil engineering, and is a certified professional civil engineer. She doesn't mince words when she acknowledges that the Clearwater has a problem with its road system, and she seems almost grateful to the 1995–96 floods for the lessons they brought, noting, "Natural events such as flood and fire can make us much more sensitive to the impacts we have caused."[81] The floods also gave the Clearwater engineers a pulse of much-needed funding—the vast majority from a special National Forest Emergency Supplemental appropriation and a portion from the Emergency Relief for Federally Owned (ERFO) roads program administered by the Federal Highway Administration (discussed in Chapter 4). Connor and her team applied the money to taking out damaged roads.

Road obliteration is not cheap and the Clearwater has proven not only efficient with its work but also resourceful in its funding. Road obliteration money has come from annual appropriations in watershed, fisheries, and road maintenance, as well as the emergency funds following the 1996 floods. Since that time, the Clearwater has also worked cooperatively with the Nez Perce Tribe, which has funded 12 to 50 percent of the costs of the obliteration work.

The Nez Perce retain fishing and hunting rights to more than 13 million acres of "ceded lands"in north-central Idaho, including most of the Clearwater National Forest, and have a vested interest in the maintenance of water quality and fisheries in the watershed.[82]

While the working relationship between the Nez Perce Tribe and Clearwater National Forest continues to evolve, the Tribe views its role as that of comanagers of the ceded lands. In addition to providing essential funding for road removal work, the Nez Perce are helping to set the priorities for fisheries restoration, working with Clearwater officials on an environmental watershed assessment, and putting money and effort into a monitoring and evaluation program. At times, they have also taken the Forest Service to task administratively or in court to press for stronger habitat protection. As Ira Jones, the Nez Perce watershed director says, "We're all going through times of change and we need to find new ways of doing business. . . . When you look back it's been over a hundred years of mismanagement. We're looking a hundred years in the future. There's nothing short-term about what were doing."[83]

Road obliteration costs on the Clearwater National Forest vary depending upon the treatment, but range from $2,000 per mile to recontour a road entrance to restrict vehicle access, to more thǎn $10,000 per mile for recontouring the majority of the road.[84] On a recent project on the West Fork of Wawaatamnima (Fishing) Creek, for example, the Clearwater obliterated 8.9 miles of road for a total cost of $85,096. Of this sum, $3,290 went to project planning, surveying, and compliance with the National Environmental Policy Act; $28,403 to technical support, inspection, and labor; $9,403 to materials and overhead; and $44,000 to pay for the obliteration equipment.[85] As photos 7-4, 7-5, and 7-6 show, road obliteration on the Clearwater can transform the character of heavily roaded watersheds.

Equipment costs, in this case and many other road obliteration projects, are for the same types of heavy machinery such as excavators and large bulldozers that were used to build the road in the first place. Such an aggressive approach makes some people cringe at the impacts, but the officials in the Clearwater and other sites across the country have learned

Photo 7-4

Photo 7-5

Road removal and recontouring on the West Fork of Wawíaatamnima (Fishing) Creek, Clearwater National Forest, Idaho. Notice the rock circled as a reference point in each photo. (Courtesy of Clearwater National Forest.)

Photo 7-6

some important lessons about road obliteration. For many of these lessons they point to work under way at Redwood National Park.

The Redwood Experience

"Basically, I'm a road killer."

When I heard that job description, I knew I ought to meet Mike Sanders. With degrees in both physics and geology, Sanders has been working as a hit man—taking out roads—for Redwood National Park since 1995. When it comes to road removal, it is tough to find anyone who moves more dirt than Mike Sanders.

Sanders works as part of a team of geologists, hydrologists, engineers, and heavy equipment operators who for more than two decades have established Redwood National Park as the premier living laboratory for large-scale road obliteration and habitat restoration.

By many accounts, Redwood National Park is the most severely degraded of any unit in the scenic national park system. Despite this reputation, what I saw still took me aback when I finally made it to Northern California to see the park firsthand. Even the park's South Operations Center, where Sanders and the road removal team work, is marked by a massive charred redwood stump that towers some forty feet above the park offices in broken testimony of what once was.[86]

Congress first designated a Redwood National Park in 1968 in an effort to save some of the last stands of ancient forest. The trees here grow like no others in the world. At more than 360 feet, they stand as the world's tallest living things and some live for more than 2,000 years.

With the first round of national park protection at Redwood Creek, timber corporations in the area realized that more set-asides were on the way. For the next ten years, Georgia-Pacific, Arcata Redwood, and other companies cut with abandon to get to as many of the valuable large old redwoods as possible before the federal government put them off-limits to the saw. By the time Congress acted again, doubling the size of Redwood National Park in 1978, loggers had managed to cut all but 9,000 of the 48,000 acres added to the park. All told, the expanded park protected some prize stands of old trees, but also included more than 300 miles of logging roads and more than 3,000 miles of roadlike "skid trails" where heavy machinery had dragged the large trees from their stumps to the logging trucks.[87]

The park itself came at a purchase price that approached $2 billion. Using an initial allocation of $33 million for restoration and road removal that came with the 1978 park designation, Redwood Park officials have now worked to treat nearly 200 miles of road. It is a task that could easily engage Mike Sanders and his colleagues for the rest of their working lives.

When the Park Service first took over management of the lower Redwood Creek basin, they took care with their restoration efforts to avoid the heavy impacts wrought upon the land by the mechanized logging industry. Crews of people pulled culvert pipes out of stream crossings by hand, hauled wheelbarrows full of eroded soil away from streamsides, and meticulously constructed wooden check dams to trap sediments and reduce erosion.

Within just a few years, however, park officials realized the hand labor was not enough. Flooding streams blew out check dams and the roaded lands continued to drop soils into the creeks where Pacific salmon spawning areas were choking with sediment. The increased erosion also began to expose the roots of some of the redwoods, leading to fears that the ancient trees were protected only on paper and would soon drown, topple, or wash away.

Road restoration work began to focus on stream crossings and brought in backhoes and small dozers to pull fill material back from active water channels. In places, crews added an "outslope"to the roadbeds, which retained part of the road prism but created a more natural contour for water to sheet across road surfaces. Using a few machines and focusing attention where roads crossed streams, Park crews could treat several dozen miles of road in a summer season. This, too, proved inadequate as roads continued to collapse and create debris torrents even on slopes without any stream crossings (see photo 7-7).

Finally, in the early 1990s, park personnel turned to the same equipment that had created the roads in the first place.[88] Using large excavators and bulldozers, Redwood crews took out entire road systems by pulling fill material back into the old road prism, restoring the original contours and slopes of the land, and scouring old road crossings down to the original cobbles, stumps, and soils of the natural stream channels.

Ecologically, the goals of the roadwork focus upon providing some immediate relief to the park's fish-bearing streams. By returning the roads to the contours of their original slopes, park scientists expect soils to stay in place more securely, thereby reducing the likelihood of road-triggered

Photo 7-7: Old revegetated roads can still collapse, as shown by Mike Sanders on this road failure in Redwood National Park.

landslides. With road prisms filled in, subsurface flow and hydrologic function can also return to approximate conditions prior to road construction.[89]

Though the Redwood restoration effort is only partially completed, Redwood National Park crews have already removed more than 1 million cubic yards—the equivalent of 100,000 dump truck loads—from road stream crossings on the former roadways. The park plans to treat an additional 9.5 miles of road each year—rehabilitating stream crossings, restoring hydrologic function and topographic features, filling roadcuts, and reseeding soils. By 2005, Redwood officials expect they will have restored 10 percent of the degraded area.[90]

The work at Redwood National Park is notable not just for its lessons and its history, but also for its magnitude in space and time. The scale of the work is staggering. When Mike Sanders brought me to some of the main-stem logging roads that had been removed, he jokingly strolled into the distance to provide "a geologist for scale." Time and again I watched in amazement as he disappeared to a small speck amid the swath of recontoured road and looming stumps. In places the obliterated road *looked* far worse than the original had, since in the decades following road construction alder trees and shrubs had colonized the disturbed areas and covered the scars of heavy industry. But overgrown untreated roads have collapsed throughout the park

Photo 7-8: Large-scale road obliteration often requires the relocation of tens of thousands of cubic yards of material. For scale, note the geologist standing on the redwood stump in the lower center of the photo.

in recent years, dispelling the false impression that aesthetics contribute much to a road's stability. Visiting such a scene, we can only stand and imagine 300 hundred years from now when redwoods might once again poke through the canopy of alders and restake their claim on the park.

The cost of road removal also speaks to the size of the projects at Redwood National Park. In 1999, Sanders planned and supervised a 1.5-mile obliteration along Redwood Creek that cost $750,000. In about a month's work, heavy machinery on the project moved more than 200,000 cubic yards of soil. Although the former road now looks like an old power line cut, cluttered with alder debris and a cleared swath running through the forest, the undulations of hill and swale now match the surrounding landscape perfectly (see photo 7-8). In five years red alder will fill in the clearing, in thirty years they will stand as a sizable second-growth forest—as they do throughout much of the park—and in a century the sitka spruce and redwoods may start to take over once again.

The road obliteration program at Redwood, like most other places, comes with its share of controversies and headaches. Local residents of nearby Orick and other northern California towns originally resented the park designations and the seemingly associated decline of the area's timber industry, but feelings have softened somewhat with time and the steady trickle of tourist dollars that arrive each summer season. Furthermore, the handful of road obliteration jobs that involve heavy machinery are typically contracted out to local operators, in some cases the very same men who constructed the roads thirty or forty years ago.

Some critics have also questioned the Park Service's strategies to treat the road system. When a heavy rain in December of 1996 fell on already-saturated soils it triggered a number of debris torrents and landslides throughout the park (the rain was rated a modest "11-year event"for its probability for recurrence). The episode helped bring in $11 million in emergency funding, a badly needed supplement to the road obliteration program's paltry $180,000 base funding from annual appropriations, but it also generated concerns about how park officials were setting priorities for road obliteration. Should they treat more miles of road to a lesser degree, thereby trying to reduce the chances of major blowouts? Or should they move systematically through the park to try to restore more fully the watersheds that hold the greatest potential for productive fisheries, even at the possible expense of other areas?

Federal agencies in charge of endangered species recovery also add a layer of complexity to the road obliteration work. The National Marine Fisheries Service, in charge of anadromous salmon and steelhead recovery, generally supports the road removal and its long-term improvement of fisheries habitat, but still sets limits on the season during which work can occur (these fish spend part of their lives in freshwater streams such as Redwood Creek, and the remainder in the open ocean). Similarly, the U.S. Fish and Wildlife Service is overseeing recovery of the northern spotted owl and places certain stipulations about leaving old growth stands intact for breeding and nesting sites. Ironically, some of the areas where loggers cut redwoods three or four decades ago now contain alder forests that can provide owl habitat, causing problems for road obliteration crews planning to tear out the old roads and the aging alders that grow on top of them.

When I asked Mike Sanders why he works at the park, puts up with the hassles, and dedicates himself to road obliteration, he spoke first about his interest in "process geomorphology"and his fascination with earth movements and landslides. He recalled the day in graduate school when his current supervisor, Terry Spreiter, came to a brown bag luncheon for geology students and inspired him with her talk about restoration work on the roads at Redwood Park. He spoke of trying to make connections between geology, ecology, and park policy. Then he paused for a moment; a hint of indignation crept into his voice and he said, "I just think it's a travesty to have roads like this in a national park."

Living with Public Lands

As agencies work to adapt to changing times, the public in turn will need to respond. In the 1950s, few people concerned themselves with questions of wide-open motorized access on millions of acres of national forest and BLM land, and even national park and wildlife refuge road projects stirred few souls. Today, access looms as a critical and contentious issue. Whether we are able to move steadily into active restoration and road removal programs, as land managers have in Redwood National Park, or become bogged down in protests and legal proceedings like those surrounding the Jarbidge road controversy near Elko, Nevada, depends in many cases upon the response and participation of each of us: anglers and hunters, scientists, students, recreationists, agency officials, conservationists, and others.

Thanks in part to the evolution of law, knowledge, and technology, agency planners, students, and other citizens now have tools for change that can dramatically affect the way we manage roads and motorized access on public lands. Each of the land management agencies has recognized to some degree the changing landscapes they must serve in the twenty-first century, and new mission statements and road policies should contribute to their abilities to respond appropriately. Conservation groups, Native Americans, and other citizens have also learned to work with land managers, create new visions for the future, and when necessary, turn to the courts to press for the gradual peeling back of roads and motors from many public lands.

New branches of science, including conservation biology and restoration ecology, hold promise for research and education that will better inform our access and road management programs. We continue to discover new methods for mapping and keeping track of roads and their impacts on wildlife habitat or water quality. As digital imagery and personal computing power increase, so too may our ability to document our progress and our failures to manage the public domain for its lasting health and the public good. And, finally, as public demands and economies change, from logging and road building to recreation and road removal, we will no doubt continue to determine the outcome of this distinctly American experience of living with our public lands. Whatever the tools, we will need to keep teaching ourselves how we ought best to use them.

We are not fighting progress,
we are making it.

—Howard Zahniser

8 | The Road Ahead

The North Fork of the Boise River flows clear
and cold from its headwaters in the Sawtooth National Recreation Area
of central Idaho. From the roadless wildlands of the Sawtooths, the river
flows through multiple-use lands of the Boise National Forest. Clear water
flowing over a cobbled bed steadily changes into a turbid river coursing
through sandbars and deep drifts of sediment.

In August of 1997, Dan Funsch and I arrived at the North Fork of the
Boise River with two mountain bikes lashed to the roof of the car and one
thing on our minds: national forest roads. For two weeks, we set out to
locate, map, measure, and evaluate every mile of road that existed in the
North Fork of the Boise River basin. Such a comprehensive inventory of
roads had never before been accomplished, and to my knowledge, still has-
n't: we only made it through one-third of the river's watershed. But in
those two weeks, Funsch and I bicycled, hiked, and measured more than
450 miles of road in the Boise National Forest.

The North Fork of the Boise road inventory took us longer than we
expected for several reasons. A large fire had burned through the area the
previous year, and an active helicopter-based timber "salvage" operation
made access limited and dangerous where logging was taking place. Roads
had washed out in nearly two dozen places and caused landslides, mak-

ing travel difficult. Other roads were overgrown with trees, while in still other places the Forest Service had intentionally ripped the road surface to discourage motorized use and reduce soil density. On one occasion, I was turned back on my bicycle by a charging black bear after I accidentally treed her two cubs. But the single most challenging aspect of the inventory was simply finding the roads in the first place.

Most national forests publish a travel plan map that shows land ownership, roads, trails, recreation areas, and places where visitors can legally drive. These maps typically show only a portion of the actual roads in a particular area—usually the constructed roads that are obvious and either open to some public access or closed by a gate, earthen barrier, or other device. Many old or overgrown roads receive no public use and often the agency leaves these off of travel plan maps or has lost track of them entirely.[1]

To survey the roads and mark them on detailed maps, Funsch and I first needed to traverse every length of road, follow each spur to its end, and distinguish roads from the numerous logging skid trails.

Later, after analyzing the data, we confirmed what we suspected at the time: dozens of miles of the North Fork's roads were useless to the general public because they were too overgrown to drive or even walk along. One-fourth of the roads in the North Fork of the Boise watershed were restricted from public use and approximately 20 percent were impassable by motorized vehicle, but many of these roads were still causing problems that could affect wildlife and the water quality of the basin's streams and rivers. On multiple occasions, we came upon closed roads that were slumping or collapsing into streams or had serious structural problems.[2]

While working to find and measure all the North Fork of the Boise's roads, I sometimes reflected back to the language and purpose for first designating the national forests. Above all else, the 191-million-acre national forest system is supposed to remain loyal to the two goals of providing a long-term sustainable timber resource and protecting the birthing ground for our nation's waters.

Looking across the heavily cut mountainsides of the the North Fork and its tributaries, I had little doubt that for at least the past few decades a generous supply of timber had been coming off these Boise National Forest lands. But later, when Funsch and I drove to the upstream edge of the North Fork of the Boise River's road system and found the river flowing clear with cobbles and riffles, we were startled by the difference in water quality. Just twenty heavily roaded miles downstream, the North Fork was murky. In places, the river had visible beds of silt rising out of the water midstream. Along this stretch, road-caused landslides had also reached the river and dumped tons of sediment into the channel. I could not help but wonder how well the Boise National Forest was holding up to the second part of its mission: to protect water supplies.

Unusable, damaging roads are exactly the kind that spurred former Forest Service chief Mike Dombeck to call for new policies during his tenure with the Clinton administration. These roads offer no public goods or services, they disrupt wildlife habitat and water quality, would cost billions of dollars to repair and return to a functional condition, and are stacked like cordwood on top of each other in some of the national forests' steeper, least stable slopes. Road densities in subdrainages of the North Fork study area exceed six miles per square mile—about twice the average in national forests but nowhere near that of drainages such as the nearby Clearwater or Coeur d'Alene watersheds.

Many of these are the "easy" roads that would provide a distinct benefit to the public if removed. But road removal, like a number of public land issues, has to contend with battle lines that are firmly drawn. Conservationists, supporters of fish and wildlife, many land managers, and some fiscal conservatives recognize that excess roads are causing needless damage to our public lands, pocketbooks, and the environment. Other constituencies maintain that roads of any kind lead to better public access and better land management.

In this final chapter, we will look at how land managers can act responsibly in their position as stewards of our public domain, what kinds of choices policy makers and legislators may face that can positively influence access management, the role of citizens and conservation groups, and what we have yet to learn that will bear critically upon the decisions that loom.

Agency Officials, Laws, and Citizenship

Land managers today are often wedged firmly between two strongly polarized voices of the public. Pleasing no one has become a measuring stick for many agency officials, especially those pursuing the multiple-use agendas of the Forest Service and Bureau of Land Management (BLM). Agency planners have often told me, "If both sides are yelling at me, I figure I'm right where I should be." Whether for decisions about roads and access management, timber sales, mining projects, or recreation, many agency decisions become bracketed by the conflicting demands of the most vocal margins of society.

There are a number of problems with this approach to land management. At the individual level, it appears almost sadistically unproductive to gauge policy positions (as a success!) depending upon the perceived balance of negative feedback. Little wonder, then, that a Forest Service once legendary for its esprit de corps must at times resort to office postings with catchy slogans ("Service is job number one!") simply to keep employees from drooping with low self-esteem. Referees at sporting events may be the only other professionals in the country who go to work expecting such ready public abuse on a daily basis.

More broadly, the agencies' informal policy of mutually assured public dissatisfaction can distance land managers from the laws that *should* be dictating agency actions. Some environmental groups have gained a reputation in recent decades for hounding the land management agencies with lawsuits, but these suits are only successful when the agencies have strayed from their legal obligations. The fact that many suits prevail indicates that agency actions do not consistently meet their statutory requirements. The problem in these cases is not that the laws are overly strict or that the environmental groups are too aggressive; the problem is simply that the land management agencies neglect to follow their own standards and laws.

These laws, in fact, offer a clean escape for land managers hounded by a polarized public. With the exception of a handful of renegades on either end of the political spectrum, America remains a nation of laws and of citizens who support and respect the law. When making controversial decisions, agency personnel can tap into this culture of respect most effectively by pointing to the laws they have sworn to uphold. In this way, land managers might be able to extract themselves from the position of pleasing no one—and the subsequent abuse that engenders—in favor of a publicly supported stance of defending the laws of the land. Removing roads to meet road density standards and protect elk habitat, for instance, becomes a matter of honoring the laws that we as a nation have created, not a question of positioning the agency in some estimated middle ground of public disgruntlement.

Similarly, prohibiting off-road vehicles (ORVs) on federal lands where they are causing damage or user conflicts accords with rules established by two different presidential executive orders made by one Republican, Richard Nixon, and one Democrat, Jimmy Carter. Agencies such as the BLM would find far steadier ground if they based their actions explicitly upon this legal footing than they currently do trying to walk the quivering tightrope of local opinion.

Not coincidentally, recent decades have also witnessed a forced objectivity for public land managers that has muted many of these government employees as citizens. Land management agency employees today are commonly instructed not to take such public positions as writing letters to the editor, speaking out at public meetings, or otherwise expressing their personal views as citizens, even outside the context of their professional lives.[3] This muting of our land managers represents a partial loss of citizenship and reduces their ability to serve as civic leaders. If reinstated, these roles could prove to be personally satisfying and could also serve as an inspiration to others.

The position of government employees as silenced citizens has not always been the case. In fact, some of America's most revered conservation figures came from within the ranks of the Forest Service, U.S. Fish and Wildlife Service, and other agencies. Aldo Leopold was a high-ranking regional forester in the 1920s even as he spoke against threats of road building and motorization to the Gila Mountains of New Mexico.[4] As a direct consequence of Leopold's efforts, the Forest Service set aside the Gila as the country's first protected wilderness where roads and motorized vehicles were expressly forbidden.

Rachel Carson worked as a scientist for the U.S. Fish and Wildlife Service throughout her career as an author, and was admirably supported by many colleagues and superiors in the agency when the agrochemical industry launched vitriolic attacks on her following the publication of *Silent Spring* in 1962.[5] Carson spoke out not *despite* her position with the Fish and Wildlife Service, but rather, at least in part, *because* of the sense of duty and responsibility she gained from her work.

Bob Marshall was an outspoken proponent of wilderness and civil liberties during a distinguished government career cut short by his death at age 38. Even as he helped found The Wilderness Society and openly criticized government programs in forestry and labor, Marshall held supervisory positions in Washington, D.C., for the Bureau of Indian Affairs and the U.S. Forest Service. Marshall addressed his duty as government official and U.S. citizen directly, writing, "I cannot conceive why a person working for the public must accept an inferior position as a citizen to one who receives a salary from private enterprise. The real danger to American institutions and American democracy will come, not when government officials participate as citizens in the democratic determination of politics, but when a large body of American citizens who are government workers become permanently muzzled."[6]

Fortunately, Leopold, Carson, and Marshall are not mere historical footnotes to today's practices. In response to concerns he developed while working for the agency as a timber planner in the 1980s, Jeff DeBonis founded the Forest Service Employees for Environmental Ethics (FSEEE). The group strives to create a solid network of support and encouragement for agency employees in order "to forge a socially responsible value system for the Forest Service." Operating with the belief that "land is a public trust, to be passed with reverence from generation to generation," FSEEE holds the Forest Service accountable to work for an ecologically and economically sustainable future.[7] In addition to publishing the bimonthly *Forest Magazine*, FSEEE has created a middle school curriculum, monitoring reports, brochures, and an activist alert network to support its 12,000 members and its mission.

In 1992, DeBonis expanded his vision and started Public Employees for Environmental Responsibility (PEER). PEER now boasts thousands of members from federal and state agencies and "promotes environmental ethics and government accountability."[8]

These two organizations work from within the agencies as well as by applying external pressure. In this way, federal employees gain an increased ability to lead secure professional lives without suffering undue consequences if they speak out as "whistle blowers" against unethical, inappropriate, or illegal agency activities. The active membership of these groups bears witness to the critical role they play in protecting government employees' rights to free speech, but too many land managers continue to feel pressured to abdicate their positions as citizens in order to carry out the terms of their occupation.[9]

Groups such as PEER and FSEEE may help land managers turn to a more positive approach for their jobs—one that emphasizes a devotion to the law and agency missions rather than the appeasement of vocal minority constituencies—and provide a healthy support network for land managers who have the temerity to act as citizens as well as civil servants.

Although a newly activated corps of land managers might still not produce hordes of Leopolds, Carsons, and Marshalls, many people who work for the Forest Service, Park Service, and other agencies were first attracted to their profession because of a personal commitment to public lands, wildlife, or the environment. These people are, in other words, primed from the outset to work for conservation and thoughtful management. In some cases this initial passion is dampened by the culture of bureaucratic neutrality that pervades the agencies, but the background, training, or activism of agency employees can also be inhibited by the simple fact that land managers want to get along with their neighbors.

In many places, district offices for the Forest Service, BLM, Park Service, and wildlife refuges are located in small towns where the prevailing view may differ markedly from that of Americans nationwide or from more urban areas where managers grew up, attended college or were trained. In towns such as Elko, Nevada, or Troy, Montana, locals have relied upon grazing, mining, or logging for many decades and the prospect of change is frightening and infuriating. When a recently arrived land manager speaks out in favor of protecting fish or wildlife interests, for instance, instead of promoting road-based logging or mining projects, local relations can become chillingly hostile.

As we saw in Chapter 7, Humboldt-Toiyabe National Forest supervisor Gloria Flora resigned during the Jarbidge Road controversy near Elko, citing a pervasive atmosphere of intimidation and isolation in which she no longer felt safe.[10] Other land managers have faced local hostilities ranging from the harassment of their children at school to death threats and having their offices firebombed.[11] Even where there is no overt threat to officials' safety, the views of the townsfolk can be difficult to ignore.

In 1997, I attended an agency hearing in Troy, Montana, where officials from the Forest Service and U.S. Fish and Wildlife Service were presenting—and inviting public comment on—a plan that would involve closing a number of old logging roads. Land managers and wildlife biologists considered road closures one of the best ways to protect the two dozen or so grizzly bears struggling for survival in the nearby Kootenai National Forest. I had met with some of the Forest Service planners earlier in the year and generally found them concerned about the plight of the grizzlies and supportive of the federal laws that provided for the species' protection.

When speaking in a high school gymnasium packed with most of Troy's 500 residents, however, these same officials veered dramatically away from any pro-bear, road-closing statements and instead tried to appease their assembled neighbors with apologies or by stating their own dissatisfaction with the federal mandates. At one point in the hearing, when a sizable Trojan stood up and bellowed, "Who in this room even wants grizzly bears around?" I felt the full force of local sentiment as my own arm held the only hand extending toward the rafters and a thousand eyes turned upon me in disgust. I left the meeting feeling exposed and uneasy, but had the relief of knowing that my own home lay 200 miles distant.

While there may be no quick answer to these situations, as a society and as neighbors we need to at least renounce acts of violence or intimidation. Regardless of policy disagreements we may have as individuals, we should still manage to live respectfully together in our communities. I may not like it if my old neighbor Gary still drives his motorcycle on national forest trails that are closed to motorized use or if my college roommate vacations with a snowmobile in Yellowstone, but surely we could still manage to live together in a community.

Public officials also need to feel genuinely supported by local and federal law enforcement officials in order to conduct the work for which they are chartered. Far too often, law enforcement funds are not available to conduct the basic monitoring and control work to support road closure orders and limits on motorized access.

If employees' personal and professional interests are defended more carefully, both the pride and the performance of agencies will surely benefit. Liberated and supported agency employees could serve as an important catalyst for sound policies that honor the laws of the land and restrict motorized access, protect habitat, and conserve soil and water.

Land managers need to have the confidence in their own actions—and the support of their agencies—to make effective decisions and be able to implement them. Transportation planners often complain of their powerlessness to prevent illegal use by ORVs detouring earthen barriers or passing beneath and around gates. A number of these agency employees have lost faith in their ability to contain a rebellious motorized public or see little help on the way, and as a result they sometimes stop trying (or repeatedly install devices that are promptly vandalized). This need not be the case.

If a road is closed to public use but essential for administrative access, strategically placed, reinforced steel gates with multiple rails ("ranch gates") can provide easy passage to key-wielding officials. When constructed and placed properly in a fence line, on a bridge, or in thick forest, certain temporary devices such as reinforced steel gates or anchored guardrails can keep out all but the most determined motorized trespasser. Wherever possible, more permanent measures such as road removal and recontouring to match original slopes are superior, and these can remedy most of the original impacts of a road and its accompanying motorized access. In other words, there are ways of closing roads effectively; agencies simply need to provide land managers with the guidance, funding, training, and tools to accomplish the task. And when violations do take place, law enforcement needs to be swift, effective, and well-publicized to discourage further transgressions.

Citizens Guard the Gates

On a March day in 1903, a Florida orange grower and part-time boat builder named Paul Kroegel set out for the first-ever patrol of a national wildlife refuge. Using his own boat and shotgun, and for a salary that at first varied from nothing at all to $1.00 per month, Kroegel worked to protect the roseate spoonbills, egrets, ibises, and eponymous birds of Pelican Island, Florida.[12] For several years Kroegel had rallied for protection of Pelican Island and its birds, and with the help of the Florida Audubon Society and Ornithologists' Union, Inc., he finally persuaded President Theodore Roosevelt to create the first National Wildlife Refuge with an executive order on March 14, 1903.[13]

From even before that day to the present, the citizens of this country have established a long, proud history as conservators of wildlife, the land, and its waters. Of course, Americans have also acted with extreme carelessness and disregard for our natural environment—otherwise the conservators could never have kept so busy—but perhaps from the first crossings of the Bering land bridge and, certainly, the much later landings at Roanoke or Plymouth, there have been those who lifted their voices or acted to protect the features of the continent they came upon.

Kroegel, for example, not only lobbied President Theodore Roosevelt for several years about the importance of protecting egrets, pelicans, and other birds at Pelican Island, he also remained active in the Fish and Wildlife Service until his death in 1948.[14] To this day, citizens are stepping forth in similarly devoted ways. Without this citizen presence and activism we would have lost many of the land, water, and wildlife features of our nation in the past century's blitz of development.

The actions of early opponents of unbridled motorization such as Aldo Leopold and Bob Marshall are well documented and popularly known. But the hero's wreath we sometimes place around these figures can obscure the fact that they acted, first and foremost, as concerned citizens (as noted earlier, they also worked for land management agencies).

Working frequently alone and from her own resources, in the 1930s Rosalie Edge proved herself a determined champion of conservation. To this day she is given primary credit for preserving the Hawk Mountain Sanctuary in Pennsylvania and Washington's Olympic National Park, but she also published a pointed critique of public lands roads policies at the time. In the pamphlet *Roads and More Roads in the National Parks and National Forests* Edge commented, "[A] road into a wild region is the prelude to its destruction, its forests, its scenery and its wild life. An increase of roads in the National Forests spells the doom of the last of the great timber."[15] It was with a clear mix of admiration and trepidation that one of Edge's occasional collaborators called her, "the only honest, unselfish, indomitable hellcat in the history of conservation."[16]

Working in an era before the "professional environmentalist" quite existed, these conservationists helped define a tradition that both amateurs and professionals maintain to this day.

In many parts of the country, citizen activists working for little or no pay tend the front lines of the debate over roads and motorized recreation. In the 1980s, a former logger and Forest Service employee named Keith Hammer grew concerned about the effect of ORVs and road access on grizzly bears in the Flathead National Forest near his home in western Montana. Hammer designed and conducted a study in which he documented road conditions and checked road closures in the 2 million acre Flathead National Forest. When he compiled his results he found that far more roads existed in grizzly bear habitat than the national forest's management plan permitted. With photos and documentation in hand, he confronted agency officials with the news that they were out of compliance with their own laws. As a direct result of Hammer's work, the Flathead closed some 400 miles of abandoned roads.[17] In 1995, the Flathead National Forest agreed to a 10-year program of road removal and habitat restoration to meet its obligations to help recover threatened grizzly bears.[18] By 1999, the Flathead Forest had "reclaimed" 273 miles of road out of a planned 617 miles. As long as road reclamation work continues to treat stream crossings and remove culverts, the effort to protect bear habitat should also prove beneficial to water quality and the recently listed bull trout. Hammer, who now works as an artist and kayak guide as well as an activist, remains devoted to efforts to improve conditions in the Flathead Forest, but notes that it requires, "constant vigilance."[19]

In Duluth, Minnesota, Jeff Brown grew concerned about the "noise, fumes, and danger" caused by snowmobile use on nearby lands. Rallying around the human and social impacts of this motorized winter recreation, Brown helped create the group Minnesotans for Responsible Recreation. In an effort to decrease the number of accidents and user conflicts with snowmobiles in the North Woods, Minnesotans for Responsible Recreation has introduced a bill to the state legislature that requires snowmobiles to register and display license plates similar to automobiles, creates an enforceable code of ethics to reduce user conflicts, and provides for increased law enforcement. The bill has drawn praise for its promise to decrease deadly accidents and reduce public safety costs.[20]

In the hardwood forests of Illinois and the southern Midwest, Jim Bensman, a former retail manager, works with a coalition of conservationists in an effort to protect some of the nation's most diverse forests from damage caused by logging, road building, and ORV use. Bensman became interested in environmental activism in high school when he started attending Sierra Club meetings for extra credit in his biology class. Though he is not an attorney, Bensman has taught himself enough about law to file successful *pro se* cases, presented as a citizen without an attorney. Among other victories, Bensman and Heartwood, the group with whom Bensman now works, have curtailed the Forest Service's use of categorical exclusions and battled ORV abuse by insisting that the agency adhere to its requirements for monitoring environmental impacts. Bensman's efforts have focused largely on the Shawnee National Forest in Illinois, but some of his efforts have affected forest policy nationally.[21]

Although the actions of these individuals are exemplary, citizens in every state in the nation are making a difference as they work to contain the impacts of roads and motorized recreation on public lands. From the Big Cypress Preserve in Florida to the Izembek National Wildlife Refuge in the Bering Sea of Alaska, the work of citizens and the agency officials they support (or confront) carries the fight to protect these public lands from recurring threats of new roads and increasing ORV use.

Land Management Traditions, Revisited

On a recent trip I took to Jacksonville, Florida, a cab driver struggled to place my home state of Montana: "Is that near Utah?" When I mentioned that Yellowstone National Park was located partially in Montana, the cabby's eyes lit up and he exclaimed, "Oh! I've read about *that* place!"

For many decades now, Americans have read about or visited Yellowstone, the Great Smokies, Acadia, the Grand Canyon, and Yosemite because we know that these places are special. Our actions—and those of our fellow visitors—are bounded by the necessity to protect the qualities we find there. Particularly in these national parks, as well as in national wildlife refuges, motorized access is generally very restricted. This does not make these places less appealing to visit; to the contrary, we go out of our way to find these places because of their very special qualities, including their limits on motorized access.

In Yellowstone National Park, where controversy promises to rage for some time over winter use, snowmobilers have long accepted restrictions on where and how they will travel. Yellowstone snowmobilers have been restricted to the same paved road loops available in summer to cars, have had to limit speeds to forty-five miles per hour, and only use the park from mid-December to mid-March. None of these restrictions exist on the adjacent national forest lands, yet snowmobilers still flock to Yellowstone by the thousands. The prospect of seeing the bison, trumpeter swans, rivers, geysers, and other natural features of Yellowstone makes snowmobilers willing to accept certain restrictions on their behavior and the use of their machines.

Millions of visitors come to public lands each year even though they understand that their activities in these places are subject to restrictions. Especially on the more tightly controlled park and refuge lands, we know what to expect, anticipate a certain amount of law enforcement, and understand that observing the regulations will help to preserve the experiences we seek. Furthermore, as visitors we are generally able to distinguish between areas that have different land use prescriptions. In Glacier National Park, for example, tourists heading for the Apgar

Vistor Center can expect to park their car within a short walk of the rest rooms, have easy access to hot and cold running water, and stroll over to a nearby cafe for a meal. In the same national park, visitors will need to hike twelve miles to reach a backcountry campsite near Buffalo Woman Lake, and once there they will need to use a pit toilet, fetch water from the lake (and sterilize it before drinking), and cook their own food using a campstove they carried in their backpack. We are able to discern that in different areas of the park different types of activities and access are appropriate.

This same tenet holds for many of the multiple-use national forest and BLM lands, but the baseline expectations are different here. Because ORVs have had unlimited access to many BLM lands for the past few decades, motorized recreationists often assume that this privilege should continue regardless of environmental impacts, social conflicts, or changing values in land management. Similarly, national forest users have grown accustomed to a virtually unlimited road network and the perception that with a potent enough vehicle few places would be out of reach. Where regulations do exist, they are sometimes applied inconsistently or appear on travel maps that can confuse inexperienced visitors.

In many cases, expectations are based upon the false assumption that motorized access is a fundamental right on public lands. In others, they come from the translation of a few decades of ORV access into a claim of "traditional" use. But in fact, from the early days of their designation, public lands have restricted motorized access to varying degrees, and the oldest traditions for access include only hiking and horsepacking.

In hearings on the National Forest Management Act in the mid-1970s, Arkansas senator Dale Bumpers testified, "Unfortunately, the building of permanent roads in many areas has created new problems by encouraging uncontrolled access to remote, lightly patrolled forest areas with an attendant increase in litter, vandalism, fire danger, and an increased encroachment on the solitude which these areas once offered the hunter, the fisherman, the hiker, and the naturalist. Nor is simply closing off such roads, once they are constructed, an adequate remedy."[22] As our lives become increasingly mechanized and automated, public lands will become more and more valuable for what they do not have—unlimited motorized access, noise and air pollution, the constant whir of machines—

as well as for the spectacular features, wildlife habitat, and soil and water that they contain.

In the future, we will likely consider it ever more appropriate to restrict motorized access and remove roads even on public lands where these have grown relatively abundant in recent years. Early American explorers such as Jim Bridger and Jedediah Smith once hunted and trapped in the area now protected as Yellowstone National Park, where these same activities are now expressly prohibited. Few voices rise in protest that we can no longer hunt Yellowstone's elk, waterfowl, or bison. To the contrary, in a controversy that continues to this day, when the State of Montana offered a limited hunt to shoot bison migrating out of the park in the late 1980s, public protests quickly sent wildlife managers scrambling for cover.[23] In this same way, Americans in the future will almost surely appreciate BLM and national forest lands that are *less* motorized and roaded than these same areas are today. As we have already seen, the mission statements for each of the land management agencies cite long-term goals to protect resources or natural conditions "for future generations." As the progenitors of these generations to come, those of us living today should work to ensure that our land management agencies are abiding by their own pledges to duty.

Conservation biologists, land managers, natural resource economists, and nonmotorized recreationists have all pointed to roads and access management as top concerns, but for many Americans roads and ORVs sound like marginally insignificant topics. People overlook these issues, in part, because roads and motor vehicles have grown so common in our lives that we now take them for granted. Beyond this familiarity, which has not bred contempt so much as it has fostered neglect, many Americans have also adopted a free-market–influenced view that denigrates the role of regulations in society.

As we explored in Chapter 6, the idea that we each have the right to act as we please, regardless of the consequences to the environment or our neighbors, comes in direct opposition to the laws that created our public lands or those that we follow each day in our communities. I am allowed to play loud music in my home, but when I crank it beyond a certain level or time of day, my neighbors may come and ask me to turn it down—or call the police to enforce local noise regulations. Similarly, people generally have access to their public lands, but only within certain constraints that help ensure that other visitors and the places themselves are not excessively disturbed. We are, in short, a society governed by legal, environmental, and social restraints. These terms apply to our actions within our own homes as well as on public lands.

Policy Makers Weigh In

Citizens can initiate studies, propose legislation, and sharpen the legal focus on roads and ORV use, but ultimately certain changes will also need to occur in the places where decisions and laws are made—on the desks of agency leaders and in the state and federal legislatures. Some policy makers have already taken important steps: recall the leadership of Forest Service chief Michael Dombeck in moving the agency toward some dramatically new directions for road management and removal. Though subsequent agency leaders may not share Dombeck's vision, if some of the changes he set in motion can survive they should lead to lasting improvements in national forest transportation planning. Dombeck may have at least shifted the agency's status quo, so that new road construction— especially in areas currently free of roads and other developments—will be seen as an aberration rather than the norm.

In addition to legislation such as that proposed by Minnesotans for Responsible Recreation, license and registration programs for snowmobiles and all-terrain vehicles (ATVs) can be strengthened at the state level. Most states already charge a registration fee for snowmobiles and ATVs. Requiring full-sized license plates for all ORVs would help create higher expectations for users of these motor vehicles and would facilitate safety programs and law enforcement efforts. Such registration requirements could also include driving and written tests, and emissions and noise standards similar to those already in place for automobiles in many states. Many of the impacts of ORVs will remain even when these machines come with four-stroke engines and mufflers, but enforceable standards could help reduce the disproportionate amount of pollution currently generated by summer and winter ORV use. In this regard, policy makers can make it very clear: ORVs will not be permitted anywhere, even on existing road systems, until they pollute no more than standard passenger cars.

Actions such as these would offer some mitigation of ORV impacts. If we are willing to accommodate ORV use in certain places, we will need to acknowledge that the recreational benefits to the users of these machines—as well as the economic gain of manufacturers, retailers, and agency partners—come as a compromise carrying ecological and social impacts.

Legislation proposed at the national level could establish a more progressive, protective stance for roaded and unroaded lands and ORV management in selected regions. A multistate proposal called the Northern Rockies Ecosystem Protection Act (NREPA) includes programs for road removal and the restoration of critical wildlife habitat currently fragmented by logging roads, as well as the protection as wilderness of 17 million acres of public land.[24]

In southern Utah, America's Redrock Wilderness bill seeks to protect as wilderness some 9.1 million acres of sandstone canyons and sagebrush mesas currently managed by the BLM. The Utah bill has received significant national support, with more than 160 cosponsors in the House and fourteen in the U.S. Senate, but like its northern Rockies cousin has not yet found enough congressional will to counter hostile treatment from its in-state legislators.[25] Both NREPA and the Utah wilderness bill would permanently protect vast areas from road building and ORV use.[26]

Not all progressive legislation focuses on wilderness designations. The National Forest Protection and Restoration Act, which gained more than ninety Congressional cosponsors in 2000, would prohibit commerical logging on federal lands. With the majority of new road miles in the past five decades coming in tandem with timber sales on national forests and BLM lands, a logging prohibition would eliminate one of the key incentives for new road construction or reconstruction on public lands. The act would also create a Natural Heritage Restoration Corps—directed to remove roads, improve soil, and restore natural fish passage in rivers and streams—and emphasizes the rehiring and retraining of dislocated timber industry workers.[27] The bill's chief sponsors, Rep. Cynthia McKinney (D-GA) and James Leach (R-IA), note that by reclaiming funds that currently subsidize timber industry operations on public lands, the United States would save enough money to provide $25,000 in worker retraining for every public lands timber employee, and would still have cash left over to contribute $200 million toward retiring the national debt.[28]

The emergence of new alliances, such as the Green Scissors Coalition's fiscal conservatives and more liberal environmentalists, has also brought some new clout to Congress. The overhaul of the timber purchaser road credit program, though more symbolic than substantive, suggests that even long-established roads programs can give way to new priorities and values.

Corporate Citizenship and Incentives

Although we occasionally hear about "responsible corporate citizens" participating in our communities, we should hold few expectations that the ORV industry will work to protect public lands out of some innate sense of civic duty. Corporations tend to be accountable primarily to their shareholders, and nearly always accountability equates to turning a profit. To nudge the motorized recreation industry toward positions of broader public responsibility, we need to demonstrate that their profits depend upon it.

Snowmobile manufacturers have begun to develop quieter, cleaner four-stroke machines in response to public demand and the prospect of being ousted from the snowmobile meccas of Yellowstone and other national parks. In January 2000, Arctic Cat emerged as the first of the major snowmobile makers to release a prototype four-stroke machine.[29] With much fanfare, the company promptly donated two of the new sleds to Yellowstone officials for administrative use and testing, and later donated fifty of the "Yellowstone Special" to the park for public use.[30] Arctic Cat officials promised to make the four-stroke snowmobiles commercially available by the 2001–2002 season, and declared the cleaner machines, "absolutely" the sleds of the future.[31]

During the 2000 winter season, the Society of Automotive Engineers also initiated a yearly contest among college students to design and test new breeds of snowmobile that could meet both environmental and performance standards. The first year's winner, a snowmobile modified by students from Buffalo University, was the only machine of seven entered that was powered by a four-stroke engine.[32]

A similar trend is emerging with summer ORVs. Honda has exclusively produced four-stroke ATVs for a number of years, but a 2001 industry product review featured sixty-three new models of ATV, only six of which were powered by two-stroke engines.[33] Nearly all of these production changes in the ORV industry are occurring because of pressure applied by a mix of citizen groups, regulatory agencies, and consumers. Manufacturers are beginning to recognize that if they fail to convert to cleaner, quieter machines they may feel a public backlash that will drastically reduce riding opportunities—and consequently, sales—for ORVs on public and private lands across the country.

Keeping in mind this same prospect of losing recreational opportunities and sales, a program called Tread Lightly encourages motorized recreationists to cause minimal impact and respect the rights of others and the environment. Although it began in the mid-1980s as a Forest Service– and BLM-sponsored effort to educate ORV drivers, Tread Lightly incorporated as a private organization in 1990 "to maximize its effectiveness." In addition to its agency, media, and affiliate members, the nonprofit group relies upon, in its own words, an "elite group of sponsors (a veritable Who's Who of truck, sport utility vehicle, and powersport manufacturers)."[34] The claim is scarcely overstated, as corporate sponsors include American Honda, American Suzuki, Arctic Cat, Bombadier, Ford, Hummer, Kawasaki, Land Rover, Mazda, Mitsubishi, Nissan, Porsche, Subaru, Yamaha, and many others. Tread Lightly asks ORV drivers to stay on designated roads and trails, and believes that user conflicts will decrease if motorized users avoid cross-country travel and reckless behavior.[35]

While the conversion to cleaner engines and programs such as Tread Lightly's can obviously mitigate the current impacts of ORVs on public lands, we should recognize these changes for the self-interested acts they are. Many of the problems already caused by ORVs will continue, even if the fleet converts entirely to four-stroke engines and if drivers are flawlessly courteous. Drivers will still be able to access remote habitat areas and disturb wildlife, tires will compact soils and cause erosion, air and noise pollution may be reduced but will certainly not be eliminated, and user conflicts will continue to emerge. Tread Lightly emphasizes responsible use of ORVs, but as these machines become more popular—which is precisely what Tread Lightly's sponsors seek—they will invariably roam into more and more areas where their impacts are heavy indeed.

The Conservative View

Two dictionaries I use at home shed some light onto the conflict we currently face over roads and recreational access on public lands. The first, a cheap paperback, defines "conservation" as "the wise use of natural resources."[36] In this version of conservation, a host of groups from the Blue Ribbon Coalition to the American Petroleum Institute can rally around their own view of "wise use" and label themselves as "conservationists." Thus emerged the "wise use movement," which has systematically worked to open areas to ORV use, promoted road building, and encouraged extractive industrial use unencumbered by environmental regulations.[37]

The second dictionary, a hefty, two-volume hardcover with more than a half-million definitions, describes conservation as, "The action of keeping from harm, decay, loss, or waste; careful preservation."[38] Here we find conservation in the form practiced by John Muir, Aldo Leopold, Rosalie Edge, and many modern environmental groups.

As we search for a suitable destiny for roads and motorized vehicles on our public lands, these two versions of conservation offer a glimpse at two different futures. One appears much like the policies of the past: we will build roads and drive vehicles in order to use these lands, and the wisdom of that use will be guided by our views and desires at the time. For a timber-hungry nation in the 1950s or an adrenalin-seeking snowmobiler in the 1990s, a wide-open policy on road building and motorized access might easily seem appropriate and passably wise. We need not condemn these views—they fit the pleasures and the practices of the time or person—but we also need not embrace them.

The second definition offers a different way to conserve the public lands, manage road and motorized access, and act wisely. With this approach, we are not cast freely to the whims of each day's or each individual's wisdom, but rather receive a steadier guide to prevent harm, avoid loss, and protect our lands against decay and waste. In a society where the meaning of "wise use" has become tainted deeply by cynicism, we have with this second definition a crisper vision of what it means to be careful with the lands and waters in our custody.

This second, genuinely conservative view of roads and motorized recreation can support efforts to remove roads and restore damaged habitat, not as a rejection of what has come before but as a step of progress toward real conservation. In their current condition, thousands of miles of roads decay the stability of mountainsides and waste their soils. Poorly planned or ill-maintained roads harm municipal water supplies and wild fisheries and contribute to the loss of biodiversity, aesthetics, and integrity of our public lands. Conservation of these lands—their careful preservation for future generations as prescribed in the laws that first designated them—charges us with the duty to act with a wisdom that extends beyond that of any one time or individual. Conservation calls for a collective wisdom that necessarily uses resources cautiously and works to preserve or restore public lands wherever possible.

Although for a number of decades we determined our nation's progress by the number of new roads built, wildlands cleared for development, and the ease of motorized access, it is time now to revise our standards of success. Our public lands can no longer support a management agenda that adds miles of road without concern for long-term costs and maintenance, ecological effects, or other values and uses. The increasing motorization and mechanization of our daily lives no longer calls for motorized vacations as the highest recreational pursuit on the limited base of public lands. Unlike the 1920s, when an automotive journey through a national park was extraordinary both for the marvel of the automobile as well as the nature of the park, today's parks become all the more splendid when we are able finally to leave behind the ubiquitous noise, fumes, and metal of our vehicles.

The future of access management on our public lands does not boil down to a simple dichotomy that roads and motors are bad, wildlands and muscle power are good. There are, of course, roads that are located, constructed, and maintained responsibly. A number of these cause relatively minor impacts and can provide widespread, popular use. These are the roads that should stay as the backbone of the public lands road system for the future.

Likewise, ORVs represent a technology that, if used carefully and within limits, can be appropriate. In their current form and application, however, many of these ORVs unfortunately fail to meet such terms. As public lands grow increasingly valuable as places distinctive for their clean water, standing forests, arid ecosystems, fish and wildlife habitat, opportunities for solitude and reflection, or discovery of the wonders of the natural world, we may grow less and less comfortable with "sacrifice areas" where ORVs can shred soils or snowmobiles can penetrate winter's quiet shroud.

There should always be room for the family outing, puttering along a road to find a picnic spot or a berry patch, or the horse-paced driving tour of an open-road system, but for ridge-pummeling snowmobiles or ATVs, we should feel little remorse at their final passing. Much like advocates for "quiet trails" who offer the refrain, "Roads are for vehicles, trails are for animals and people,"[39] we should learn to manage our public lands not for vehicles, but for people, other animals and plants, clean water, beauty, and intact functioning ecosystems. These are, in fact, the purposes we continue to identify for national parks, national forests, national wildlife refuges, and the public domain of BLM lands.

Requiem for the North Fork

One day I hope to return to the North Fork of the Boise River. Perhaps in twenty or thirty years I will go back and find that two weeks is plenty of time to map every road in the river basin. The roads I find then will be different from those that exist now. In places where the hillsides today appear candy-striped with roads, I imagine slopes restored to their natural, stable contours. Maybe the cutover forests will start to grow back. Where yesterday's logging trucks rumbled down a mountain, tomorrow a family will hike along a restored trail and reach out to touch pine seedlings.

When I go back to the North Fork—maybe it will be in forty years and my bad knee will have finally given out so I'll need to drive—the roads that still exist will be well-maintained and I won't come upon narrow spots where today's roads have slumped and collapsed into ruin. Where roads are open only seasonally for wildlife or administrative needs, the road closures will be solid and well placed. Even on these closed roads—the few that haven't been removed and recontoured—culverts and stream crossings will be well built and cared for. I will smile, incredulous, to see that there are no ORV tracks detouring the solid gates. Later, when I get out of the car to limp down to the river's edge, the water will flow clear over smooth cobbles and there in the fading light I might catch a glint of bull trout as it fins in the current.

I do not dream of a pristine landscape in the North Fork of the Boise watershed. We have already dispensed with that future in this place. What I foresee, instead, is a river basin that looks lived in and used, but more like a home than an abandoned shack, more loved than abused. Here, and elsewhere, we can find places in our lives where machines belong and also places where they do not. There will always be roads in and around the North Fork basin, just as there will always be roads on public lands across the country. But unlike today, the roads I envision in my old age are the roads we want, the roads we truly need, and the roads we can afford to take care of year after year. And, every now and then, perhaps we will round a bend in the road, hear a thrashing in the bushes, and feel that great thrill of wonder as a bear or a deer or a cottontail rabbit bounds away into a thicket. The end of the road, after all, is where the rest of the world begins.

Appendix: Contact Information for Selected Organizations

National

The Bluewater Network
300 Broadway, Suite 29
San Francisco, CA 94133
(415) 788-3666
www.earthisland.org/bw/

Wild Wilderness
248 NW Wilmington Ave.
Bend, OR 97701
(541) 385-5261
www.wildwilderness.org

The Wilderness Society
1615 M Street
1101 14th Street N.W., Suite 1400
Washington, D.C. 20003
(202) 429-2643
www.wilderness.org

Wildlands Center for Preventing Roads (Wildlands CPR)
PO Box 7516
Missoula, MT 59807
(406) 543-9551
WildlandsCPR@wildlandscpr.org
www.wildlandscpr.org

Forest Service Employees for Environmental Ethics (FSEEE)
PO Box 11615
Eugene, OR 97440
(541) 484-2692
www.afseee.org

Public Employees for Environmental Responsibility (PEER)
2001 S Street NW, Suite 570
Washington, D.C. 20009
(202) 265-7337
www.peer.org

Rocky Mountains

**Biodiversity Associates and
  Friends of the Bow**
PO Box 6032
Laramie, WY 80273
(307) 742-7978
www.biodiversityassociates.org

Montana Wilderness Association
PO Box 635
Helena, MT 59624
(406) 443-7350

Predator Conservation Alliance
PO Box 6733
Bozeman, MT 59771
(406) 587-3389
www.predatorconservation.org

Southern Rockies Forest Network
2260 Baseline Rd., Suite 200
Boulder, CO 80302
www.southernrockies.org

Southwest

Forest Guardians
312 Montezuma, Suite A
Santa Fe, NM 87501
(505) 988-9126
www.fguardians.org

Sky Island Alliance
PO Box 41165
Tucson, AZ 85717-1165
(520) 624-7080
www.skyislandalliance.org

Southern Utah Wilderness Alliance
1471 S. 1100 East
Salt Lake City, UT 84105-2423
(801) 486-3161
www.suwa.org

Far West

California Wilderness Coalition
2655 Portage Bay, Suite 5
Davis, CA 95616
(530) 758-0380
www.calwild.org

Klamath-Siskiyou Wildlands Center
PO Box 332
Williams, OR 97544
(541) 846-9273
www.kswild.org

Pacific Rivers Council
PO Box 10798
Eugene, OR 97440
(541) 345-0119
www.pacrivers.org

Washington Trails Association
1305 Fourth Ave., Suite 512
Seattle, WA 98101
(206) 625-1367
www.wta.org/wta

Midwest

Heartwood (multiple chapters)
PO Box 1424
Bloomington, IN 47402
(812) 337-8898
www.heartwood.org

Minnesotans for Responsible Recreation
PO Box 111
Duluth, MN 55801
(218) 525-0584
www.cpinternet.com/~mrr

Southeast

Florida Biodiversity Project
PO Box 220615
Hollywood, FL 33022
(954) 922-5828

Georgia Forest Watch
15 Tower Rd.
Ellijay, GA 30540
(706) 635-8733
www.gafw.org

Southern Appalachian Forest Council
46 Haywood St., Suite 323
Asheville, NC 28801-2838
(828) 252-9223
www.safc.org

Wild Alabama
PO Box 117
Moulton, AL 35650
(256) 974-6166
www.wildalabama.org

Northeast

Restore: The North Woods
PO Box 1099
Concord, MA 01742
(978) 287-0320
www.restore.org

The Wildlands Project
PO Box 455
Richmond, VT 05477
(802) 434-4077
www.twp.org

Alaska

Alaska Center for the Environment
807 G. Street, Suite 100
Anchorage, AK 99501
(907) 274-363621
www.akcenter.org

Southeast Alaska Conservation Council
419 Sixth St., Suite 200
Juneau, AK 99801
(907) 586-6942
www.seacc.org

Notes

Chapter 1. Introduction

1. *Divided Highways: The Interstate Highway System and the Transformation of American Life,* video produced by Larry Hott and Tom Lewis, 1997.
2. In 1996, the Forest Service reported 37,205 employees. Available online: http://www.fs.fed.us/pl/pdb/96report/table54.html [21 February 2001]. In 1999, the National Park Service employed 15,729 permanent and 5,548 temporary/seasonal workers. Available online: http://www.nps.gov/pub_aff/e-mail/faqs.htm [21 February 2001]. The BLM reported 8,700 employees. Available online: http://www.blm.gov.nhp/pubs/rewards/2000/letter.htm [21 February 2001]. The U.S. Fish and Wildlife Service employed 6,247 people in 1994 for work on wildlife refuges. U.S. Fish and Wildlife Service employee numbers and land acreage figures for agencies taken from Zaslowsky and Watkins, *These American Lands,* pp. xi, 325 and passim.
3. http://www.nps.gov/pub_aff/e-mail/faqs.htm [21 February 2001].
4. Laitos and Carr, The transformation on public lands, pp. 161–162.
5. *Fulfilling the Promise: The National Wildlife Refuge System,* p. 43.
6. http://refuges.fws.gov/centennial/index.html [21 February 2001].
7. Visitor numbers from Laitos and Carr, Transformation on public lands, pp. 161–162.
8. *Forest Service Roadless Area Conservation: Final Environmental Impact Statement,* pp. 1–5.

9. The Federal Highway Administration (FHWA) also keeps track of road miles on lands managed by the Bureau of Indian Affairs, Army Corps of Engineers, and Bureau of Reclamation. These totals include: BIA—5,500 paved, 17,500 unpaved, 25,600 other (48,600 total); COE—4,800 paved, 3,600 other (8,400 total); and BOR—1,000 paved, 980 unpaved, 8,000 other (9,980 total). See *1999 Status of the Nation's Highways, Bridges and Transit: Conditions and Performance Report to Congress*, Appendix E: Conditions and Performance of the Transportation System Serving Federal and Indian Lands, p. E-3. Washington, D.C.: U.S. Department of Transportation, Federal Highway Administration, Federal Transit Administration.

10. Zaslowsky and Watkins, *These American Lands*, p. xi.

11. Culpin, *The History of the Construction of the Road System in Yellowstone National Park, 1872–1966*, pp. 9–11, notes that by 1878 there were 103 miles of road in Yellowstone (some of these were more trail than road), and by 1879 the road and trail mileage within the park had more than doubled to 234. These wagon or horse roads were later converted to accommodate automobiles after cars were allowed into the park in 1915 (Culpin, p. 83).

12. Leopold, *A Sand County Almanac*, p. viii. See also, Glover, *A Wilderness Original: The Life of Bob Marshall*, pp. 145–195 and passim.

13. See settlement reached in Pikes Peak suit, 15 April 1999. Available online: http://www.cnn.com/NATURE/9904/15/pikes.peak.cnn/ [1 June 2001].

14. Scientists are fairly unequivocal about roads being a liability for bears. A study in Yellowstone found that the park bears essentially split into two groups: road habituated and road averse bears. The habituated bears suffered higher mortality than the road averse bears and were deemed a "sink" population. In other words, even though visitors might see bears or their tracks and scat near roads, these bears are declining in number faster than they can breed. See Pease and Mattson, Demography of the Yellowstone bears, pp. 957–975. According to the Interagency Grizzly Bear Committee, "Roads probably pose the most imminent threat to grizzly habitat today." *Grizzly Bear Recovery Plan*, p. 21.

15. Forman and Alexander, Roads and their major ecological effects, p. 213. Roadkill and roadsalt attractants are most common on paved roads with higher vehicle speeds.

16. Poll: Most Montanans support roadless plan, 2000, p. A-4, reported support for the Forest Service's roadless protection measure by 53 percent of the voters in Montana, 57 percent in Idaho, 72 percent in California, 71 percent in New Mexico, 69 percent in Michigan, 75 percent in Colorado, 72 percent in Tennessee, 76 percent in Minnesota, 83 percent in Wisconsin, 72 percent in Washington, and 67 percent in Oregon.

17. Possessing a firearm is generally prohibited in the national park system, though a few parks such as Grand Teton do have controlled hunting seasons, and national preserves in Alaska have fewer restrictions. Secondary uses are

permitted in wildlife refuges, but these must be deemed compatible with the system's primary purpose of protecting fish and wildlife and their habitats.
18. Taylor, *The Transportation Revolution, 1815–1860,* pp. 19–20.

Chapter 2. From Bicycles to Board Feet: A History of Public Land Roads

1. See Rae's *The American Automobile: A Brief History.* The Fish and Wildlife Service was created in 1940 and the BLM in 1946.
2. A number of roads already existed on lands that were part of the public domain, but with the designation of Yellowstone as a national park the United States began to depart from a policy of public land disposal. Although more than 100 miles of rough road and trail etched across Yellowstone as early as 1878, the road developments that began in 1883 represented the first planned construction on lands specifically identified as permanent federal land reserves. See Sellars, *Preserving Nature in the National Parks: A History,* p. 19; Culpin, *History of the Construction of the Road System,* pp. 9–11.
3. Culpin, p. 46.
4. In the video *Divided Highways,* historian Ronald Edsforth states that 40 million cars and trucks existed in the U.S. by 1929; according to the American Automobile Manufacturers Association, American car registrations (not including trucks) in 1930 numbered slightly more than 23 million.
5. From *Statistical Abstract of the United States, 1998,* pp. 631–632 .
6. Perry, *Bike Cult: The Ultimate Guide to Human–Powered Vehicles,* p. 243.
7. From *Divided Highways.*
8. Perry, p. 243.
9. See Gutfreund, Twentieth–century sprawl: Accommodating the automobile and the decentralization of the United States, p. 11.
10. Fuller, *RFD: The Changing Face of Rural America,* p. 182.
11. Fuller, p. 189.
12. Fuller, p. 244.
13. Hoyt Jr., The good roads movement in Oregon: 1900–1920, p. 42.
14. *Oregon Journal,* 16 October 1902, from Hoyt, p. 48.
15. Preston, *Dirt Roads to Dixie: Accessibility and Modernization in the South, 1885–1935,* Knoxville: University of Tennessee Press, 1991, p. 30.
16. Belasco, *Americans on the Road,* pp. 12–35.
17. Gutfreund, Twentieth-century sprawl, pp. 17–18.
18. Shaffer, Negotiating national identity: Western tourism and "See America First," pp. 122–151.
19. Taylor, *The Transportation Revolution,* pp. 19–20.
20. Jackson, *Wagon Roads West,* p. 319. See also *The National Road* by Philip D. Jordan as cited in Hoyt, The good roads movement in Oregon, p. 3.
21. Jackson, *Wagon Roads West,* pp. 169–328.

22. Hoyt, The good roads movement in Oregon, p. 32.

23. Hoyt, p. 24.

24. The Transfer Act of 1905 moved the existing Division of Forestry from the Department of the Interior to the Department of Agriculture; one month later the division was renamed.

25. Woodrow Wilson signed the National Park Service Organic Act into law on 25 August 1916.

26. Sellars, *Preserving Nature,* pp. 26–27.

27. Sellars, pp. 7–9. The Northern Pacific connected rail service to Cinnabar, at the edge of the Yellowstone Park boundary north of Mammoth, in 1883; see Culpin, *History of the Road System,* p. 15. See also Runte, *Trains of Discovery: Western Railroads and the National Parks,* and Runte's *National Parks: The American Experience,* 2nd ed., especially pp. 82–105.

28. 16 USC §1.

29. Sellars, *Preserving Nature,* p. 49.

30. Wilkinson, *Crossing the Next Meridian,* p. 126.

31. Runte, *Public Lands, Public Heritage: The National Forest Idea,* pp. 47–55. According to Runte, by the end of 1893 President Harrison had set aside 17.6 million acres as forest reserves. President Cleveland added 22.4 million acres by 1897, and President McKinley chipped in 7.2 million acres before his assassination in 1901. The national forest landbase has fluctuated slightly over the ensuing decades due to land withdrawals for national parks, monuments, and Indian reservations; railroad, state, and homestead claims; Weeks Act purchases; land swaps; and donations.

32. Sellars, *Preserving Nature,* p. 11. Three of these original parks, Sully's Hill, Platt, and General Grant, were later reclassified or dropped from the national park system. See also *Encyclopedia Americana,* v. 19, pp. 771–772, for a list of parks, acreages, and dates of designation.

33. As cited by Wilkinson and Anderson, *Land and Resource Planning in the National Forests,* p. 18.

34. *Roads in the National Forests,* USDA, Forest Service, May 1988, cites the Weeks Act of 1911 as one reason for roads on national forest lands. The act allowed for the purchase of private timber lands for conversion to national forests. Many of these private lands were already logged and roaded prior to purchase, so the agency inherited the roads along with the land.

35. Belasco, *Americans on the Road,* p. 76.

36. Belasco, p. 72, citing Elon Jessup, *The Motor Camping Book.*

37. Belasco, p. 74.

38. Graves, A crisis in national recreation, pp. 391–400.

39. Graves, p. 393.

40. Graves, p. 391.

41. Graves, p. 399.

42. Sutter, Driven wild: The intellectual and cultural origins of wilderness advo-

cacy during the interwar years (Aldo Leopold, Robert Sterling Yard, Benton MacKaye, Bob Marshall), p. 88.

43. Sutter, p. 88, citing O.C. Merrill, Opening up the National Forests by road building, *Yearbook of the Department of Agriculture, 1917,* pp. 521–529. See also Gilligan, The development of policy and administration of Forest Service Primitive and Wilderness Areas in the western United States, p. 73. See U.S. Forest Service annual reports for 1916 and 1939 for mileage accounts. The 1939 report noted that more than 50 percent of the roads were of less-than-satisfactory condition.

44. Gilligan, Development of policy, p. 76.

45. Sutter, Driven wild, p. 92; Allin, Wilderness policy, p. 174.

46. Paul Sutter's Ph.D. dissertation, Driven Wild, explores this nicely.

47. Sutter, pp. 85–86.

48. Sutter, p. 92

49. Sutter, pp. 97–98.

50. Sutter uses this term to include "automotive technology, road-building, and other infrastructural provisions which accompanied the automobile," p. 5.

51. Sellars, *Preserving Nature,* p. 59.

52. Sellars, p. 58.

53. Sellars, p. 59, citing Mather, Ideals and policies of the National Park Service, p. 81.

54. Sellars, p. 59.

55. As quoted in Culpin, *History of the Road System,* p. 116.

56. Sellars, *Preserving Nature,* p. 61.

57. *Divided Highways.*

58. Anne Mitchell's Ph.D. dissertation, Parkway and Politics, offers a well-written, in-depth look at the creation and conflicts of the Blue Ridge Parkway.

59. Sellars, *Preserving Nature,* p. 135, citing W. Wharton from *National Parks Bulletin* 14 (June 1938): 5.

60. See Mitchell, Parkway and politics, p. 58, citing Margaret Lynn Brown, Smoky Mountains story: Human values and environmental transformation in a southern bioregion, 1900–1950, Ph.D. dissertation, University of Kentucky, pp. 99–115.

61. Mitchell, p. 58.

62. Mitchell, pp. 29–30; *Divided Highways.*

63. Mitchell, pp. 30–58, citing D. E. Simmons, 1978, "The Creation of Shenandoah National Park and the Skyline Drive," Ph.D. Dissertation, University of Virginia, pp. 63–69, 77–80, 83, 90, 150–152.

64. *World Almanac and Book of Facts, 1999,* p. 506.

65. Sutter, Driven wild, pp. 18–19.

66. See Merrill, *Roosevelt's Forest Army: A History of the Civilian Conservation Corps 1933–1942,* p. vii; *Roads in the National Forests,* p. 6; *National Forests for All Uses . . . Keeping Natural Resource Quality . . . Building the Right Road,* p. 2.

67. Merrill, *Roosevelt's Army,* pp. 42–50.
68. Merrill, p. 196.
69. Edge, *Roads and More Roads in the National Parks and National Forests,* p. 8.
70. *Report of the Chief,* 1942, p. 22.
71. Sellars, *Preserving Nature,* p. 182.
72. Wilkinson, *Crossing the Next Meridian,* p.136.
73. Steen, *The U.S. Forest Service: A History,* p. 314; *Roads in the National Forests,* p. 7. The *Report of the Chief* indicates 100,414 road miles in national forests in 1946 and 199,042 miles in 1969. Note that in earlier Forest Service reports, such as 1939's figure of 140,000 miles, more than half of the miles included roads deemed "nonexisting" or of "unsatisfactory standard." Later reports, such as the 1946 figure of 100,414 miles, apparently dropped many of these substandard roads from the count.
74. Steen, *U.S. Forest Service,* pp. 284–314, citing William B. Greeley, Memorandum on the need for rapid construction of access logging roads in the national forests of the Northwest, 2 March 1946.
75. Clary, *Timber and the Forest Service,* p. 117.
76. *Report of the Chief,* 1946 and 1956, p. 19, report receipts of $10,534,332 and $107,073,158 respectively.
77. *Roads in the National Forests,* pp. 8–9.
78. *Annual Report of the Chief,* 1952, p. 22.
79. Steen, *U.S. Forest Service,* p. 284.
80. Steen, p. 284.
81. Clary, *Timber and the Forest Service,* p. 158.
82. Bryner, *U.S. Land and Natural Resources Policy,* p. 153.
83. Clawson, *The Bureau of Land Management.*
84. Rosenberg, *Wilderness Preservation: A Reference Handbook,* p. 5.
85. Mileage from the *1999 Status of the Nation's Highways, Bridges and Transit,* p. E-3. Recall that the actual number *crossing* BLM lands is more than 90,000 miles, but only 83,000 of these are directly under the agency's jurisdiction.
86. Clawson, *Bureau of Land Management,* p. 103.
87. This is true with the significant exception of the Oregon and California Railroad lands discussed in note 89 and in Chapter 4.
88. *The Federal Land Policy and Management Act: An Interim Report, October 21, 1976 to June 30, 1977,* p. 2.
89. The important exception comes from roads on the Oregon and California Railroad lands managed by the BLM in the Pacific Northwest. Of these roads Clawson writes, "[T]here is no other aspect of all BLM operations about which there have been more controversies," p. 103.
90. Clawson, *Bureau of Land Management,* p. 103.
91. *Digest of Federal Resource Laws of Interest to the U.S. Fish and Wildlife Service,* p. 35. The Fish and Wildlife Act of 1956 (16 USC §§742a–742j-2) confirmed the consolidation of bureaus and creation of the Fish and

Wildlife Service as directed in Reorganization Plan No. III, 30 June 1940 (54 Stat. 1,232).

92. *Digest of Federal Resource Laws,* p. 63 (16 USC §668dd–668ee). This act is also considered the "organic act" for the National Wildlife Refuge System.

93. Executive Order 12996 of 25 March 1996, U.S. Fish and Wildlife Service; see also Laughlin and Caudill's *Banking on Nature: The Economic Benefits to Local Communities of National Wildlife Refuge Visitation.*

94. Cawley and Freemuth, A critique of the multiple-use framework in public lands decisionmaking, p. 40, make this distinction between multiple-use agencies and dominant-use agencies (which in their estimation include the U.S. Fish and Wildlife Service and National Park Service). Wilkinson and Anderson, *Land and Resource Planning,* p. 11, also discuss the "dominant-use statutes" governing the National Park Service and Fish and Wildlife Service.

95. The Refuge Recreation Act of 1962 granted the secretary of the interior the authority to allow incidental or secondary uses of refuges as long as the primary function of the refuge is not deemed impaired as a result (16 USC §460k–460k-4). Also see Williams, Seeking refuge, pp. 34–45; and Grove, *Wildlands for Wildlife: America's National Wildlife Refuges.*

96. Personal communication with Thomas Hawkins, Realty Specialist, USFWS, Division of Realty, Washington Office, 11 August 1999 and 30 October 2001. Hawkins identified 43,000 road miles on refuge lands, but later clarified that this figure included trails, dikes, and any other linear feature managed by the Fish and Wildlife Service. Personal communication with Sean Furniss (19 September 2000, USFWS Refuge Program Specialist), Jim Amenta (21 September 2000, Federal Highway Administration), and the FHWA's *1999 Status of the Nation's Highways, Bridges and Transit,* reported the number at 9,000 miles. As discussed earlier, the lower number represents the road mileage under the jurisdiction of the Fish and Wildlife Service.

97. Line, A system under siege, reported 26,000 cars in 1994, pp. 10–17. Also, Riley and Riley, *Guide to the National Wildlife Refuges,* pp. 61–64.

98. Crupi, Roads to nowhere imperil Alaska's wildness, p. 4; personal communication with Tom Reed, Assistant Refuge Manager, Red Rock Lakes National Wildlife Refuge, Montana, 8 July 1999.

99. Wilkinson and Anderson, *Land and Resource Planning,* p. 151.

100. Wilkinson and Anderson, pp. 29–30.

101. NFMA was actually an amendment of the Forest and Rangeland Renewable Resources Planning Act of 1974, which is commonly known as RPA. For an in-depth treatment of this legislation and its history, see Wilkinson and Anderson, pp. 36–45. According to the Forest Service's *Report of the Chief,* timber harvest in national forests increased from 9.4 billion board feet in 1959 to 13.4 billion board feet in 1970.

102. 16 USC §1608(b) as written in the Forest Service Manual 7703.1, cited in Hammer, *The Road-Ripper's Guide to the National Forests,* p. 3. See also *Forest*

Service Roadless Area Conservation Final Conservation Impact Statement, p. 3–28.
103. *Report of the Forest Service,* FY 1985, pp. 31–32.
104. *Roads in the National Forests,* May 1988; *Roads in the Rocky Mountain Region,* 1988.
105. *Administration of the Forest Development Transportation System: Temporary Suspension of Road Construction in Roadless Areas,* U.S. Department of Agriculture, Forest Service, p. 2.
106. Even the moratorium that applied to roadless area developments had its loopholes: areas smaller than 5,000 acres were excluded, as were all forests that had recently completed forestwide planning documents.
107. *Report of the Chief,* 1935, p. 36.
108. *1999 Status of the Nation's Highways, Bridges and Transit,* p. E-3.
109. Adams, Treadmarks on the virgin land: The appropriate role of off-road vehicles in national forests, provides good background information on the development of off-road vehicle technology.
110. According to Cartographic Technologies in Brattleboro, Vermont, Thorofare in Wyoming is 20 miles distant, the second most remote location is 18 miles in the Bob Marshall Wilderness complex of north-central Montana, while a point in Idaho's Frank Church–River of No Return Wilderness comes in third at 16 miles. These rankings do not include Alaska. See also, Black, Yellowstone outpost most remote in U.S., p. A-2; also, personal communication with Susan Boswell, Cartographic Technologies Inc., 14 December 2000.

Chapter 3. The Ecological Effects of Roads

1. Forman and Alexander, Roads and their major ecological effects, p. 213. Countless insects also die each day from vehicle impacts. Note that this figure includes highways and other roads generally beyond the scope of this book.
2. Trombulak and Frissell, Review of ecological effects of roads on terrestrial and aquatic communities, p. 24.
3. See, for example, the Boone and Crockett Club's summer 1999 issue of *Fair Chase,* or the summer 2000 issue of *Mule Deer,* published by the Mule Deer Foundation. The Rocky Mountain Elk Foundation has also sponsored work parties to reduce road densities in big game habitat.
4. For recreation as nonconsumptive use, see for example Laitos and Carr, The transformation on public lands, p. 144.
5. See Trombulak and Frissell, Review of ecological effects, p. 19, for square mileage of road surfaces. Massachusetts has an area of 8,257 square miles, Connecticut 5,009, Rhode Island 1,214, and Delaware 2,057.
6. Assuming an average road width of twelve feet, the 550,000 miles of road on these lands amounts to 1,250 square miles.
7. Romin and Bissonette, Deer–vehicle collisions: Status of state monitoring activities and mitigation efforts, pp. 276–277, report that approximately 120 people

die from vehicle–deer collisions in an average year. Over a four-year period, Michigan recorded 3,289 injuries to motorists as a result of collisions with deer; between 1981 and 1991, the State of Vermont registered more than $31 million of property damage (primarily to automobiles) from cars hitting deer.

8. Most roadkill studies relate to interstate highways, state or county roads, and other paved routes where high speed and high traffic volumes make a particularly lethal combination.

9. Bangs, Bailey, and Portner, Survival rates of adult female moose, pp. 557–563.

10. Noss, *The Ecological Effects of Roads or the Road to Destruction*, p. 11, reports that more than ninety black bears were killed by vehicle collisions in Pennsylvania in 1985; Romin and Bissonette, Deer–vehicle collisions, p. 278, report 43,002 deer killed by vehicles in Pennsylvania in 1990.

11. Adams and Geis, *Effects of Highways on Wildlife, Final Report*, p. 105.

12. Adams and Geis sampled 118 miles of interstate highway and 120 miles of country roads; 85 percent of the roadkills they recorded were on or along the interstate highways, pp. 101, 105.

13. Adams and Geis, pp. 106–110.

14. Varland, Klaas, and Loughlin, Use of habitat and perches, causes of mortality and time until dispersal in post-fledging American kestrels, pp. 169–178; Loos and Kerlinger, Road mortality of saw-whet and screech owls on the Cape May Peninsula, 210–213. Despite its limitations of scope and size, the Loos and Kerlinger study found multiple vehicle-caused mortalities to sharp-shinned hawks, broad-winged hawks, American kestrels, red-tailed hawks, great horned owls, and barred owls.

15. Gibbs, Amphibian movements in response to forest edges, roads and streambeds in southern New England, p. 584.

16. Fahrig et al., Effect of road traffic on amphibian density, p. 177, citing G. Heine, 1987, Einfache Meß- und Rechenmethode sur Ermittlung der Überlebenschance wandernder Amphibien bein Überqueren von Straßen, *Beihefte zu den Veröffentlichungen för Naturschutz und Landschaftspflege in Baden-Württemberg* 41: 175–186.

17. Fahrig et al., p. 177, citing J. Kuhn, 1987, Straßentod der Erdkröte (*Bufo bufo L.*): Verlustquoten und Verkehrsaufkommen, Verhalten auf der Straße, *Beihefte zu den Veröffentlichungen för Naturschutz und Landschaftspflege in Baden-Württemberg* 41: 175–186.

18. Fahrig et al., p. 177.

19. Rosen and Lowe, Highway mortality of snakes in the Sonoran Desert of southern Arizona, p. 143.

20. Rosen and Lowe, p. 147; Dalrymple and Reichenbach, Management of an endangered species of snake in Ohio, USA, pp. 195–200.

21. Noss, *Ecological Effects*, pp. 11–12; Jenkins, *Texas Department of Transportation Wildlife Activities*, pp. 199–231; Kushlen, Conservation and management of

the American crocodile, p. 783. See also Noss et al., Conservation biology and carnivore conservation in the Rocky Mountains, p. 958, citing L.D.Harris and P.B. Gallagher, 1989, New initiatives for wildlife conservation: The need for movement corridors. In *Preserving Communities and Corridors,* G. MacKintosh, ed., pp. 11–36. Washington, D.C.: Defenders of Wildlife; and Willams, The ghost cat's ninth life, p. 76.

22. McMillion, At least five grizzlies mistakenly killed by black bear hunters, pp. A-1, A-8.

23. Dood, Brannon, and Mace, *Final Programmatic Environmental Impact Statement: The Grizzly Bear in Northwestern Montana;* Aune and Kasworm, *Final Report East Front Grizzly Studies.*

24. See Jamison, National Park Service makes resource protection top priority, pp. A-1, A-7 for NW Montana figures; McMillion, At least five grizzlies mistakenly killed, pp. A-1–A-8 for Yellowstone data.

25. *Grizzly Bear Recovery Plan,* p. 22.

26. Weaver and Dale, Trampling effects of hikers, motorcycles, and horses on meadows and forests, pp. 451–457; Seney, Erosional impact of hikers, horses, off-road bicycles, and motorcycles on mountain trails; Freddy, Bronaugh, and Fowler, Responses of mule deer to disturbance by persons afoot and snowmobiles, pp. 63–68. See also generally, Hammitt and Cole, *Wildland Recreation: Ecology and Management.*

27. Devlin, Open valve dumps sewage into Lake McDonald, pp. A-1, A-3; Moen, Yellowstone sewage system overwhelmed, p. B-5.

28. Sutter, "A blank spot on the map": Aldo Leopold, Wilderness, and U.S. Forest Service Recreational Policy, 1909–1924, p. 196.

29. Anthony and Isaacs, Characteristics of bald eagle nest sites in Oregon, pp. 148–159; Trombulak and Frissell, Review of ecological effects, p. 21, citing C. Fernandez, The choice of nesting cliffs by golden eagles *Aquila chrsaetos:* the influence of accessibility and disturbance by humans, *Alauda* 61: 105–110.

30. Norling, Anderson, and Hubert, Roost sites used by sandhill crane staging along the Platte River, Nebraska, pp. 253–261.

31. Brody and Pelton, Effects of roads on black bear movements in North Carolina, pp. 5–10.

32. Rost and Bailey, Distribution of mule deer and elk in relation to roads, pp. 634–641. Lyon, Road density models describing habitat effectiveness for elk, pp. 592–595.

33. Sovada, Roy, and Woodward, Swift fox mortality in grassland and cropland landscapes of western Kansas; Hines and Case, Diet, home range, movements, and activity periods of swift fox in Nebraska, pp. 131–138.

34. Cowardin, Gilmer, and Shaiffer, Mallard recruitment in the agricultural environment of North Dakota, pp. 17–20.

35. Adams and Geis, Effects of roads on small mammals, p. 403.

36. Mech, Wolf population survival in an area of high road density, pp. 387–389.

37. See Horejsi, Gilbert, and Craighead, *British Columbia's Grizzly Bear Conservation Strategy: An Independent Review of Science and Policy*, p. 9.

38. Trombulak and Frissell, Review of ecological effects, pp. 22–23, citing M.D. Haqus and H.A. Hameed, Lead content of green forage growing adjacent to expressways and roads connecting Erbil City (northern Iraq), *Journal of Biological Science Research* 17: 151–164.

39. Motto et al., Lead in soils and plants: Its relationship to traffic volume and proximity to highways, pp. 231–238.

40. Noss, *Ecological Effects*, pp. 13–14.

41. A.M. Farmer, The effects of dust on vegetation: A review, pp. 63–75.

42. Noss, *Ecological Effects*, p. 14. This treatment is still relatively common on private roads. See also Payne and Martins, Crankcase oils: Are they a major mutagenic burden in the aquatic environment? pp. 329–330.

43. Noss, *Ecological Effects*, p. 14.

44. Trombulak and Frissell, Review of ecological effects, p. 23.

45. Trombulak and Frissell, p. 23.

46. Wood, Roads and toxic pollutants, p. 11, bibliography notes citing A.M. Fleck, M.J. Lacki, and J. Sutherland, Response by white birch (*Betula papyrifera*) to road salt applications at Cascade Lakes, New York, *Journal of Environmental Management* 27(4): 369–378; and G. Hofstra and D.W. Smith, The effects of road de-icing salt on the levels of ions in roadside soils in southern Ontario, *Journal of Environmental Management* 19: 261–271.

47. Wood, Roads and toxic pollutants, p. 11, bibliography notes citing E. McBean and S. Al-Nassri, Migration pattern of de-icing salts from roads, *Journal of Environmental Management* 25(3): 231–238; and W.S. Scott and N.P. Wylie, The environmental effects of snow dumping: a literature review, *Journal of Environmental Management* 10: 219–240.

48. Noss, *Ecological Effects*, p. 14.

49. Information from U.S. Department of Agriculture fact sheets on Clopyralid and Picloram, available online: http://www.fs.fed.us/foresthealth/pesticide/clopyralid.html and http://www.fs.fed.us/foresthealth/pesticide/picloram.html. Clopyralid is often marketed under the trade names Transline, Stinger, or Reclaim, while picloram is marketed as Tordon.

50. Personal communication with Lolo National Forest Missoula District Ranger Andy Kulla, 19 July 2000. The Lolo NF treated 871 acres with herbicide in 1999, at an average application of one pint/acre for picloram (other chemicals are applied in different quantities, but picloram is the one most commonly used on the Lolo). Kulla reports 280,000 acres of weeds on the Lolo National Forest.

51. *Administration of the Forest Development Transportation System: Advance Notice of Proposed Rulemaking*, p. 2. Conservationists contend that even this figure

underrepresents the actual number of user-created routes on national forests, and the Forest Service acknowledges this as well: "It is anticipated that future inventories will verify the existence of substantially more miles of unclassified roads" (National Forest System Facts, http://www.fs.fed.us/news/roads/factsheet.shtml [18 July 2000]).

52. Trombulak and Frissell, Review of ecological effects, p. 24, citing J.M.B. Smith, Feral fruit trees on New England roadsides, in *Ecology of Biological Invasions*, ed. R.H. Groves and J.J. Burdon, p. 158.

53. Ebersberger, Roads and exotic plants, pests and pathogens, pp. 12–13, citing J. Kollmeyer, Tansy ragwort control project: Proposed action plan, U.S. Forest Service, Flathead National Forest, MT.

54. Trombulak and Frissell, Review of ecological effects, p. 24, citing D.B. Zobel, L.F. Roth, and G.M. Hawk, Ecology, pathology, and management of Port Orford Cedar (*Chamaecyparis lawsoniana*), General Technical report PNW-184, U.S. Forest Service, Portland, OR; also, Ebersberger, Roads and exotic plants, pp. 12–13, citing J.D. Castello, D.J. Leopold, and P.J. Smallidge, Pathogens, patterns, and processes in forest ecosystems, *BioScience* 45: 16–24.

55. Perry, Landscape pattern and forest pests, p. 219.

56. Gelbard, Roads as conduits for exotic plant invasions, presented at the Society of Conservation Biology annual meeting, Missoula, Montana.

57. Forman, Estimate of the area affected ecologically by the road system in the United States, pp. 31–35.

58. Belnap, Surface disturbances: Their role in accelerating desertification, pp. 39–57; Wilshire et al., *Geologic Processes at the Land Surface*, pp. 1–41.

59. Vora, Potential soil compaction forty years after logging in northeastern California, p. 117.

60. Riley, Effect of clearing and roading operations on the permeability of forest soils, Karuah Catchment, New South Wales, Australia, p. 290.

61. Vora, Potential soil compaction, p. 117; and Trombulak and Frissell, Review of ecological effects, p. 21, citing J.D.Helvey and J.N. Kochenderfer, Soil density and moisture content on two unused forest roads during first thirty months after construction, Research paper NE-629, U.S. Forest Service, Northeast Forest Experiment Station, Broomhall, PA.

62. Trombulak and Frissell, Review of ecological effects, citing P.C. Whitford, Bird behavior in response to the warmth of blacktop roads, *Transactions of the Wisconsin Academy of Sciences Arts and Letters* 73: 135–143.

63. Haskell, Effects of forest roads on macroinvertebrate soil fauna of the southern Appalachian Mountains, pp. 59–61.

64. Reed, Johnson-Barnard, and Baker, The contribution of roads to forest fragmentation in the Rocky Mountains, pp. 1098–1106.

65. Rich, Dobkin, and Niles, Defining forest fragmentation by corridor width: The influence of narrow forest-dividing corridors on forest-nesting birds in southern New Jersey, pp. 1109–1121.

66. Van Dyke et al., Reactions of mountain lions to logging and human activity, pp. 95–102; Lyon, Road density models for elk, pp. 592–595; Thiel, Relationship between road densities and wolf habitat suitability in Wisconsin, pp. 404–407; Mech et al., Wolf distribution and road density in Minnesota, pp. 85–87.

67. Gibbs, Amphibian movements in response to forest edges, roads, and streambeds in southern New England, pp. 584–589.

68. Oxley, Fenton, and Carmody, The effects of roads on populations of small mammals, p. 57; Mader, Animal habitat isolation by roads and agricultural fields, pp. 85–86; Swihart and Slade, Road crossing in *Sigmodon hispidus* and *Microtus ochrogaster,* p. 357.

69. Mader, Animal habitat isolation, p. 85.

70. Van Dyke, Brocke, and Shaw, Use of road track counts as indices of mountain lion presence, pp. 102–107, determined that mountain lions avoided crossing improved dirt and hard-surfaced roads, and that lions lived in areas where such roads were "underrepresented"; Bruns, Winter behavior of pronghorns in relation to habitat, p. 564, found that pronghorns avoided crossing roads with traffic volume of 0 to 6 cars/day; Brody and Pelton, Effects of roads on black bear movements, pp. 5–10, ascertained a barrier effect of roads on black bears, but the strength of the effect varied according to road use.

71. Yellowstone Science interview: Mary Meagher "The Biology of Time," p. 16. These larger herds are subsequently trying to expand beyond the boundaries of the national park, which has led to the controversial bison shootings each winter by the Montana Department of Livestock (DOL). Montana's DOL killed more than 1,000 Yellowstone bison during the winter of 1996–1997.

72. Trombulak and Frissell, Review of ecological effects, p. 20, citing A.W.F. Banfield, The relationship of caribou migration behavior to pipeline construction, in *The Behavior of Ungulates and Its Relation to Management,* ed. V. Geist and F. Walther, pp. 797–804.

73. Haskell, Effects of forest roads, p. 62.

74. Baxter, Frissell, and Hauer, Geomorphology, logging roads, and the distribution of bull trout (*Salvelinus confluentus*) spawning in a forested river basin: Implications for management and conservation, pp. 854–867.

75. Rieman and McIntyre, *Demographic and Habitat Requirements for Conservation of Bull Trout.* Also, introduction presented at bull trout hearings for listing under the Endangered Species Act, Missoula, MT, 1997.

76. Megahan, *Effects of Silvicultural Practices on Erosion and Sedimentation in the Interior West: A Case for Sediment Budgeting,* pp. 174–175.

77. Edwards and Burns, *Relationships among Fish Habitat Embeddedness, Geomorphology, Land Disturbing Activities, and the Payette National Forest Sediment Model,* p. 1–6.

78. Megahan, *Effects of Silvicultural Practices,* p. 169.
79. Megahan and Kidd, Effects of logging and logging roads on erosion and sediment deposition from steep terrain, pp. 136–141; and Megahan and Kidd, Effects of logging roads on sediment production rates in the Idaho Batholith.
80. *Forest Service Roadless Area Conservation: Draft Environmental Impact Statement Summary and Proposed Rule,* pp. S–4.
81. North Fork Boise River watershed inventory, p. 2.
82. Elliot et al., Hydrologic and sedimentation effects of open and closed roads, p.8.
83. Personal communication with Tom Reed, assistant refuge manager, Red Rocks National Wildlife Refuge, Montana, 8 July 1999.
84. Jones and Grant, Peak flow responses to clear-cutting and roads in small and large basins, western Cascades, Oregon, p. 970.
85. Jones and Grant, p. 968.
86. Trombulak and Frissell, Review of ecological effects, pp. 25–26.
87. Findlay and Bourdages, Response time of wetland biodiversity to road construction on adjacent lands, pp. 86–94.
88. Findlay and Bourdages, pp. 92–93.

Chapter 4. The Cutting Edge: Money, Politics, and Access

1. *Transportation Equity Act for the 21st Century: A Summary,* p. 20.
2. Federal Lands Highway, Federal Lands Highway Programs, U.S. Department of Transportation, Federal Highway Administration, available online: http://www.fhwa.dot.gov/flh/flhprog.htm, visited August 16, 2000. The Federal Lands Highway Program came with the passage of the Surface Transportation Assistance Act in 1982 that later led to 1998's TEA-21.
3. Federal Lands Highway, Overview, available online: htttp://www.fhwa.dot.gov/flh/flhprog.htm [16 August 2000].
4. Federal Lands Highway, available online: wysiwyg://284/http://fhwa.dot.gov/flh/index.htm [16 August 2000].
5. Federal Lands Highway, Federal Lands Highway Programs, available online: http://www.fhwa.dot.gov/flh/flhprog.htm [16 August 2000]. See also, *Transportation Equity Act for the 21st Century: A Summary,* pp. 44–45.
6. Personal communication with Sean Furniss, U.S. Fish and Widlife Service, Refuge Program Specialist, 19 September 2000.
7. U.S. House of Representatives, *Future Maintenance and Repair of the Going-to-the-Sun Road in Glacier National Park: Field hearing before the Subcommittee on National Parks and Public Lands.*
8. Glacier National Park, press release, 4 February 2000.
9. Personal communication with Mike Roy, U.S. Fish and Wildlife Service, June 2000.
10. P.L. 105-78, sec. 115(e)(k)(1). According to the Fish and Wildlife Service's

Sean Furniss, the provision that money could not be used to construct new roads was included in order to preclude a proposal to build the controversial road into the Izembek National Wildlife Refuge in western Alaska, not from any broader congressional concern about road impacts.

11. Sean Furniss noted that refuge lands are administered by a relatively small corps of employees—approximately 2,500—compared to the other land management agencies, and that "traditionally we've been at the low end" for agency funding.

12. *Transportation Equity Act for the 21st Century: A Summary,* p. 20; also, Federal Lands Highway Programs, Emergency Relief for Federally Owned Roads, available online: http://www.fhwa.dot.gov/flh/erfo.htm [16 August 2000].

13. Walder, ERFO fact sheet, Wildlands Center for Preventing Roads; Personal communication with Anne Connor, Clearwater National Forest, 29 March 2001; personal communication with Mike Sanders, Redwood National Park, April 2001. ERFO funds can be applied to road obliteration up to the amount it would have cost to replace the damaged road segment.

14. *Public Land Statistics,* U.S. Department of the Interior, BLM, annual reports from 1949 to 1999.

15. Purchaser credits were not to exceed a minimum price required for the sale, and a 10 percent performance bond was required in advance. Purchasers also had to pay approximately 20 to 25 percent of the sale price as a downpayment on the sale.

16. Much of this information comes from an interview with Charlie Sells, USFS Region One timber sale contract specialist, Missoula, MT, 15 September 2000.

17. The Federal Wage and Concessions Act, for example, requires the Forest Service to calculate costs using union wage scales. Private logging companies are not so bound.

18. Personal communication, July 1994, with timber crew foreman, Anita Bay, Etolin Island, Alaska.

19. U.S. House, *Financing of Roads in the National Forests: Hearing before the Subcommittee on Forestry, Resource Conservation, and Research,* noting a Price Waterhouse study submitted to subcommittee, p. 9.

20. *Financing of Roads,* p. 9.

21. See Clawson, *The Bureau of Land Management,* for background on the O & C Lands; O & C Lands road mileage from 1999 *Public Land Statistics,* Table 6-2.

22. Personal communication with Joe Casey, BLM Forester, Dillon, MT, 20 September 2000.

23. See, *Financing of Roads.*

24. *Financing of Roads,* p. 5, testimony from Congressman George E. Brown Jr., D-California.

25. Charlie Sells, 15 September 2000.

26. President Clinton signed The Secure Rural Schools and Community Self-Determination Act of 2000 on 30 October 2000 (PL 106-393), available online: http://www.fs.fed.us/news/2001/01/01jan18-FS-Final-FY2000-Payments-to-States.htm [24 January 2001].

27. Personal communication with Capitol Reef superintendent Al Hendricks, 18 June 2001. See also U.S. District Court, District of Utah, Judge Bruce Jenkins's ruling dated 24 October 2000 (Case Civil No. 2: 96-CV-450J).

28. 43 U.S.C. §932 (RS-2477), as cited in the *Federal Register*, v. 59, no. 146, Monday, 1 August 1994, Proposed Rules, Revised Statute 2477 Rights-of-Way, p. 39,216.

29. Title VII of the Federal Land Policy Management Act of 1976 (90 Stat. 2793) repealed RS 2477, but claims preexisting at that time remained valid. See RS 2477 bill would permit rampant roading, p. 1.

30. See *Report to Congress on RS 2477: The History and Management of RS 2477 Right-of-Way Claims on Federal and Other Lands*, pp. 16–19. See also U.S. Secretary of the Interior Bruce Babbitt to assistant secretaries, 22 January 1997 [memorandum], Subject: Interim Departmental Policy on Revised Statute 2477 Grant of Right-of-Way for Public Highways; Revocation of December 7, 1988 Policy.

31. Utah: RS 2477, again, p. 8.

32. Milstein, Roads to Ruin, pp. 29–33; *Road-RIPorter*, 1(1).

33. Memorandum from Secretary of the Interior Donald Hodel to Assistant Secretaries, Subject: Departmental Policy on Section 8 of the Act of July 26, 1866, Revised Statute 2477 (Repealed), Grant of Right-of-Way for Public Highways (RS-2477).

34. Memorandum from Secretary Hodel.

35. The Hodel memorandum states, "Removing high vegetation, moving large rocks out of the way, or filling low spots, etc., may be sufficient as construction."

36. Several passages in the Hodel memorandum suggest that such paths or trails can qualify as RS 2477 highways: "A public highway is a definitive route or way that is freely open for all to use. It need not necessarily be open to vehicular traffic for a pedestrian or pack animal trail may qualify." And, "Construction is a physical act of readying the highway for use by the public according to the available or intended mode of transportation—foot, horse, vehicle, etc."

37. *Federal Register*, 1 August 1994, p. 39216.

38. Personal communication with T.J. Brown, The Wilderness Society/Coalition to Fight Phantom Roads, 29 January 2001. See Public Law 104-208, 30 September 1996, 110 Stat. 3009-200, Section 108. The notice for the proposed rule in the *Federal Register*, 1 August 1994, p. 39220, gave the following definitions for road construction: "The proposed rule, therefore, would require that intentional physical acts be performed with the achieved purpose of preparing a durable, observable, physical modification of land and that

this modification be suitable for highway traffic." "Construction of a highway cannot be accomplished solely by any of the following activities: continual passage over a surface that has not previously been intentionally constructed, even if the continual passage eventually creates a defined route; clearing of vegetation; or removal of large rocks."

39. Memorandum from Secretary Babbitt.

40. This road's reconstruction may cost as much as $210 million for thirty miles of pavement.

41. From 1991 to 1996, the average cost per mile of forest road construction was slightly more than $84,000. This includes recreation roads, general purpose roads, and timber roads. If average replacement costs came to $1.25 million/mile, the total cost of the national parks' 8,000 road miles would reach $10 billion. Road miles totaling 550,000 at $85,000/mile comes to $46.8 billion.

42. Road Management Website—News and Information, Q & As, available online: http://www.fs.fed.us.news/roads/qanda.shtml [21 June 2001].

43. See Swanson and Loomis, *Role of Nonmarket Economic Values in Benefit–Cost Analysis of Public Forest Management*, p. 29.

44. The agency's *Administration of the Forest Development Transportation System: Advance Notice of Proposed Rulemaking,*, p. 7, estimated the backlog to be over $10 billion. In its *Forest Service Roadless Area Conservation: Draft Environmental Impact Statement*, p. S-4, the agency estimated a backlog of $8.4 billion.

45. *Administration of the Forest Development Transportation System*, p. 7.

46. *Financing of Roads*, p. 6.

47. Zion, Grand Canyon, Denali, Acadia, and Yosemite National Parks have already committed to such changes, while other parks such as Yellowstone are looking into alternatives. More on this in Chapter 7.

48. Refuge Roads Home Page, Scope of Improvements, USFWS fact sheet, available online: http://bluegoose.arw.r9.fws.gov/roads/guidance/improvements.html [16 August 2000].

49. *Forest Service Roadless Area Conservation*, p. S-40, Washington Office; also, personal communication with Jim Sauerbier, USFS Region One road engineer, 9 December 1997, who estimated maintenance costs ranging up to $15,000 per mile.

50. *Forest Service Roadless Area Conservation*, p. 3-22.

51. *Forest Service Roadless Area Conservation*, Figure 3-10, p. 3-23.

52. Personal communication with ranger district personnel on the Helena, Kootenai, Idaho Panhandle, and Colville National Forests, May 1997.

53. Romin and Bissonette, Temporal and spatial distribution of highway mortality of mule deer in newly constructed roads at Jordanelle Reservoir, Utah, pp. 1–11.

54. Romin and Bissonette (and I) use $2,500 per deer–vehicle collision as an average value. See Romin and Bissonette, Deer–vehicle collisions, pp. 276–283, for descriptions of studies that attempt to quantify the value of deer–vehicle collisions. Using hunting figures, the 1996 value of a mule deer was estimated

at $1,313; average property damage estimates ranged from $500 in Colorado to $1,800 in Vermont; the FHWA placed a $1.5 million value on each of the 120 human lives lost annually as a result of animal–vehicle collisions; other studies have found that 4 to 5 percent of deer–vehicle collisions result in some human injury. The $1.3 billion figure applies to collisions on all roads, not just those found on public lands.

55. The national forests' century-old charter includes "the purpose of securing favorable conditions of water flows . . . [to] the citizens of the United States." 16 U.S.C. §471. The Organic Act of 1897 also listed furnishing a "continuous supply of timber" as one of the forest reserves' two fundamental purposes.

56. Minbashian, Reclaiming the concept of resoration, p. 5; and personal communication with Jim Erchmann, Seattle public utilities watershed ecosystem manager, 19 June 2001.

57. Minbashian, p. 5; and personal communication with Erchmann and Marti Spencer, Seattle public utilities civil engineering supervisor, 19 June 2001.

58. *Statistical Abstract of the United States 1999*, p. 267.

59. *Statistical Abstract 1999*, p. 262. These relatively recent figures do not adequately reflect the century-long decline of the Pacific salmon industry. Salmon catches on the Columbia River, for example, have charted a steady drop from the 33.9 million pounds/year from 1880–1930, to 23.8 million pounds/year from 1931–1948, to 10.9 million pounds/year from 1949–1973, and finally, a mere 1.4 million pounds/year in 1994. See Richard White, 1995, *The Organic Machine*, p. 97, New York: Hill and Wang.

60. See Quigley and Cole, *Aquatic Strongholds and Areas of Predicted Road Density: Highlighted Scientific Findings of the Interior Columbia Basin Ecosystem Management Project*, p.19.

61. *Statistical Abstract*, p. 262, for example, shows that mechanized travel and viewing scenery claim 35.8 percent of the recreational visits, compared to 25.5 percent for camping, picnicking, and swimming; 9.7 percent for hiking, horse, and water travel; 5.8 percent for winter sports; and less than 6 percent each for hunting and fishing. Note that the vast majority of the mechanized travel occurs on road systems. The popularity of motorized off-road recreation consistently ranks far below hiking, camping, skiing, and other nonmotorized activities.

62. *1999 Public Land Statistics*, Table 4-1. Of a total of 62.2 million recreational visitor days, trail-related activities recorded 23.2 million, educational opportunites 20.1 million, driving for pleasure 19.9 million, fishing and hunting 12.0 million, and camping 11.4 million (totals do not add up since many visitors engage in multiple activities).

63. Hebert, Firefighting bill nears $1 billion, p. A-2.

64. This visceral and largely negative response to fire fails to recognize the historic and ecologically important role that fire has played in many natural landscapes.

65. Devlin, Racicot, officials spar on TV, quoting Agriculture Secretary Dan Glickman, p. A-10.

66. Morrison et al., Assessment of summer 2000 wildfires: History, current condition and ownership, Pacific Biodiversity Institute, 16 September 2000. Available online: http://www.pacificbio.org/Projects/fires2000/fire2000. htm [24 January 2001].

67. See U.S. Senate, Committee on Interior and Insular Affairs.

68. Personal communication with Rob Alt, University of Montana School of Forestry, 2 April 2001.

69. According to U.S. Forest Service statistics from all regions between 1984 and 1989, personal communication between Bethanie Walder and Andrea Wojtasek, USFS, 18 September 1997.

70. Show et al., A planning basis for adequate fire control on the southern California national forest, *Fire Control Notes* 5: 28.

71. Wilson, Roadsides: Corridors with high fire hazard and risk, p. 576, citing *Fire Hazard Reduction Guide for Roadsides,* California Dept. of Conservation and U.S. Department of Agriculture, Forest Service, 1968.

72. Interim Rule Suspending Road Construction in Unroaded Areas of National Forest System Lands, Environmental Assessment, p. 16.

73. Interim Rule, p. 16.

74. Lopez, *The Rediscovery of North America,* p. 45.

75. Garrity, Economic analysis of the conservation biology alternative for grizzly bear restoration in the Salmon–Selway region, p. 19.

76. Garrity identifies 1501 jobs associated with 3,482 miles of road obliteration. More broadly, see Power, *Environmental Protection and Economic Well-being: the Economic Pursuit of Quality.*

77. See generally, Power, *The Economic Pursuit of Quality,* or Power, The economics of wilderness preservation in Utah, pp. 1–8. Such trends do not necessarily address the fundamental flaws in equating economic wealth with growth—a problem exemplified by thoughtless sprawl or traffic jams.

78. Vaughan, *Endangered Species Act Handbook,* p. 3, supra 5, citing Stephen M. Meyer, Environmentalism and economic prosperity: Testing the environmental impact hypothesis, Cambridge, MA: MIT Project on Environmental Politics and Policy.

79. See also, Goodstein, *Jobs and the Environment: The Myth of a National Trade-Off,* and Bezdek, Environment and economy: What's the bottom line? pp. 7–32.

Chapter 5. Industrial Revolutions: The Motorized Recreation Boom

1. Personal communication with Howard Wilshire, 8 May 2000; see also Wilkinson, *Science under Siege: The Politicians' War on Nature and Truth,* pp. 295–335.

2. *Off-Road Recreation Vehicles: U.S. Department of the Interior Task Force Study,* p. 42.

3. Wilshire et al., *Impacts and Management of Off-Road Vehicles,* 2–3.

4. Sheridan, *Off-Road Vehicles on Public Land,* p. iii.

5. See Forman, Estimate of the area affected ecologically by the road system in the United States, pp. 31–35.

6. *Trails Management Handbook,* USDA, Forest Service. 10 January 1991.

7. In 1983, Suzuki was the first company to come out with a 4-wheeled, fat-tired ATV similar to those common today. By 1985, Yamaha, Kawasaki, and Honda were also marketing 4-wheelers. See *Popular Mechanics,* August 1985, pp. 80–83, 131. See also, Adams, Treadmarks on the virgin land.

8. *Dealernews,* 31(9): 46.

9. *Dealernews,* 35(10): 96, based on expected sales at the time.

10. The International Snowmobile Manufacturers Association cites 147,867 unit sales in 1999, down from a peak of 174,000 in 1997, which ISMA attributes to poor snow conditions in 1998 and 1999; from ISMA fact sheets and online: http://www.snowmobile.org.

11. *Statistical Abstract of the United States, 1999,* p. 273.

12. Advertisement in *Sports Afield,* November 1998, p. 48.

13. Advertisement in *North American Hunter,* September 1998, p. 13.

14. According to the *ATV News,* "2001 Buyer's Guide," average retail price for a new ATV was $5,285.

15. U.S. Consumer Product Safety Commission, Consumer product safety alert, p. 1.

16. *The Missoulian,* 19 October 1999, p. B-2.

17. All-terrain vehicle–related deaths—West Virginia, 1985–1997, p. 2, citing U.S. Consumer Product Safety Commission, All-terrain vehicle exposure, injury, death, and risk studies.

18. All-terrain vehicle–related deaths.

19. Many studies document the environmental impacts of ORVs, for example see Lodico, *Environmental Effects of Off-Road Vehicles: A Review of the Literature*; Sheridan, *Off-Road Vehicles on Public Land*; and Webb and Wilshire, *A Bibliography on the Effects of Off-Road Vehicles on the Environment.*

20. Wilshire et al., *Impacts of ORVs,* pp. 2–3.

21. Wilshire et al., *Geologic Processes at the Land Surface,* p. 21.

22. Iverson et al., Physical effects of vehicular disturbances on arid landscapes, pp. 915–917.

23. Kay et al., Evaluating environmental impacts of off-road vehicles, pp. 10–18.

24. Webb et al., Environmental effects of soil property changes with off-road vehicle use, pp. 219–233; Eckert et al., Impacts of off-road vehicles on infiltration and sediment production of two desert soils, pp. 394–397; Belnap, Surface disturbances: Their role in accelerating desertification, p. 50; Knott, Reconnaissance Assessment of Erosion and Sedimentation in the Cañada de los Alamos Basin, Los Angeles and Ventura Counties, California, U.S., pp. 1–26; Webb et al., p. 228.

25. Harper and Marble, A role for nonvascular plants in management of arid and semiarid rangelands, pp. 135–169; Johansen, Cryptogamic crusts of semi-arid and arid lands of North America, pp. 140–147.

26. Wilshire et al., *Geologic Processes*, p. 21.

27. Webb and Wilshire, Recovery of soils and vegetation in a Mojave desert ghost town, Nevada, U.S.A., pp. 291–303.

28. Willard and Marr, Recovery of alpine tundra under protection after damage by human activities in the Rocky Mountains of Colorado, pp. 181–190.

29. Slaughter et al., Use of off-road vehicles and mitigation of effects in Alaska permafrost environments: A review, pp. 63–72.

30. Wanek, *A Continuing Study of the Ecological Impact of Snowmobiling in Northern Minnesota*, pp. 10–27; Neumann and Merriam, Ecological effects of snowmobiles, pp. 207–212.

31. Bess, The effect of snowmobile engine noise on the hearing mechanism, pp. 147–159.

32. Bess, p. 157.

33. Brattstrom and Bondello, Effects of off-road vehicle noise on desert vertebrates, pp. 190–192.

34. Brattstrom and Bondello, pp. 190–192. See also Bondello, The effects of high-intensity motorcycle sounds on the acoustical sensitivity of the desert iguana, *Dipsosaurus dorsalis.*

35. Brattstrom and Bondello, passim.

36. Reported in Brasher, Government wants emission standards for snowmobiles, ATVs.

37. Reported in *The Missoulian* (AP), 21 October 1999, p. A-11.

38. Snook, An investigation of driver exposure to carbon nonoxide while traveling in the wake of a snowmobile, pp. 2, 87.

39. Snook Fussell, Exposure of snowmobile riders to carbon monoxide, p.1.

40. Snook Fussell, p. 1, citing Air quality criteria for carbon monoxide, U.S. Environmental Protection Agency-60018-90-045A.

41. D.J. Schubert, Petition to enhance and expand regulations governing the administration of recreational off-road vehicle use on national forests, citing C.C. Chan et al., Comparing tail pipe emissions from motorcycles and passenger cars, *Journal of Air and Waste Management Association* 45:116–124.

42. Schubert, pp. 101–102, citing J.T. Oris, Toxicity of ambient levels of motorized watercraft emissions to fish and zooplankton in Lake Tahoe, California/Nevada; Occupational Safety and Health Administration/U.S. Department of Labor, Material Data Safety Sheet. See also Hoffman, Eastin Jr., and Gay, Embryotoxic and biochemical effects of waste crankcase oil on birds' eggs, pp. 230–241; and Payne and Martins, Crankcase oils: Are they a major mutagenic burden in the aquatic environment? pp. 329–330.

43. Tahoe Research Group, *The Use of 2-Cycle Engine Watercraft on Lake Tahoe: Water Quality and Limnological Considerations*, p. 4, notes that "studies have

shown that 4 percent to more than 50 percent of the fuel and oil mixture passes through a two cycle engine . . . uncombusted." The Montana Department. of Environmental Quality reports 20 to 30 percent unburned fuel from two-stroke engines (Howard J. Haines, MT DEQ, May 1996 memo); and the U.S. EPA reports 25 percent unburned fuel from these engines, cited in Schubert.

44. In 1987, the Forest Service estimated ORV use at 80 million visitor days. With 25 percent discharge of unburned fuels, an ORV running at an efficient rate of .25 gallons/hour for six hours of a twelve-hour "visitor day" would dump approximately .33 gallons of fuel into the aquatic or terrestrial system. Multiplied by 1987's 80-million-visitor days, it is realistic that 30 million gallons or more of fuel might be dumped each year on national forests.

45. Ingersoll et al., Snowpack chemistry as an indicator of pollutant emission levels from motorized winter vehicles in Yellowstone National Park, pp. 103–113.

46. Hagen and Langeland, Polluted snow in southern Norway and the effect of the meltwater on freshwater and aquatic organisms, pp. 45–57; Harte and Hoffman, Possible effects of acidic deposition on a Rocky Mountain population of tiger salamander *Ambystoma tigrinum,* pp. 149–158.

47. Hynes, *The Ecology of Running Waters,* pp. 443–450; Murdoch and Cheo with O'Laughlin, *Streamkeeper's Field Guide: Watershed Inventory and Stream Monitoring Methods,* p. 49 and passim.

48. Unpublished data from Wild Rockies Field Institute's "Restoration Ecology in Greater Yellowstone" course, 1997–1998, Missoula, MT. Roaded streams scored lower on the "EPT Index" of mayflies, stoneflies, and caddis flies, and had higher numbers of worms, leeches, and diptera (true flies) that are more tolerant of anoxic conditions.

49. Neumann and Merriam, Ecological effects of snowmobiles, pp. 207–212; Duck, The effects of off-road vehicles on vegetation in Dove Springs Canyon.

50. Liebhold et al., *Invasion by Exotic Forest Pests: A Threat to Forest Ecosystems;* Vitousek et al., *Biological invasions as global environmental change.*

51. Liddle, A selective review of the ecological effects of human trampling on natural ecosystems, pp. 17–36.

52. Belnap, Surface disturbances, p. 50.

53. Neumann and Merriam, Ecological effects of snowmobiles, pp. 209–219.

54. Wanek, *Ecological Impact of Snowmobiling* p. 32.

55. Neumann and Merriam, Ecological effects of snowmobiles, pp. 208–209; Wanek, *Ecological Impact of Snowmobiling* p.32.

56. Lacey et al., *Controlling Knapweed on Montana Rangeland.*

57. Bury, Luckenbach, and Busack, *Effects of Off-Road Vehicles on Vertebrates in the California Desert.*

58. Baldwin, *The Off-Road Vehicle and Environmental Quality,* includes correspondence from agency officials citing such actions; see also Lazon, The thrill

killers, pp. 6–7, 36; and Olsen, Bad show out in the snow, pp. 28–30, 33–35 for examples of snowmobilers running down and killing wildlife.

59. http://www.bowsite.com/pbs [19 July, 2000].

60. *The Silent Majority: Public Attitudes toward Trail Use on the Gallatin National Forest,* p. 10.

61. Sheridan, *Off-Road Vehicles on Public Land,* p. 12, citing B. Hoover, Off-road vehicle problems on federal lands, *Proceedings Annual Meeting, Association of Midwest Fish and Game Commission,* 40: 37–49; and P. Jorgensen, Vehicle use at a desert bighorn watering area, *18th Annual Bighorn Council Transactions,* pp. 18–24; Bury, Luckenbach, and Busack, *Effects of Off-Road Vehicles,* pp. 3, 16; Luckenbach, An analysis of off-road vehicle use on desert avifaunas; Dorrance, Savage, and Huff, Effects of snowmobiles on white-tailed deer, pp. 563–569; Moen, Whittemore, and Buxton, Effects of disturbance by snowmobiles on heart rate of captive white-tailed deer, pp. 176–183; Brattstrom and Bondello, Effects of off-road vehicle noise, pp. 183–200; Copeland, Biology of the wolverine in central Idaho.

62. Neumann and Merriam, Ecological effects of snowmobiling, p. 211; Dorrance, Savage, and Huff, Effects on deer, p. 568; Moen, Whittemore, and Buxton, Effects of disturbances, p. 181.

63. Stebbins, Off-road vehicles and the fragile desert, pp. 203–208, 294–304; Bury, Luckenbach, and Busack, *Effects of Off-Road Vehicles,* p. 16.

64. Altmann, The flight distance in free-ranging big game, pp. 207–209; Freddy, Bronaugh, and Fowler, Responses of mule deer to disturbance by persons afoot and snowmobiles, pp. 63–68. Freddy, Bronaugh, and Fowler also cite Horejisi, Behavioral response of barren ground caribou to a moving vehicle, pp. 180–185; A.L. Ward et al., *Effects of Highway Construction and Use on Big Game Populations;* Richens and Lavigne, Response of white-tailed deer to snowmobiles and snowmobile trails in Maine, pp. 334–344; R.A. MacArthur, V. Geist, and R.H. Johnston, 1982, Cardiac and behavioral responses of mountain sheep to human disturbance, *Journal of Wildlife Management* 46: 351–358.

65. Freddy, Bronaugh, and Fowler, Responses of mule deer, p. 63.

66. Marchand, *Life in the Cold: An Introduction to Winter Ecology,* p. 102 and passim.

67. Schmid, Modifications of the sub-nivean microclimate by snowmobiles, pp. 251–257.

68. Schmid, pp. 251–257; Wanek, *Ecological Impact of Snowmobiling;* Neumann and Merriam, Ecological effects of snowmobiling, pp. 210–211.

69. Wilkinson, The Forest Service sets off into uncharted territory, pp. 8–12.

70. Citizen comment received in 1998 FOIA request. See Roaring from the past: Off-road vehicles on America's national forests, quoted as written, p. 10.

71. Caldwell and Shrader-Frechette, *Policy for Land: Law and Ethics,* p. 234.

72. Caldwell and Shrader-Frechette, p. 234, citing E. Mishan, 1969, *Technology and Growth: The Price We Pay,* p. 39, New York: Praeger.

73. See Roaring from the past, pp. 9–12.
74. Freedom of Information Act request submitted to all national forests by Wildlands CPR in October 1998. See Roaring from the past, p. 2, Executive summary.
75. According to the online source http:// atvsource.com [21 January 2000], when asked, "Have you ever trespassed illegally on your ATV?" 55.6 percent responded "yes," 33.9 percent responded "no," and 10.5 percent responded "don't know."
76. Wilshire and Nakata, Off-road vehicle effects on California's Mojave Desert, 123–132.
77. Personal communication with Howard Wilshire, 8 May 2000.
78. Personal communication with Las Vegas District BLM Outdoor Recreation Planner Bob Bruno, 21 June 2001.
79. Bruno, personal communication.
80. Executive Order 11644, signed by President Richard Nixon, 8 February 1972.
81. Executive Order 11989, signed by President Jimmy Carter, 24 May 1977.
82. 36 CFR §4.10a-b states, "Operating a motor vehicle is prohibited except on park roads, in parking areas and on routes and areas designated for off-road vehicle use. . . . Routes and areas may be designated only in national recreation areas, national seashores, national lakeshores and national preserves."
83. Kolman, No ban yet on snowmobiles at Yellowstone, pp. A-1, A-6. The NPS subsequently issued a separate decision to ban snowmobiles in Yellowstone by 2003–2004. At the end of June 2001, the Bush administration announced plans to review the NPS's decision in Yellowstone, leaving the fate of national park snowmobiling uncertain at the time this book goes to press.
84. Galvin quoted in Kolman, pp.A-1, A-6.
85. 50 CFR §27.31 states, "Travel or use of any motorized or other vehicles, including those used on air, water, ice, snow, is prohibited on national wildlife refuges except on designated routes of travel." Also, personal communication with Ken Edwards, refuge program specialist, 2 June 2000; Ed Loth, chief of refuge operations for the Southeast Region, 6 June 2000 and 19 July 2000; Dom Ciccone, Southwest regional director, 2 June 2000; and many refuge managers.
86. Wilkinson and Anderson, *Land and Resource Planning in the National Forests,* p. 30 and passim. Uses prescribed under the Forest Service's Multiple Use-Sustained Yield Act of 1960 include outdoor recreation, wildlife and fish, watershed management, range, and timber. The BLM received similar guidance with the 1976 passage of the Federal Land Policy Management Act.
87. Roaring from the past, and Freedom of Information Act request file.
88. Roaring from the past, and Freedom of Information Act request file.
89. Personal communication with Bill Kerr, Monongahela Forest Program Manager for Recreation, 1 June 2000.

90. Recreation trail damage memo, 3 November 1998, Athens Ranger District, Wayne National Forest.
91. *Annual Monitoring Report,* Wayne National Forest, 1998.
92. *Trails Management Handbook,* USDA, Forest Service. 10 January 1991.
93. 42 U.S.C.A. §4321. In addition to providing federal funding for motorized routes, the National Recreational Trails Fund (discussed later in this chapter) also proposed that most trail widening projects should qualify as "Categorical Exclusion" projects under NEPA.
94. See 40 CFR §1508.4 for further description of categorical exclusion provisions.
95. The Washington Trails Association and other groups have won court decisions to block ORV trail projects in both the Dark Divide and Entiat areas, while the Southern Utah Wilderness Alliance recently gained an administrative decision to restore a widened trail to its former pack-saddle nonmotorized condition. See United States District Court, Western District of Washington at Seattle, *Washington Trails Association, et al. v. United States Forest Service, et al.,* filed 12 June 1996, Intervener-Defendent, No. C95-877R; United States District Court, Western District of Washington at Seattle, *North Cascades Conservation Council, et al. v. United States Forest Service, et al.,* filed 31 August 1999, No. C99-889R; and Israelsen, Newly carved "Road" will be a trail again, p. B-1.
96. Some ambiguity remains. For example, Florida's Big Cypress National Preserve's enabling legislation states, "While the use of all-terrain vehicles must be carefully regulated by the Secretary (of the Interior) to protect the natural wildlife and wilderness values of the preserve, the bill does not prohibit their use along designated roads and trails." *Final Recreational Off-Road Vehicle Management Plan Supplemental Environmental Impact Statement: Big Cypress National Preserve, Florida,* p. v.
97. Personal communication with Heidi McIntosh, Southern Utah Wilderness Alliance, 1 June 2000.
98. ORV ban may aid plovers, p. 23; Primack, The plovers' paradise, pp. 9–10.
99. The National Recreation Trails Fund, often referred to as the Symms Act, was included in the passage of the Intermodal Surface Transportation Efficiency Act (ISTEA).
100. Legislative update, 1998, *Road-RIPorter,* 3(4): 6; American Recreation Coalition issue summary: National Recreational Trails Fund, available online: http://www.funoutdoors.com/policy.html.
101. This was included in the 1998 Transportation Equity Act for the 21st Century, or TEA-21.
102. U.S. Department of Transportation, TEA-21 fact sheet: Recreational Trails Program, 13 February 2000, available online: htttp://www.fhwa.dot.gov/tea21/factsheets/rec-trl.htm.
103. Walder, Money for motors from the halls of Congress, p. 1.
104. Several studies in Montana have found that motorized users generally are not disturbed by nonmotorized use, but that hikers, equestrians, and cross-

country skiers consistently avoid motorized "shared use" trails. *Statewide Comprehensive Outdoor Recreation Plan,* Montana Department of Fish, Wildlife and Parks, August 1994; *Montana Trail Users Survey,* University of Montana Institute for Tourism and Recreation Research, August 1994; *The Silent Majority: Public Attitudes toward Trail Use on the Gallatin National Forest,* 1999, Predator Project.

105. Washington State bills to limit allowances for ORVs, p. 15.

106. *Off-Road Montana! A Summary of OHV Laws, Regulations, and Tips for Responsible Off-Roading,* Montana Fish, Wildlife and Parks, undated pamphlet.

107. *Montana Off-Highway Vehicle Program, Project Application and Grant Program Information,* Montana Department of Fish, Wildlife and Parks, 1998.

108. Adams, Treadmarks on the virgin land, citing William T. Jobe, Snowmobiling in the 1980's: Continued progress for a mature recreational activity, Outdoor Recreation Trails Symposium; and International Snowmobile Manufacturers Association, *Snow Facts,* available online: http://www.snowmobile.org/snowfacts.html [November 2001].

109. Statement by Clark Collins, executive director Blue Ribbon Coalition, printed from http://www.sharetrails.org, 10 November 1998. See also, Poet, Blue Ribbon Coalition: Big corporate dollars, p. 18.

110. Information on Blue Ribbon Coalition funding sources may not be current, but accurately depicts past or present sponsors according to information from the Environmental Working Group's Clearinghouse on Environmental Advocacy and Research (CLEAR). See also Poet, Blue Ribbon Coalition, p. 18.

111. *Draft Environmental Impact Statement for the Revised Land and Resource Management Plan, Rio Grande National Forest,* 1995; Greg Thompson, recreation forester for the Rio Grande, personal communication, 28 January 2000.

112. *DEIS Rio Grande NF,* 1995, pp. 3-296–299, B-5–6.

113. *DEIS Rio Grande NF,* p. B-25.

114. Green Mountain–Finger Lakes National Forests Recreation Staff Officer Greg Wright, personal communication, 21 January 2000.

115. From U.S. House, *To Establish the Lee Metcalf Wilderness and Management Area in the State of Montana, and for Other Purposes: Transcript from Hearing on S. 96,* 17 May 1983, p. 67; see also, Adams, Treadmarks on the virgin land.

116. See 36 CFR §4.10b and Alaska National Interest Lands Conservation Act.

117. Clifford, Land of the fee, pp. 1, 6–10; Durbin, Land of the fee: The Forest Service says no pay no play, pp. 8–14.

118. *Off Road Recreation Vehicles: U.S. Department of the Interior Task Force Study.*

119. Sheridan, *Off-Road Vehicles on Public Lands,* p. 8.

120. From Lyons's speech at the Western Summit on Tourism and Public Lands, as quoted by Silver, From chainsaws to chassis: Motorizing the public lands, *Road-RIPorter,* p. 1. See also Christensen, The shotgun wedding of tourism and public lands.

121. Laitos and Carr, Transformation on Public Lands, pp. 140–242.
122. American Recreation Coalition fact sheet, available online: http://www. funoutdoors.com/facts.html [15 February 2000].
123. This is only a partial list of American Recreation Coalition members, as cited on ARC's website, http://www.funoutdoors.com [15 February 2000].
124. Clifford, America's eroding atolls of nature, p. A-1.
125. Clifford, America's eroding atolls of nature, p. A-20.
126. Clifford, America's eroding atolls, p. A-20; as of July 2000, Slavik remained on the Board of the San Bernardino Forest Association, personal communcation with SBFA, July 2000.
127. Randall O'Toole's *Reforming the Forest Service,* Washington, D.C.: Island Press, 1998, is one of the canonical works for "free marketeers" in this vein. Scott Silver, director of Wild Wilderness, applies these three terms as something of a mantra in his efforts to combat corporate dominance of public lands.
128. For more on Wild Wilderness, see www.wildwilderness.org.
129. On 10 October 2001, Congress passed compromise legislation for an Interior Appropriations bill that included a two-year extension of the Fee Demo program. President Bush was expected to sign the bill, even though he originally requested a four-year extension of Fee Demo. Others, including Chair of the House Resources Committee Jim Hansen (R-UT), continue to advocate permanent authorization of Fee Demo. In June 2001, Senator Bob Graham (D-FL) introduced the National Parks Stewardship Act (S. 1011) that, if passed, would establish a permanent fee program; meanwhile, state and local governments from New Hampshire to Oregon have come out against Fee Demo and the program's legal authority continues to face challenges in court. See www.freeourforests.org/newsflash.htm [24 October 2001] for more information and updates.
130. http://refuges.fws.gov/centennial/index.html [21 February 2001].
131. Laitos and Carr, Transformation on Public Lands, pp. 161–162.
132. http://www.nps.gov/pub_aff/e-mail/faqs.htm [21 February, 2001].
133. Laitos and Carr, Transformation on Public Lands, p. 161.
134. Laitos and Carr, p. 146, citing the Natural Resources Law Center's *Resource Law Notes,* summer 1998, p. 7, University of Colorado Law School.
135. Recreational Fee Demonstration Project: Progress report to Congress, fiscal year 1999, available online: http://www.doi.gov/nrl/Recfees/2000R/ 2000Report.html [15 February 2000] ("Report to Congress" hereafter).
136. Report to Congress.
137. Interview with Jake Cebula, supervisory resource specialist, Uwharrie National Forest, Troy, NC, 27 March 2001.
138. Though still a National Forest by title, the Uwharrie is managed as a ranger district within the four administratively clustered national forests of North Carolina. All figures provided by Jake Cebula, interview 27 March 2001.

139. Report to Congress. Revenues increased each year as more demonstration sites were added, approaching the project's limit of 100 per agency: FY 1996—$93.3 million, FY 1997—$147.2 million, FY 1998—$180.2 million, and FY 1999—$193.2 million. Per agency in FY 1999, Fee Demo brought in $141.4 million to the NPS, $3.6 million to USFWS, $6.7 million to the BLM, and $26.5 million to the USFS.
140. See Clifford, Land of the fee.
141. U.S. Forest Service recreation, heritage and wilderness resources, available online: http://www.fs.fed.us/recreation/fee_demo/fee_intro.shtml [15 February 2000].
142. Duncan and Maughan, Feet vs. ORVs: Are there social differences between backcountry users? pp. 478–480.
143. Duncan and Maughan, pp. 478–480, citing Burch and Wenger, 1967, USDA-FS Research Paper PNW-48, 29 pp.; and Merriam and Ammons, 1967, The social characteristics in three styles of family camping in three Montana areas, University of Minnesotas School of Forestry, 54 pp.
144. Knopp and Tyger, A study of conflict in recreational land use: Snowmobiling vs. ski-touring, pp. 6–17.
145. Alston, The Individual vs. the Public Interest: Political Ideology and National Forest Policy, p. 12.
146. This example oversimplifies the formula, but corresponds to the "Travel Cost Method" for estimating recreation demand and benefits as described in Swanson and Loomis, Role of Nonmarket Economic Values in Benefit–Cost Analysis of Public Forest Management, p.14.
147. These methods reflect what Swanson and Loomis call, respectively, the "Contingent Valuation Method" and "option value," pp. 14–15.
148. From Laitos and Carr, Transformation on Public Lands, pp. 228–239.
149. Laitos and Carr, p. 235, citing Costanza et al., The value of the world's ecosystem services and natural capital, p. 253.
150. Laitos and Carr, pp. 237–239.
151. For example, see Swanson and Loomis, Role of nonmarket values, p. 13.
152. Alston, Individual vs. Public Interest, p. 40, citing Aristotle's Ethics 1.2, J.A.K. Thompson translation.
153. Caldwell and Shrader-Frechette, Policy for Land, p. 7, citing the Works of Thomas Jefferson, vol. 11, 1904, ed. P.L. Ford, New York: Putnam and Sons, p. 298.
154. Caldwell and Shrader-Frechette, p. 231.
155. Nixon, Environmental Quality: The First Annual Report of the Council on Environmental Quality, pp. xii–xiii.
156. Caldwell and Shrader-Frechette, Policy for Land, p. 94; Caldwell, The National Environmental Policy Act, pp. xiv–xv.
157. Sax, Mountains without Handrails, p. 33.
158. Bleich, Chrome on the range: Off-road vehicles on public lands, p. 171, citing a Cape Cod study by S.P. Leatherman and P.J. Godfrey, 1979, The impact

of off-road vehicles on coastal ecosystems in Cape Cod National Seashore: An overview. National Park Service Cooperative Research Unit Report No. 34, Amherst, MA: University of Massachusetts, 34 pp.

Chapter 6. Public Values, Public Lands

1. Craig and Chenoweth, Tank Traps and the Forest Service, p. 65.
2. For instance, the so-called 40-inch rule, which restricted trail use in national forests to motor vehicles no wider than 40 inches, was rescinded in 1990 without any environmental analysis. As a result, four-wheeled ATVs are now legal on many national forest trails even though their impacts on the land, other forest users, water, and wildlife have not been assessed in any systematic way.
3. The two executive orders signed by Presidents Nixon and Carter applied specifically to limiting damage from ORVs, while in 1976 the Federal Land Policy Management Act and National Forest Management Act created more specific management guidance for BLM and national forest lands respectively.
4. Palmer, in *Environmental Ethics*, p. 6, defines ethics as, "how we should live and what we ought to do; what kind of behavior is right and wrong; what our moral obligations might be."
5. In *Conserving Natural Value*, p. 154, Holmes Rolston III writes, "A person may be doing what would be, taken individually, a perfectly good thing, a thing he has a right to do, were he alone, but which, taken in collection with thousands of others doing the same thing, becomes a harmful thing, which he has no right to do because it destroys the commons and irreversibly destroys natural values."
6. Rolston, *Conserving Natural Value*, p. 165.
7. A vocal minority of Americans still press for state or private control of federal lands, typically to promote resource extraction, generate private revenues, or avoid federal regulations. Thus far, efforts such as the "Sagebrush Rebellion" in the 1980s have been stifled by the majority public view that federal lands should remain in federal control.
8. Leopold's oft-quoted lines describe this condition as, "A thing is right when it tends to preserve the integrity, stability, and beauty of the biotic community. It is wrong when it tends otherwise," *A Sand County Almanac*, p. 262.
9. Leopold, p. 204.
10. See, for example, Stone, *Earth and Other Ethics*, pp. 26–35.
11. Such a view obviously failed to consider the long-time native inhabitants of the land, human and otherwise.
12. Total landbase figure taken from U.S. Census Bureau, *Statistical Abstract of the United States, 1999*, p. 240. Roadless lands constitute approximately 230 million acres, or 10 percent, out of 2.3 billion acres of U.S. landbase. The

Wilderness Preservation System currently includes 105 million acres. The Forest Service identified (and sought to protect) 58 million acres of roadless land remaining under its management in 2000; the other three agencies were not able to provide ready acreage counts, but their "best guess" estimates suggest another 100 to 150 million acres would qualify as roadless using a standard similar to that used for wilderness designations. Personal communication with Nancy Roeper, U.S. Fish and Wildlife Service, 11 December 2000; Jeff Jarvis, Bureau of Land Management, 14 December 2000; Theresa Ely, National Park Service, 3 January 2001.

13. For example, Poll: Most Montanans support roadless plan, (AP) March 31, 2000, *Missoulian,* A-4, reported support for the Forest Service's roadless protection measure by 53 percent of the voters in Montana, 57 percent in Idaho, 72 percent in California, 71 percent in New Mexico, 69 percent in Michigan, 75 percent in Colorado, 72 percent in Tennessee, 76 percent in Minnesota, 83 percent in Wisconsin, 72 percent in Washington, and 67 percent in Oregon. In 1999–2000, the Clinton administration asked the Forest Service to create a policy to prohibit further road building on nearly 60 million acres of national forest from Alaska to Florida. This was enacted in January 2001 but remains clouded by threats that the new Bush administration will undermine or overturn the protections.

14. Steen, *U.S. Forest Service,* pp. 22–23, citing F.J. Turner, The significance of the frontier in American history, speech presented on 12 July, 1893 at the Columbian Exposition in Chicago.

15. Quoted in Culpin, *History of the Construction of the Road System,* p. 111.

16. Culpin, p. 111.

17. Thorofare is 20 miles distant, the second most remote location is 18 miles in the Bob Marshall Wilderness complex of north-central Montana, personal communication with Susan Boswell, Cartographic Technologies Inc., 14 December 2000.

18. Quoted in Culpin, *Construction of the Road System,* p. 31.

19. Quoted from a letter from Interior Secretary Franklin Lane to National Park Service Director Stephen Mather (likely written by Mather) in Dilsaver, ed., *America's National Park System: The Critical Documents,* Secretary Lane's letter on National Park management, p. 49

20. Quoted on p. 261 in Pinchot, *Breaking New Ground,* 1972 edition; the original letter was written by Pinchot and signed by Secretary of Agriculture James Wilson on 1 February 1905.

21. *Fire Management Plan for Big Oaks National Wildlife Refuge* states, "All areas of Big Oaks National Wildlife Refuge are considered contaminated with UXO [unexploded ordnance]," p. 11.

22. Quoted from Lane letter in Dilsaver, *America's National Park System: The Critical Documents,* p. 48.

23. Pinchot, *Breaking New Ground,* p. 261.

24. Executive Order 12,996, 25 March 1996. It seems safe to assume that the generations mentioned here are human. This mission statement was essentially reiterated by Congress in the National Fish and Wildlife Refuge Improvement Act of 1997. Available online: http://www.nara.gov/fedregeo1996.html#12996 [25 October 2001].

25. BLM created and adopted its mission statement in 1994, with its "Blueprint for the Future" document and planning process, available online: http://www.blm.gov.nhp/facts/index.htm [24 October 2001].

26. In *Atlas of the New West* geographer William Riebsame notes, "[T]he New West is a post-industrial, high-tech society riding hard in the saddle of a beautiful but fragile landscape," p. 46; see also Laitos and Carr, Transformation on public lands, p. 146.

27. For example, in a speech titled, A Gradual Unfolding of a National Purpose: A National Resource Agenda for the 21st Century, Forest Service Chief Michael Dombeck stated in March 1998, "We are committed to providing superior customer service and ensuring that the rapid growth of recreation on national forests does not compromise the long-term health of the land." Quoted from http://www.fs.fed.us/news/roads [21 November 2000]. Under the Bush administration and the new Forest Service chief, Dale Bosworth, it now seems less clear how diminished logging activities, at least, will remain.

28. "The Recreation Agenda," dated September 2000 (FS-691), available online: http://www.fs.fed.us/news/roads [21 November 2000].

29. The U.S. Fish and Wildlife Service's "100 on 100" campaign tacitly acknowledged this point in 1995 when it set a goal to have 100 percent of Americans be aware of the national wildlife refuges by the system's 100th anniversary in 2003. By 1999, the Fish and Wildlife Service had already conceded that the campaign was "unrealistic." See *Fulfilling the Promise*, pp. 57 and 59.

30. Barker, *Saving all the Parts: Reconciling Economics and the Endangered Species Act*, pp. 93–95; Lichatowich, *Salmon without Rivers*, pp. 60–66, discusses some of the historic impacts of logging on Columbia River salmon. See also, for example, Goodstein, *Jobs and the Environment*, and Bezdek, Environment and economy, cited in Chapter 4, supra 79.

31. Godfrey-Smith, The value of wilderness, pp. 309–319.

32. Katz, Utilitarianism and preservation, pp. 357–364.

33. Sumner, The need for a more serious effort to rescue a few fragments of vanishing nature, p. 248. Sumner held that conservation should rest solely upon the value of nature to humans, but he advocated for a broader consideration of value.

34. Thompson, *Agricultural Ethics: Research, Teaching, and Public Policy*, p. 17.

35. Quoted in Nash, *Wilderness and the American Mind*, p. 126.

36. According to Nash, p. 231, the ads ran nationally on 25 July 1966.

37. See for example online: http://www.leaderu.com/orgs/probe/docs/ecology.htm for article by Dr. Ray Bohlin, Christian environmentalism [November 21, 2000].

38. Other laws control grazing, conserve fish and wildlife, manage national forests, establish wilderness, define a national environmental policy, and place constraints on mining practices.

39. Steen, *U.S. Forest Service,* pp. 24–25; Wilkinson and Anderson, *Land and Resource Planning in the National Forests,* p. 17.

40. *Annual Report of the Secretary of the Interior,* 1874, p. xvi.

41. *Annual Report of the Secretary of the Interior,* 1877, p. xvi (also cited in Wilkinson and Anderson, *Land and Resource Planning,* p. 17).

42. Sax, *Defending the Environment,* p. 169. See also Sax, Liberating the public trust from its historical shackles, pp. 185–194; Dunning, ed., *The Public Trust Doctrine in Natural Resources Law and Management: Conference Proceedings*; and Wilkinson, The headwaters of the public trust: Some thoughts on the source and scope of the traditional doctrine, pp. 425–472.

43. Sax, The public trust doctrine in natural resource law: Effective judicial intervention, pp. 492–494.

44. Sax, *Defending the Environment,* p. 165.

45. Sax, Public trust doctrine in natural resource law, pp. 562–565.

46. Dunning, *Public Trust Doctrine,* p. 177.

47. 376 F. Supp. 90 (N.D. Calif 1974); 398 F. Supp (N.D. Calif 1975); 424 F. Supp. 172 (N.D. Calif. 1976).

48. Jawetz, The public trust totem in public land law: Ineffective—and undesirable—judicial intervention, pp. 482–483. Congress expanded the park boundaries in 1978 to include much of the land in question.

49. Jawetz, pp. 482–483.

50. Jawetz, quoting from *Light v. U.S.* (1911); and *Van Brocklin v. Tennessee* (1886).

51. Sax, Public trust doctrine in natural resource law, p. 486.

52. Sax, Public trust doctrine in natural resource law, p. 514.

53. Personal communication with Joseph Sax, 4 June 2001.

54. Executive Order 11,644, 1972.

55. P.L. 91-190, January 1, 1970.

56. National Environmental Policy Act of 1969, As Amended. Pub. L. 91-190, 42 U.S.C. §§4,321 4,347, January 1, 1970, as amended by Pub. L. 94-83, August 9, 1975.

57. Sax, Liberating the public trust, p. 188.

58. Sax, Public trust doctrine in natural resource law, pp. 562–565. Sax describes "natural purpose" in this context as a natural resource being left in its natural state; that is, is a lake being used "as a lake."

59. Clifford, Land of the fee, pp. 1, 6–10.

60. Sax, Public trust doctrine in natural resource law, p. 565.

61. Sax, Public trust doctrine in natural resource law, p. 565.

62. This resembles Holmes Rolston III's assertion that laws such as the Endangered Species Act should be considered "liberating policy" rather than "prohibitive policy," as they allow us to become more sensitive to environmental and cultural values instead of solely economic value. See Rolston's *Conserving Natural Value*, p. 156. In a similar fashion, Rolston supports wilderness designations: "No one is locked out of wilderness, if they are prepared to come on wilderness terms. . . . Wilderness designations open up access; this permits access over many generations to come and all comers. Designation prevents taking possession of property there (ores, wildlife, timber, forage, water) and removing public goods at public loss. . . . It makes the commons comprehensive in the fullest sense—not a commons for people only, but for squirrels and trilliums as well (p. 191)."

63. Other large scenic parks included in this pre-agency span included Yosemite (1890), Sequoia (1890), Mount Rainier (1899), Olympic (1909), and Glacier (1910).

64. From the Lane letter in Dilsaver, *America's National Park System: The Critical Documents*, p. 48.

65. See Wilkinson and Anderson, *Land and Resource Planning in the National Forests*, for an overview of this trend, as well as more details on many of the specific acts. The full title of the Resources Planning Act (RPA) is the Forest and Rangeland Renewable Resources Planning Act of 1974; NFMA, in 1976, was passed as an amendment to RPA.

66. *Forest Service Manual*, 7,703.1. The Forest Service Manual represents the agency's legal interpretation of how to implement the National Forest Management Act statutes. See also, 16 USC §1608(b) and 36 CFR §219.27 (a)(11) for the full progression from congressional action to agency implementation. See also, Hammer, *Road-Ripper's Guide to National Forests*, p. 3

67. 36 CFR §295.2 (b), as cited in Wikinson and Anderson, *Land and Resource Planning*, p. 329.

68. FLPMA was passed on 21 October 1976; NFMA a day later on 22 October 1976.

69. NFMA established forest planning requirements and the conservation of native vertebrate species for the Forest Service; FLPMA required the BLM to conduct surveys and make recommendations for wilderness designations, as well as to avoid "unnecessary or undue degradation" to lands in its care. See Coggins, The developing law of land use planning on the federal lands, pp. 307–353.

70. PL 93-205; 16 USC §1531 et seq., as amended.

71. Greenwalt, The power and potential of the act, pp. 31–42; see also, Rolston, Life in jeopardy on private property, pp. 43–61.

72. Rolston, Life in jeopardy, p. 46.

73. See Vaughan, *Endangered Species Act Handbook*, p. 1. Rolston, Life in jeopardy, pp. 43–44, asserts that the ESA does, in fact, "ask whether animals, plants,

species, and ecosystems count morally," but such questions are implied and not as explicit as the text of the law that clearly emphasizes "value to the Nation and its people."

74. See Palmer, *Environmental Ethics,* p. 113; and more generally, Stone's *Earth and Other Ethics.*

75. Leopold, *A Sand County Almanac,* p. viii.

76. Leopold, p. 204.

77. Quoted in Brooks, *Rachel Carson: The Writer at Work,* p. 321.

78. Stone, Should trees have standing? Toward legal rights for natural objects, pp. 450–501. Singer, All animals are equal, pp. 213–257, presents a similar progression in advocating rights for animals; as does Thompson in *Agricultural Ethics: Research, Teaching, and Public Policy,* p. 14; and, of course, Leopold, *A Sand County Almanac,* pp. 201–203.

79. NPS Organic Act, 16 U.S. Code Annotated, sec. 1.

80. On 19 June 1998, the 10th U.S. District Court ordered Canyonlands National Park to close Salt Creek to motorized vehicle use and that the Park Service had a legal obligation to manage preferentially for preservation, even at the prospective expense of public enjoyment. On 15 August 2000, the 10th Circuit Court of Appeals remanded this decision back to the 10th Circuit, where it now awaits further consideration. Subsequently, Canyonlands Superintendent Jerry Banta issued a temporary closure order for motorized use of Salt Creek until the Park Service can complete a formal rulemaking process, which is expected to extend well into 2001. Until further court or agency action, Salt Creek remains closed to motorized use. On 8 September 2000, National Park Service Director Robert Stanton issued Director's Order 55, which states that preservation is, in fact, the overriding obligation of the National Park Service. See Chapter 7.

81. Quoted from the Lane letter in Dilsaver, *America's National Park System: The Critical Documents,* p. 48.

82. This is particularly interesting in contrast to the emerging views of "ecological modernism" during this same period. For example, according to D. Harvey, 1996, *Justice, Nature and the Geography of Difference* (Cambridge, MA: Blackwell), p. 377, ecological modernism became popular during the progressive era of Gifford Pinchot and "depends upon and promotes a belief that economic activity systematically produces environmental harm."

83. See Subcommittee on Public Lands of the Senate Committee on Interior and Insular Affairs, 92nd Cong., 2nd sess., *Clearcutting on Federal Timberlands* 3-4 (Committee Print 1972) reprinted in *Forest and Rangeland Management: Joint Hearings before the Subcommittee on Environment, Soil Conservation, and Forestry of the Senate Committee on Agriculture and Forestry and the Subcommittee on the Environment and Land Resources of the Senate Committee on Interior and Insular Affairs,* 94th Cong., 2nd sess. 953-954 (Committee Print 1976), p. 260, as cited in Wilkinson and Anderson, *Land and Resource Planning,* p. 292.

84. 36 CFR §219.19, in *Code of Federal Regulations* 36, parts 200 to 299, revised as of 1 July 2000, Parks, forests, and public property, p. 79. Recent administrations have worked to revise the NFMA regulations, but to date these efforts have not been finalized and implemented.
85. 36 CFR §219.19, p. 79.
86. See Wilkinson and Anderson, *Land and Resource Planning*, p. 299.

Chapter 7. Changing Landscapes: Society, Technology, and Road Removal

1. Personal communication with Doug Edgerton, 27 June 2001.
2. *Ecosystem Management: Annual Report of Forest Service*, p. 46. Many of the available roads are considered appropriate only for high-clearance vehicles.
3. See Forest Service Roadless Area Conservation, Final Environmental Impact Statement, November 2000, U.S. Department of Agriculture, Forest Service.
4. In January 2001 the BLM released its *National Management Strategy for Motorized Off-Highway Vehicle Use on Public Lands*.
5. Personal communication with Bill Weaver, Pacific Watershed Associates, 29 June 2001. Contact PWA at PO Box 4433, Arcata, CA 95518; pwa@northcoast.com.
6. For more on the creation of the Wilderness Society and the motives of its founders, see Paul Sutter's dissertation, Driven Wild (also forthcoming as a book, University of Washington Press). Wildlands Center for Preventing Roads began as the Road Removal Implementation Project (Road-RIP), and in 1997 was renamed Wildlands CPR.
7. See *Roaded Lands, Eroded Habitats: Findings and Implications of the Roads Scholar Project, 1994–1997*, p. 16.
8. *Roaded Lands, Eroded Habitats*, p. 16.
9. Personal communication with Mary Dalton, Sierra Vista Ranger District, Coronado National Forest, 28 January 2000; and David Hodges, Sky Island Alliance, 27 January 2000.
10. Personal communication with Dalton and Hodges. The Coronado's Dalton reports that the current road density on her ranger district is 1.82 miles/square mile, compared to the forest's guideline of 1.0 mile/square mile.
11. Dalton, personal communication.
12. *Winter Use Plan: Final Environmental Impact Statement for the Yellowstone and Grand Teton National Parks and John D. Rockefeller Jr. Memorial Parkway*.
13. The status of this decision remains in question at the time of this writing. In late June 2001, the National Park Service agreed to produce a supplemental environmental impact statement that would reconsider all alternatives for winter use in Yellowstone, including cleaner or quieter snowmobiles. A final decision is not expected until at least the end of 2001.
14. Motorized recreation groups also make use of cooperative work parties to establish relationships with land managers and to help promote a reputation

of responsibility for ORV users. Motorized recreation groups often point to such collaborative efforts to support their claims that they should retain the privilege to ride on public lands.

15. *National Management Strategy for Motorized Off-Highway Vehicle Use on Public Lands,* p. 1.

16. *Off-Highway Vehicle Environmental Impact Statement and Proposed Plan Amendment for Montana, North Dakota, and Portions of South Dakota,* January 2001; and *Off-Highway Vehicle Record of Decision and Plan Amendment for Montana, North Dakota, and Portions of South Dakota,* January 2001. This policy also applies to national forest lands in these states.

17. President Clinton's Executive Order 12,996, 25 March 1996; National Wildlife Refuge Improvement Act of 1997, PL 105-57, signed 9 October 1997.

18. The National Fish and Wildlife Foundation, for example, offers several different grant programs for conservation and preservation work on refuge lands.

19. Personal communication with George Nickas, executive director of Wilderness Watch, 29 June 2001.

20. *Fulfilling the Promise: The National Wildlife Refuge System,* p. 15.

21. National Wildlife Refuge System Improvement Act of 1997 fact sheet.

22. Director's Order 125, 12 July 2000. Personal communication with Nancy Roeper, U.S. Fish and Wildlife Service, 11 December 2000.

23. Warren, Zion takes tourists out of their cars; Alder, A park rediscovers a surprising asset.

24. Alder, A park rediscovers.

25. National Park Service, South Rim transit, available online: http://www.nps.gov/grca/transit/southrim.htm [16 December 2000].

26. According to Shankland, *Steve Mather of the National Parks,* p. 151, Mt. Rainier was the first park to receive automobile use, followed by General Grant in 1910, Crater Lake in 1911, Glacier in 1912, and Yosemite and Sequoia in 1913. Yellowstone did not permit automobile traffic to enter until 1915.

27. See South Rim transit.

28. Visitor numbers from *The World Almanac and Book of Facts, 2000,* p. 573.

29. Lutz and Morrison, Gentlemen, stop your engines!

30. http://www.nps.gov/acad/bus.htm [12 December 12, 2000].

31. http://www.charlier.org/company.html [21 January 2001].

32. Lutz and Morrison, Gentlemen, stop your engines!

33. http://www.earthisland.org/bw/jetskisettlepress.html [24 January 2001]. This decision may be stalled by actions from Secretary of the Interior Gale Norton and the Bush administration.

34. E. Klim, EPA proposes new emission standards for snowmobiles; manufacturers preparing comments to proposed rule, available online: http://www.snowmobile.org/responsetoepa.html [1 November 2001].

35. *Winter Use Plan Final Environmental Impact Statement,* pp. 12–15.

36. *Winter Use Plan,* pp. 112, 187.

37. *Winter Use Plan,* p. 111. Snowmobiles obviously create major impacts on national forest and private lands too, but use in these areas has not yet received the same scrutiny as that within the national park.

38. *Winter Use Plan,* p. 408.

39. *Winter Use Plan,* p. 112.

40. Bush presidency would put snowmobile ban in doubt, p. A-2.

41. National Park Service Director's Order 55, 8 September 2000. See also, Jamison, National Park Service makes resource protection top priority, pp. A-1, A-10.

42. Quoted from the Lane letter in Dilsaver, *America's National Park System: The Critical Documents,* p. 48. The Lane letter also stated, "Every activity of the Service is subordinate to the duties imposed upon it to faithfully preserve the parks for posterity in essentially their natural state."

43. Director's Order #55, section 3.3.

44. *Ecosystem Management: Annual Report of Forest Service,* 1993, p. 46.

45. *Report of the Forest Service,* 1998, p. ii.

46. The Forest Service's new roads policy describes this in some detail. See http://www.fs.fed.us/new/roads for the full policy [24 January 2001].

47. http://www.fs.fed.us/news/roads/20010104-final-road-management-policy-2.htm [24 January 2001].

48. Devlin, Roadless rage: 2,000 attend rally against proposed ban, pp. A-1, A-4.

49. See Nijhuis, A county in Nevada assaults a river; Christensen, Nevada rebellion ends with a whimper; Christensen, Nevadans drive out forest supervisor; and Mider, Kicking and screaming in Nevada.

50. Walder, Bulltrout rebellion?! Elko road rage erodes democracy, pp. 1, 4–5.

51. Commissioners sign accord to end road feud (AP), 10 March 2001, *Las Vegas Review Journal,* available online: http://www.lvrj.com/lvrj_home/2001/Mar-10-Sat-2001/news/15611443.html [1 November 2001].

52. *A Guide for Road Closure and Obliteration in the Forest Service,* p. 9.

53. Hammer, An on-site study of the effectiveness of the U.S. Forest Service road closure program in Management Situation One Grizzly Bear Habitat, Swan Lake Ranger District, Flathead National Forest, Montana; Platt, Cabinet-Yaak grizzly bear ecosystem: 1992 Forest Service road closure program compliance inventory.

54. Havlick, Closing forest roads for habitat protection: A northern Rockies case study, pp. 327–330.

55. For examples, see Wildland CPR's 1999 report, Roaring from the past, available online: www.wildlandscpr.org.

56. *Guide for Road Closure,* p. 9.

57. Hegman, "The Location, Design, Construction and Reclamation of Low Volume Roads."

58. *Report of the Chief,* 1932, USDA-FS.
59. *Report of the Chief,* 1935, USDA-FS, p. 36.
60. *Report of the Chief,* 1966, USDA-FS, p. 46.
61. Projects include the Maine Woods National Park proposal by Restore: The North Woods; the North Cascades International Park complex proposal by the Northwest Ecosystem Alliance; the Florida Biodiversity Project's reserve design; Minnesota Ecosystem Recovery Project; The Wildlands Project; Southern Rockies Ecosystem Project; Alliance for the Wild Rockies' Northern Rockies Ecosystem Protection Act; and the Yellowstone to Yukon Initiative.
62. Personal communication, Jim Amenta, Federal Highway Administration, 21 September 2000.
63. See for example, Zuckerman, Pitfalls on the way to lasting restoration, p. 6.
64. *Promoting Ecological Restoration to the World as a Science, Art, and Conservation Strategy,* Society for Ecological Restoration pamphlet, 21 September 2000. See also http://www.ser.org.
65. *Guide for Road Closure.*
66. *Guide for Road Closure,* p. 3.
67. 6 June 1997 letter from Pierce District Ranger Douglas Gober, Clearwater NF. The *Guide for Road Closure,* p. iv, also states, "Roads to be treated by the process have already been placed in an unneeded category. . . . If unneeded for a specific amount of time, the road is in 'closure' status; if never needed again, the road will undergo natural or mechanical 'obliteration,' given effective access control."
68. Quoted in Oregon: Siuslaw NF closing roads, p. 8.
69. Siuslaw closing roads, p. 8.
70. See Siuslaw National Forest website: http://www.fs.fed.us/r6/siuslaw/floods1.htm#torrents [30 June 2001].
71. Personal communication with Doug Edgerton, West Yellowstone, MT, 27 June 2001.
72. Personal communication with Anne Connor, Clearwater National Forest, Orofino, Idaho, 29 March 2001.
73. Clearwater National Forest road obliteration fact sheet, p.5.
74. Road obliteration fact sheet, p. 3.
75. Connor, Bradbury, and Taylor, Removing roads and restoring watersheds on the Clearwater National Forest.
76. Anne Connor, personal communication.
77. Personal communication with Brooks Beegle, Clearwater National Forest, Orofino, ID, 29 March 2001.
78. McClelland et al., *Draft Assessment of the Effects of the 1995 and 1996 Flood on the Clearwater National Forest: A Report to the Regional Forester,* p. 2.
79. McClelland et al., p. 3. See also specific public notices, such as 6 June 1997 letter from Pierce District Ranger (Clearwater NF) Douglas Gober, that announces road obliteration and treatment projects.

80. Road obliteration fact sheet, p. 1.
81. Anne Connor, personal communication.
82. This claim to the "ceded lands" is recognized by the U.S. Indian Claims Commission, Docket No. 175, 1967. The Treaty of 1855 pared the Nez Perce Reservation down to 7.8 million acres. The Treaty of 1863 then carved the reservation down to the 770,470-acre plot that appears on most road maps. Many Nez Perce chiefs did not sign the latter treaty, and the tribe to this day recognizes the boundaries of the Treaty of 1855 as their rightful lands. See also, *The Nez Perce Tribe: Ensuring Our Future Honoring Our Past* and other publications by the Nez Perce Tribe, Lapwai, ID.
83. Personal communication with Ira Jones and Emmitt Taylor, Nez Perce Tribe, 12 June 2001.
84. Road obliteration fact sheet, p. 4; Clearwater National Forest Road Obliteration Fact Sheet, p. 4.
85. Project file for West Fork Squaw Creek (subsequently renamed West Fork Waw'aatamnima [Fishing] Creek), viewed at Clearwater Forest Supervisor's Office, Orofino, ID, 29 March 2001.
86. Much of the following came from a visit to Redwood National Park from 10–15 April 2001 and personal communication with Mike Sanders, Jim Howard, Neal Youngblood and Meredith Manning, in Arcata and Orick, CA.
87. http://www.nps.gov/redw [13 December 2000].
88. Spreiter, Franke, and Steensen, Disturbed lands restoration: The Redwood experience.
89. Recontouring can help restore natural hydrologic function, though many restorationists agree that, as Seattle's Marti Spencer puts it, "You're not going to erase a road . . . it's a matter of looking for stability." Personal communication, 19 June 2001.
90. Strategic plan for Redwood National and state parks—FY 2001–2005, available online: http://www.nps.gov/redw/strategic_plan.html [13 December 2000]. The degraded area identified for treatment is about 54,000 acres.

Chapter 8. The Road Ahead

1. The North Fork Boise River watershed inventory found 14 percent more roads than the Forest Service included in its own inventory.
2. See North Fork Boise River watershed inventory, Predator Project, 1998.
3. Interviews with employees of the National Park Service and U.S. Forest Service, May 2000, June 2001. See also, Wilkinson, *Science under Siege: The Politicians' War on Nature and Truth.*
4. Leopold was the assistant district forester in charge of operations, the equivalent of today's assistant regional forester. In 1921 Leopold published an article in the *Journal of Forestry,* The wilderness and its place in forest recreation

policy, and on 2 October 1922, he presented his report on the proposed Gila Wilderness to District Forester Frank Pooler. See Meine, *Aldo Leopold: His Life and Work,* pp. 175, 194, 205.

5. Brooks, *Rachel Carson: The Writer at Work,* p. 315, notes, "Secretary of the Interior Stewart L. Udall was one of Rachel Carson's staunchest supporters."

6. As quoted on p. 237 of Glover, *A Wilderness Original: The Life of Bob Marshall,* citing an unpublished letter to the *Washington Post,* 6/38, in Robert Marshall Papers, American Jewish Archives, Cincinnati, OH.

7. Information from FSEEE's website: http://www.afseee.org [21 February 2001].

8. Information from PEER's website: http://peer.org/about/index.html [21 February 2001].

9. Wilkinson's *Science under Siege* provides important illustrations of the pressures borne by land managers who speak up, including a chapter that focuses on the experiences of Howard Wilshire. More recently, the experience of Ian Thomas proved this point as well. Thomas was fired from his position with the U.S. Geological Survey in 2001 after he posted data and maps about caribou migration routes across the Arctic National Wildlife Refuge—coveted by the Bush administration for its possible oil reserves—to a website where it was available for public review.

10. Christensen, Nevadans drive out forest supervisor.

11. Christensen, Forest service bombed in Nevada, High Country News, 17 April 1995.

12. *Fulfilling the Promise: The National Wildlife Refuge System,* pp. x, 41, and 66.

13. *Final Environmental Assessment and Land Protection Plan: Proposed Expansion of Pelican Island National Wildlife Refuge—Indian River and Brevard County, FL,* p. 3.

14. *Fulfilling the Promise,* p. 66.

15. Edge, *Roads and More Roads in the National Parks and National Forests,* p 11.

16. Dr. Willard G. Van Name, quoted in *The New Yorker,* Profiles: Oh, hawk of mercy! 17 April 1948, p. 45.

17. Personal communication with Keith Hammer, 27 April 2001. Hammer helped found a grassroots group, the Swan View Coalition, with which he continues his work on roads, motorized access, and forest issues.

18. This "Amendment 19" to the Flathead Forest Plan was created in consultation with the Fish and Wildlife Service and prodded along with legal pressure from Hammer and others working with conservation groups.

19. Hammer, personal communication.

20. Personal communication with Jeff Brown, November 1998, Boulder, CO.

21. Personal communication with Jim Bensman, 13 and 18 June 2001.

22. Quoted in Hammer, *The Road Ripper's Guide to National Forests,* p. 1, from Senate legislative history for the National Forest Management Act, 1976.

23. Bison management then shifted from Montana's Division of Fish, Wildlife and Parks to the State Division of Livestock. These actions, too, have been

the subject of extended citizen protests, and the State of Montana, cattlemen, National Park Service, and citizen groups continue to quarrel about proper management of the nation's only "free roaming" herd of bison.

24. Personal communication with Jamie Lennox, Alliance for the Wild Rockies, March 2001. The Northern Rockies Ecosystem Protection Act was introduced in the 107th Congress as HR 488.

25. http://www.suwa.org [21 February 2001]. America's Redrock Wilderness Act was first introduced in Congress in 1989.

26. Many of the RS 2477 claims (see Chapter 4) filed in Utah are directed at undermining the wilderness proposals included in the Redrock Wilderness bill proposal, since designated wilderness areas are not allowed to include roads.

27. From the text of the proposed National Forest Protection and Restoration Act (HR 1494 in the 107th Congress), available online: http://www.house.gov/mckinney/hl/nfppa.htm [21 February 2001]; copy of 2001 bill also provided by Matthew Koehler, Native Forest Network, Missoula, MT, June 2001.

28. http://www.house.gov/mckinney/hl/nfppa.htm [21 February 2001].

29. Snowmobiles will be tested in Yellowstone, p. A-2.

30. Yellowstone to get cleaner snowmobiles, p. A-5; Futuristic snowmobiles take off in Yellowstone on test run, p. B-3.

31. Futuristic snowmobiles take off in Yellowstone, quoting Don Eide, manager of testing and development for Arctic Cat.

32. Buffalo U. wins contest for cleanest snowmobile, p. A-2.

33. http://www.atvnews.com [25 February 2001].

34. http://www.treadlightly.org [26 February 2001].

35. Purdy, Our scarred land: Monitoring ORVs not an easy job, pp. G-1, G-6.

36. *Random House Dictionary,* 1980, s.v. "conservation," p. 188.

37. For general coverage of the "wise use" movement, see Helvarg, *The War against the Greens: The "Wise Use" Movement, the New Right, and Anti-environmental Violence;* and Echevarria and Eby, eds., *Let the People Judge: Wise Use and the Private Property Rights Movement.*

38. *New Shorter Oxford English Dictionary on Historical Principles,* 1993, s.v. "conservation," p. 485. A third dictionary at home, *Webster's New Collegiate,* 1981, p. 239, agrees more with this latter view in defining "conservation," "a careful preservation and protection of something; especially planned management of a natural resource to prevent exploitation, destruction, or neglect."

39. The Montana Wilderness Association, for example, has developed a "Quiet Trails Campaign" that works to distinguish between the impacts of motorized recreation on trails and those of "quiet uses" such as hiking, horsepacking, or cross-country skiing.

Bibliography

Acadia National Park Official Website-Island Explorer Shuttle Bus. Available
  online: http://www.nps.gov/acad/bus.htm. U.S. Department of the Interior,
  National Park Service [12 December 2000].

Adams, J.C. 1998. Treadmarks on the virgin land: The appropriate role of off-road
  vehicles in national forests. Master's thesis, University of Montana, Missoula.

Adams, L.W., and A.D. Geis. 1981. *Effects of Highways on Wildlife, Final Report.*
  FHWA/RD-81/067. Washington, D.C.: Offices of Research and Development, Federal Highway Administration, U.S. Department of Transportation.

———. 1983. Effects of roads on small mammals. *Journal of Applied Ecology* 20: 403–415.

Administration of the Forest Development Transportation System: Advance
  Notice of Proposed Rulemaking. 4 March 1998. [RIN AB-67-0095] Washington, D.C.: U.S. Department of Agriculture, Forest Service.

Administration of the Forest Development Transportation System: Temporary
  Suspension of Road Construction in Roadless Areas. 1998. Washington,
  D.C.: U.S. Department of Agriculture, Forest Service.

Alder, Lin. 2000. A park rediscovers a surprising asset. *High Country News* 25 September. Available online: http://www.hcn.org/servlets/hcn.Article?arti-
  cle_id=6030 [November 2001].

Allin, Craig W. 1997. Wilderness policy. In *Western Public Lands and Environmental Politics*, ed. C. Davis, pp. 172–189. Boulder, CO: Westview Press.

All-terrain vehicle–related deaths—West Virginia, 1985–1997. 1999. *Morbidity and
  Mortality Weekly Report* 48(1): 1–4.

Alston, Richard M. 1983. *The Individual vs. the Public Interest: Political Ideology and National Forest Policy.* Boulder, CO: Westview Press.

Altmann, M. 1958. The flight distance in free-ranging big game. *Journal of Wildlife Management* 22: 207–209.

American Recreation Coalition fact sheet. Available online: http://www.funout-doors.com/facts.html [15 February 2000].

America's national wildlife refuge system . . . celebrating a century of conservation. Available online: http://refuges.fws.gov/centennial/index.html. U.S. Department of the Interior, Fish and Wildlife Service [21 February 2001].

Annual Monitoring Report. 1998. Athens, OH: Wayne National Forest.

Annual Report of the Secretary of the Interior. 1874. 43rd Cong., 2d sess. Washington, D.C.: Government Printing Office.

Annual Report of the Secretary of the Interior. 1877. 45th Cong., 2d sess. Washington, D.C.: Government Printing Office.

Anthony, R.G., and F.B. Isaacs. 1989. Characteristics of bald eagle nest sites in Oregon. *Journal of Wildlife Management* 53(1): 148–159.

Aune, K.A., and W. Kasworm. 1989. *Final Report East Front Grizzly Studies.* Helena, MT: Department of Fish, Wildlife, and Parks.

Baldwin, M.F. 1970. *The Off-Road Vehicle and Environmental Quality: A Report on the Social and Environmental Effects of Off-Road Vehicles, Particularly Snowmobiles, with Suggested Policies for Their Control.* Washington, D.C.: Conservation Foundation.

Bangs, E.E., T.N. Bailey, and M.F. Portner. 1989. Survival rates of adult female moose. *Journal of Wildlife Management* 53(3): 557–563.

Barker, R. 1993. *Saving All the Parts: Reconciling Economics and the Endangered Species Act.* Washington, D.C.: Island Press.

Baxter, C.V., C.A. Frissell, and F.R. Hauer. 1999. Geomorphology, logging roads, and the distribution of bull trout (*Salvelinus confluentus*) spawning in a forested river basin: Implications for management and conservation. *Transactions of the American Fisheries Society* 128: 854–867.

Belasco, W.J. 1979. *Americans on the Road: From Autocamp to Motel, 1910–1945.* Cambridge, MA: MIT Press.

Belnap, J. 1995. Surface disturbances: Their role in accelerating desertification. *Environmental Monitoring and Assessment* 37: 39–57.

Beschta, R.L. 1978. Long-term patterns of sediment production following road construction and logging in the Oregon Coast Range. *Water Resources Research* 14(6): 1011–1016.

Bess, F.H. 1971. The effect of snowmobile engine noise on the hearing mechanism. In *Proceedings of the Snowmobile and Off the Road Vehicle Research Symposium,* ed. M. Chubb, 147–159. College of Agriculture and Natural Resources, Department of Park and Recreation Resources, Recreation Resources and Planning Unit, Technical Report 8. East Lansing: Michigan State University.

Bezdek, R.H. 1993. Environment and economy: What's the bottom line? *Environment* 35(7): 7–32.

Black, R.W. 2000. Yellowstone outpost most remote in U.S. *Missoulian* (AP) 29 June: A-2.

Bleich, J.L. 1988. Chrome on the range: Off-road vehicles on public lands. *Ecology Law Quarterly* 15(1): 159–187.

Bluewater Network and National Park Service reach agreement over Jet Ski lawsuit. 20 December 2000. Available online: http://www.earthisland.org/bw/jet-skisettlepress.html. Bluewater Network Press Release [24 January 2001].

Bohlin, R. 1992. Christian environmentalism. Available online: http://www.leaderu.com /orgs/probe/docs/ecology.htm [21 November 2000].

Bondello, M.C. 1976. The effects of high-intensity motorcycle sounds on the acoustical sensitivity of the desert iguana, *Dipsosaurus dorsalis*. M.S. thesis, California State University–Fullerton, 38 pp.

Brasher, P. 1999. Government wants emission standards for snowmobiles, ATVs. *Seattle Times* 19 February. Available online: http://www.seattletimes.nwsource.com [November 2001].

Brattstrom, B.H., and M.C. Bondello. 1983. Effects of off-road vehicle noise on desert vertebrates. In *The Environmental Effects of Off-Road Vehicles: Impacts and Management in Arid Regions,* ed. R.Webb and H. Wilshire, pp. 167–206. New York: Springer-Verlag.

Brody, A.J., and M.R. Pelton. 1989. Effects of roads on black bear movements in North Carolina. *Wildlife Society Bulletin* 17: 5–10.

Brooks, P. 1989. *Rachel Carson: The Writer at Work.* Rev. ed. San Francisco: Sierra Club Books.

Bruns, E.H. 1977. Winter behavior of pronghorns in relation to habitat. *Journal of Wildlife Management* 41: 560–571.

Bryner, G.C. 1998. *U.S. Land and Natural Resources Policy: A Public Issues Handbook.* Westport, CT: Greenwood Press.

Buffalo U. wins contest for cleanest snowmobile. 2000. *Missoulian* (AP) 1 April: A-2.

Bury, R.B., R.A. Luckenbach, and S.D. Busack. 1977. *Effects of Off-Road Vehicles on Vertebrates in the California Desert.* Wildlife Research Report 8. Washington, DC: U.S. Department of the Interior, U.S. Fish and Wildlife Service. 23 pp.

Bush presidency would put snowmobile ban in doubt. 2000. *Missoulian* (AP) 6 December: A-2.

Caldwell, L. 1998. *The National Environmental Policy Act: An Agenda for the Future.* Bloomington: Indiana University Press.

Caldwell, L.K., and K. Shrader-Frechette. 1993. *Policy for Land: Law and Ethics.* Lanham, MD: Rowman and Littlefield.

Cate, D.F. 1963. Recreation and the U.S. Forest Service: A study of organizational response to changing demands. Ph.D. diss., Stanford University.

Cawley, R. M., and J. Freemuth. 1997. A critique of the multiple use framework in public lands decisionmaking. In *Western Public Lands and Environmental Politics,* ed. C. Davis, pp. 32–44. Boulder, CO: Westview Press.

Christensen, J. 1996. The shotgun wedding of tourism and public lands. *High Country News* 23 December. Available online: http://www.hcn.org/servlets/hcn.Article?article_id=2983 [November 2001].

——. 1999. Nevadans drive out forest supervisor. *High Country News* 22 November. Available online: http://www.hcn.org/servlets/hcn.Article?article_id=5393 [November 2001].

——. 1999. Nevada rebellion ends with a whimper. *High Country News* 25 October. Available online: http://www.hcn.org/servlets/hcn.Article?article_id=5352 [November 2001].

Clary, D.A. 1986. *Timber and the Forest Service.* Lawrence: University of Kansas Press.

Clawson, M. 1971. *The Bureau of Land Management.* New York: Praeger.

Clearwater National Forest road obliteration fact sheet. Undated pages. Orofino, ID: Clearwater National Forest.

Clifford, F. 1998. America's eroding atolls of nature. *Los Angeles Times* 3 November: A-1, A-20.

Clifford, H. 2000. Land of the fee. *High Country News* 14 February: 1, 6–10.

Coggins, G.C. 1990. The developing law of land use planning on the federal lands. *University of Colorado Law Review* 61: 307–353.

Collins, C. Statement by executive director of the Blue Ribbon Coalition. Available online: http://sharetrails.org [10 November 1998].

Congress passes legislation supporting snowmobiles. 19 December 2000. Available online: http://www.snowmobile.org/congresshalts.htm. Press release, International Snowmobile Manufacturers Association [20 June 2001].

Connor, A.H., C. Bradbury, and E. Taylor. 21–23 June 2000. Removing roads and restoring watersheds on the Clearwater National Forest. Presented at American Society of Civil Engineers Watershed 2000 Conference, Colorado State University, Fort Collins.

Copeland, J.P. 1996. Biology of the wolverine in central Idaho. Master's thesis, University of Idaho, Moscow. 138 pp.

Costanza, S.P., R. d'Arge, R. de Groot, S. Farber, M. Grasso, B. Hannon, K. Limburg, S. Naeem, R. O'Neill, J. Parulo, R. Ruskin, P. Sutton, and M. van den Belt. The value of the world's ecosystem services and natural capital. *Nature* 387 (6,230): 253–260.

Cowardin, L.M., D.S. Gilmer, and C.W. Shaiffer. 1985. Mallard recruitment in the agricultural environment of North Dakota. *Wildlife Monographs* 92: 17–20.

Craig, L., and H. Chenoweth. 1999. Tank traps and the Forest Service. *Range Magazine* summer: 65.

Crupi, A. 1998. Roads to nowhere imperil Alaska's wildness. *Road-RIPorter* 3(3): 1, 4–5.

Culpin, M.S. 1994. *History of the Construction of the Road System in Yellowstone National Park, 1872–1966.* Historic Resource Study, vol. 1, selections from the Division of Cultural Resources, Rocky Mountain Region, National

Park Service, No. 5. Denver: U.S. Department of the Interior, National Park Service.

Dalrymple, G.H., and N.G. Reichenbach. 1984. Management of an endangered species of snake in Ohio, USA. *Biological Conservation* 30: 195–200.

Devlin, S. 2000. Open valve dumps sewage into Lake McDonald. *Missoulian* 6 June: A-1.

———. 2000. Racicot, officials spar on TV. *Missoulian* 28 August: A-10.

———. 2000. Roadless rage: 2,000 attend rally against proposed ban. *Missoulian* 22 June: A-1, A-3.

Digest of Federal Resource Laws of Interest to the U.S. Fish and Wildlife Service. April 1992. Washington, D.C.: U.S. Department of the Interior, Fish and Wildlife Service, Office of Legislative Services.

Dilsaver, L.M., ed.1994. *America's National Park System: The Critical Documents.* Lanham, MD: Rowman and Littlefield.

Divided Highways: The Interstate Highway System and the Transformation of American Life. 1997. Florentine Films, Hott Productions and WETA, videocassette (VHS), 90 minutes.

Dombeck, M. March 1998. A gradual unfolding of a national purpose: A national resource agenda for the twenty-first century. Available online: http://www.fs.fed.us/news/agenda/sp30298.html. Statement of the Chief of the Forest Service, U.S. Department of Agriculture [21 November 2000].

Dood, A.R., R.P. Branno, and R.D. Mace. 1986. *Final Programmatic Environmental Impact Statement: The Grizzly Bear in Northwestern Montana.* Helena: Montana Department of Fish, Wildlife and Parks.

Dorrance, M.J., P.J. Savage, and D.E. Huff. 1978. Effects of snowmobiles on white-tailed deer. *Journal of Wildlife Management* 39(3): 563–569.

Draft Environmental Impact Statement for the Revised Land and Resource Management Plan, Rio Grande National Forest. 1995. U.S. Department of Agriculture, Forest Service.

Duck, T. 1978. The effects of off-road vehicles on vegetation in Dove Springs Canyon. In *The Physical, Biological, and Social Impacts of Off-Road Vehicles on the California Desert,* ed. K.H. Berry. Southern California Academy of Sciences Special Publication. Los Angeles: Southern California Academy of Sciences.

Duncan, D., and R. Maughan. 1978. Feet vs. ORVs: Are there social differences between backcountry users? *Journal of Forestry* 76(8): 478–480.

Dunning, H.C., ed. 1980. *The Public Trust Doctrine in Natural Resources Law and Management: Conference Proceedings.* Davis, CA: School of Law, University of California–Davis and University Extension, University of California–Davis.

Durbin, K. 1998. Land of the fee: The Forest Service says no pay no play. *Cascadia Times* September: 8–14.

Ebersberger, E. 1998. Roads and exotic plants, pests and pathogens. *Road-RIPorter* 3(1): 12–13.

Echevarria, J.D., and R.B. Eby, eds. 1995. *Let the People Judge: Wise Use and the Private Property Rights Movement.* Washington, D.C.: Island Press.

Eckert, R.E., M.K. Wood, W.H. Blackburn, and F.F. Peterson. 1979. Impacts of off-road vehicles on infiltration and sediment production of two desert soils. *Journal of Range Management* 32(5): 394–397.

Ecosystem Management: Annual Report of Forest Service. 1993. Washington, D.C.: U.S. Department of Agriculture, Forest Service.

Edge, R. 1936. *Roads and More Roads in the National Parks and National Forests.* Emergency Conservation Committee Publication No. 54. New York: Emergency Conservation Committee. 12 pp.

Edwards, R., and D. Burns. 1986. *Relationships among Fish Habitat Embeddedness, Geomorphology, Land Disturbing Activities, and the Payette National Forest Sediment Model.* McCall, ID: U.S. Department of Agriculture, Forest Service, Payette National Forest.

Elliot, W.J., C.H. Luce, R.B. Foltz, and T.E. Koler. 1996. Hydrologic and sedimentation effects of open and closed roads. *Natural Resource News* 6 (1): 7–8.

Fahrig, L., J.H. Pedlar, S.E. Pope, P.D. Taylor, and J.F. Wegner. 1995. Effect of road traffic on amphibian density. *Biological Conservation* 73: 177.

Farmer, A.M. 1993. The effects of dust on vegetation: A review. *Environmental Pollution* 79: 63–75.

Federal Land Policy and Management Act: An Interim Report, October 21, 1976 to June 30, 1977. 1977. Washington, D.C.: U.S. Department of the Interior, Bureau of Land Management.

Federal Lands Highway. Available online: wysiwyg://284/http://fhwa.dot.gov/flh/index.htm. U.S. Department of Transportation, Federal Highway Administration [16 August 2000].

Federal Lands Highway, Federal Lands Highway Programs. 11 July 2000. Available online: http://www.fhwa.dot.gov/flh/flhprog.htm. U.S. Department of Transportation, Federal Highway Administration [16 August 2000].

Federal Lands Highway Programs, emergency relief for federally owned roads. 11 July 2000. Available online: http://www.fhwa.dot.gov/flh/erfo.htm. U.S. Department of Transportation, Federal Highway Administration [16 August 2000].

Final Environmental Assessment and Land Protection Plan: Proposed Expansion of Pelican Island National Wildlife Refuge—Indian River and Brevard County, FL. 26 March 1991. Atlanta, GA: U.S. Department of the Interior, Fish and Wildlife Service, Southeast Region.

Final Recreational Off-Road Vehicle Management Plan Supplemental Environmental Impact Statement: Big Cypress National Preserve, Florida. July 2000. Ochopee, FL: U.S. Department of the Interior, National Park Service.

Findlay, C.S., and J. Bourdages. 2000. Response time of wetland biodiversity to road construction on adjacent lands. *Conservation Biology* 14: 86–94.

Fire Management Plan for Big Oaks National Wildlife Refuge, Madison, IN. March 2001. Washington, D.C.: U.S. Department of the Interior, Fish and Wildlife Service.

Forest Service makes final FY 2000 payments to states. Available online: http://www.fs.fed.us/news/2001/01/01jan18-FS-FINAL-FY2000-PAY-MENTS-TO-STATES.htm. U.S. Department of Agriculture, Forest Service [24 January 2001].

Forest Service Roadless Area Conservation: Draft Environmental Impact Statement Summary and Proposed Rule. May 2000. Washington, D.C.: U.S. Department of Agriculture, Forest Service.

Forest Service Roadless Area Conservation: Final Environmental Impact Statement. November 2000. Washington, D.C.: U.S. Department of Agriculture, Forest Service.

Forest transportation system notice of final administrative policy. Available online: http://www.fs.fed.us/new/roads/01_03_01_FINAL_disk_ROAD_MGMT_POLICY_NOTICE.pdf. U.S. Department of Agriculture, Forest Service, RIN 0596-AB67 [20 June 2001].

Forman, R.T.T. 2000. Estimate of the area affected ecologically by the road system in the United States. *Conservation Biology* 14: 31–35.

Forman, R.T.T., and L.E. Alexander. 1998. Roads and their major ecological effects. *Annual Review of Ecology and Systematics* 29: 207–231.

Freddy, D.J., W.M. Bronaugh, and M.C. Fowler. 1986. Responses of mule deer to disturbance by persons afoot and snowmobiles. *Wildlife Society Bulletin* 14: 63–68.

Frequently asked questions about the National Park Service. Available online: http://www.nps.gov/pub_aff/e-mail/faqs.htm. U.S. Department of the Interior, National Park Service [21 February 2001].

Fulfilling the Promise: The National Wildlife Refuge System. 22 March 1999. Washington, D.C.: U.S. Department of Interior, Fish and Wildlife Service, National Wildlife Refuge System.

Fuller, W.E. 1964. *RFD: The Changing Face of Rural America.* Bloomington: Indiana University Press.

Futuristic snowmobiles take off in Yellowstone on test run. 2000. *Missoulian* (AP) 23 December: B-3.

Garrity, M. 1996. Economic analysis of the conservation biology alternative for grizzly bear restoration in the Salmon–Selway region. In *The Conservation Biology Alternative for Grizzly Bear Population Restoration in the Greater Salmon–Selway Region of Central Idaho and Western Montana,* ed. M. Bader and T. Bechtold, pp. 19–26. Special Report No. 8. Missoula, MT: Alliance for the Wild Rockies.

Gelbard, J. 2000. Roads as conduits for exotic plant invasions. Presented at the Society of Conservation Biology annual meeting, June 5, Missoula, Montana.

Gibbs, J.P. 1998. Amphibian movements in response to forest edges, roads, and streambeds in southern New England. *Journal of Wildlife Management* 62: 584–589.

Gilligan, J.P. 1953. The development of policy and administration of Forest Service Primitive and Wilderness Areas in the western United States. Ph.D. diss., University of Michigan.

Glover, J. 1986. *A Wilderness Original: The Life of Bob Marshall.* Seattle: The Mountaineers.

Godfrey-Smith, W. 1979. The value of wilderness. *Environmental Ethics* 1(4): 309–319.

Goodstein, E.B. 1994. *Jobs and the Environment: The Myth of a National Trade-Off.* Washington, D.C.: Economic Policy Institute.

Graves, H.S. 1920. A crisis in national recreation. *American Forestry* 26 (July): 391–400.

Greenwalt, L.A. 1991. The power and potential of the act. In *Balancing on the Brink of Extinction: The Endangered Species Act and Lessons for the Future,* ed. K. Kohm, 31–36. Washington, D.C.: Island Press.

Grizzly Bear Recovery Plan. 1993. Missoula, MT: U.S. Department of the Interior, Fish and Wildlife Service.

Grove, N. 1984. *Wildlands for Wildlife: America's National Refuges.* Washington, D.C.: National Geographic Society.

A Guide for Road Closure and Obliteration in the Forest Service. June 1996. San Dimas, CA: U.S. Department of Agriculture, Forest Service, Technology and Development Program, 49 pp.

Gutfreund, O.D. 1998. Twentieth-century sprawl: Accommodating the automobile and the decentralization of the United States. Ph.D. diss., Columbia University.

Hagen, A., and A. Langeland. 1973. Polluted snow in southern Norway and the effect of the meltwater on freshwater and aquatic organisms. *Environmental Pollution* 5(1): 45–57.

Hammer, K.J. 1986. An on-site study of the effectiveness of the U.S. Forest Service road closure program in Management Situation One Grizzly Bear Habitat, Swan Lake Ranger District, Flathead National Forest, Montana. Unpublished report. Kalispell, MT: Swan View Coalition.

———. 1995. *The Road Ripper's Guide to National Forests.* Houghton, MI: ROAD-RIP (now Missoula, MT: Wildlands Center for Preventing Roads).

Hammitt, W.E., and D.N. Cole. 1987. *Wildland Recreation: Ecology and Management.* New York: John Wiley and Sons.

Harper, K.T., and J.R. Marble. 1988. A role for nonvascular plants in management of arid and semiarid rangelands. In *Vegetational Sciences Applications for Rangeland Analysis and Management,* ed. P.T. Tueller, 135–169. Netherlands: Kluwer Academic.

Harte, J., and E. Hoffman. 1989. Possible effects of acidic deposition on a Rocky Mountain population of tiger salamander *Ambystoma tigrinum. Conservation Biology* 3(2): 149–158.

Haskell, D.G. 2000. Effects of forest roads on macroinvertebrate soil fauna of the southern Appalachian Mountains. *Conservation Biology* 14(1): 59–61.

Havlick, D.G. 1999. Closing forest roads for habitat protection: A northern Rockies case study. In *Proceedings of the Third International Conference on Wildlife Ecology and Transportation,* ed. G.L. Evink, P. Garrett, and D. Zeigler, 327–330. FL-ER-73-99. Tallahassee: Florida Department of Transportation.

Hebert, H.J. 2000. Firefighting bill nears $1 billion. *Missoulian* 31 August: A-2.

Hegman, Skip. 11 December 1989. *The Location, Design, Construction and Reclamation of Low Volume Roads.* Missoula, MT: Lolo National Forest.

Helvarg, D. 1994. *The War against the Greens: The "Wise Use" Movement, the New Right, and Anti-environmental Violence.* San Francisco: Sierra Club Books.

Hines, T.D., and R.M. Case. 1991. Diet, home range, movements, and activity periods of swift fox in Nebraska. *Prairie Naturalist* 23: 131–138.

Hoffman, D.J., W.C. Eastin, Jr., and M.L. Gay. 1982. Embryotoxic and biochemical effects of waste crankcase oil on birds' eggs. *Toxicology and Applied Pharmacology* 63: 230–241.

Horejsi, B.L. 1981. Behavioral response of barren ground caribou to a moving vehicle. *Arctic* 34: 180–185.

Horejsi, B.L., B.K. Gilbert, and F.L. Craighead. 1998. *British Columbia's Grizzly Bear Conservation Strategy: An Independent Review of Science and Policy.* Calgary, Alberta: Western Wildlife Consulting, Ltd.

House legislation: The National Forest Protection and Restoration Act (HR 1396). Available online: http://www.house.gov/mckinney/hl/nfppa.htm [21 February 2001].

Hoyt, H.M., Jr. 1966. The good roads movement in Oregon: 1900–1920. Ph.D. diss., University of Oregon.

Hynes, H.B.N. 1970. *The Ecology of Running Waters.* Toronto, Ontario: University of Toronto Press.

Ingersoll, G., J. Turk, C. McClure, S. Lawlor, D. Clow, and A. Mast. 1997. Snowpack chemistry as an indicator of pollutant emission levels from motorized winter vehicles in Yellowstone National Park. In *Proceedings Western Snow Conference,* 103–113, Banff, Alberta.

Interim Rule Suspending Road Construction in Unroaded Areas of National Forest System Land, Environmental Assessment. March 1999. Washington, D.C.: U.S. Department of Agriculture, Forest Service.

Israelsen, B. 1999. Newly carved "road" will be a trail again. *Salt Lake City Tribune* 1 October: B-1.

Iverson, R.M., B.S. Hinckley, R.M. Webb, and B. Hallet. 1981. Physical effects of vehicular disturbances on arid landscapes. *Science* 212: 915–917.

Jackson, T.W. 1952. *Wagon Roads West: A Study of Federal Road Surveys and Construction in the Trans-Mississippi West, 1846–1869.* Berkeley: University of California Press.

Jamison, M. 2000. National Park Service makes resource protection top priority. *Missoulian* 6 December: A-1, A-7.

Jawetz, S.M. 1982. The public trust totem in public land law: Ineffective—and undesirable—judicial intervention. *Ecology Law Quarterly* 10: 455.

Jenkins, K. 1996. *Texas Department of Transportation Wildlife Activities.* Florida DOT Report, RL-ER-58-96, 199–231. Tallahassee: Florida Department of Transportation.

Johansen, J.R. 1993. Cryptogamic crusts of semiarid and arid lands of North America. *Journal of Phycology* 29: 140–147.

Jones, J.A., and G.E. Grant. 1996. Peak flow responses to clear-cutting and roads in small and large basins, western Cascades, Oregon. *Water Resources Research* 32: 959–974.

Katz, E. 1979. Utilitarianism and preservation. *Environmental Ethics* 1(4): 357–364.

Kay, J. and students. 1981. Evaluating environmental impacts of off-road vehicles. *Journal of Geography* 80(1): 10–18.

Knopp, T.B., and J.D. Tyger. 1973. A study of conflict in recreational land use: Snowmobiling vs. ski-touring. *Journal of Leisure Research* 5(3): 6–17.

Knott, J.M. 1980. Reconnaissance assessment of erosion and sedimentation in the Cañada de los Alamos Basin, Los Angeles and Ventura Counties, California. U.S. Geological Survey Water-Supply Paper 2061, 1–26. Washington, D.C.: U.S. Government Printing Office.

Kolman, J. 2000. No ban yet on snowmobiles at Yellowstone. *Missoulian* 28 April: A-1, A-6.

Krutch, J.W. 1957. Which men? What needs? *American Forests* 63 (April): 20–23, 44–46.

Kushlen, J.A. 1988. Conservation and management of the American crocodile. *Environmental Management* 12(6): 777–790.

Lacey, C.A., J.R. Lacey, P.K. Fay, J.M. Story, and D.L. Zamora. 1997. *Controlling Knapweed on Montana Rangeland.* Montana State University Extension Service Circular 311.

Laitos, J.G., and T.A. Carr. 1999. The transformation on public lands. *Ecology Law Quarterly* 26(2): 140–242.

Laughlin, A., and J. Caudill. July 1997. *Banking on Nature: The Economic Benefits to Local Communities of National Wildlife Refuge Visitation.* Washington, D.C.: U.S. Department of the Interior, Fish and Wildlife Service, Division of Economics.

Lazon, G. 1969. The thrill killers. *American Forests* 75 (May): 6–7, 36.

Legislative update. 1998. *Road-RIPorter* 3(4): 6.

Leopold, A. 1949. *A Sand County Almanac, and Sketches Here and There.* 1970 reprint. London: Oxford University Press.

Lessig, C.T. 1997. Automobility and social change: Mississippi, 1909–1939. Ph.D. diss., University of Mississippi.

Lichatowich, J. 1999. *Salmon without Rivers: A History of the Pacific Salmon Crisis.* Washington, D.C.: Island Press.

Liddle, M.J. 1975. A selective review of the ecological effects of human trampling on natural ecosystems. *Biological Conservation* 7(1): 17–36.

Liebhold, A.M., W.L. MacDonald, D. Bergdahl, and V.C. Mastro. 1995. *Invasion by Exotic Forest Pests: A Threat to Forest Ecosystems.* Forest Science Monograph. Wshington, D.C.: Society of American Foresters.

Line, L. 1995. A system under siege. *Wilderness* 59: 10–17.

Lodico, N.J. 1973. *Environmental Effects of Off-Road Vehicles: A Review of the Literature.* Washington, D.C.: U.S. Department of the Interior, Research Services Branch, Office of Library Services Bibliographic Series No. 29, 111 pp.

Loos, G., and P. Kerlinger. 1993. Road mortality of saw-whet and screech owls on the Cape May Peninsula. *Journal of Raptor Research* 27(4): 210–213.

Lopez, B. 1990. *The Rediscovery of North America.* New York: Vintage.

Luckenbach, R.A. 1978. Impacts of ORVs: An analysis of off-road vehicle use on desert avifaunas. *Transactions of North American Wildlife Natural Resources Conference* 43:157–162.

Lutz, C., and R. Morrison. 2000. Gentlemen, stop your engines! *High Country News* 10 April. Available online: http://www.hcn.org/servlets/hcn.Article?article_id=5692 [1 November 2001].

Lyon, L.J. 1983. Road density model describing habitat effectiveness for elk. *Journal of Forestry* 81(9): 592–595.

MacArthur, R.H., and E.O. Wilson. 1967. *The Theory of Island Biogeography.* Monographs in Population Biology I. Princeton, NJ: Princeton University Press.

Mader, H.J. 1984. Animal habitat isolation by roads and agricultural fields. *Biological Conservation* 29: 85–86.

Marchand, Peter J. 1987. *Life in the Cold: An Introduction to Winter Ecology.* Hanover, NH: University Press of New England.

McClelland, D.E., R.B. Foltz, W.D. Wilson, T.W. Cundy, C.M. Falter, C. Rahe, R. Heinemann, J.A. Sauerbier, and B. Schuster. 1997. *Draft Assessment of the Effects of the 1995 and 1996 Flood on the Clearwater National Forest: A Report to the Regional Forester.* Missoula, MT: U.S. Department of Agriculture, Forest Service, Northern Region.

McMillion, S. 2000. At least five grizzlies mistakenly killed by black bear hunters. *Bozeman Daily Chronicle* 17 June: A-1, A-8.

Mech, L.D. 1989. Wolf population survival in an area of high road density. *American Midland Naturalist* 121: 387–389.

Mech, L.D., S.H. Fritts, G.L. Raddie, and W.J. Paule. 1988. Wolf distribution and road density in Minnesota. *Wildlife Society Bulletin* 16: 85–87.

Megahan, W.F. 1980. *Effects of Silvicultural Practices on Erosion and Sedimentation in the Interior West: A Case for Sediment Budgeting.* Boise, ID: U.S. Department of Agriculture, Forest Service, Intermountain Forest and Range Experiment Station.

Megahan, W.F., and W.J. Kidd. 1972. Effects of logging and logging roads on erosion and sediment deposition from steep terrain. *Journal of Forestry* 70(3): 136–141.

——. 1972. Effects of logging roads on sediment production rates in the Idaho batholith. Research Paper INT-123. Ogden, UT: U.S. Department of Agriculture, Forest Service, Intermountain Forest and Range Experiment Station.

Meine, Curt. 1988. *Aldo Leopold: His Life and Work*. Madison: University of Wisconsin Press.

Memorandum from Secretary of the Interior Donald Hodel to Assistant Secretaries, Subject: Departmental Policy on Section 8 of the Act of July 26, 1866, Revised Statute 2477 (Repealed), Grant of Right-of-Way for Public Highways (RS-2477). 1988. Available online: http://rs2477.roads.com/2hodel.htm [27 January 2001].

Merrill, Perry H. 1981.*Roosevelt's Forest Army: A History of the Civilian Conservation Corps 1933–1942*. Montpelier, VT: Perry Merrill.

Mider, Zachary. 2000. Kicking and screaming in Nevada. *High Country News* 31 July. Available online: http://www.hcn.org/servlets/hcn.Article?article_id=5890 [1 November 2001].

Milstein, M. 1993. Roads to Ruin. *National Parks* September/October: 29–33.

Minbashian, J. 2000. Reclaiming the concept of restoration. *Road-RIPorter* 5(4): 1, 4–5.

Mitchell, A. 1997. Parkway and politics: Class, culture, and tourism in the Blue Ridge. Ph.D. diss., University of North Carolina–Chapel Hill.

Moen, A.N., S. Whittemore, and B. Buxton. 1982. Effects of disturbance by snowmobiles on heart rate of captive white-tailed deer. *New York Fish and Game Journal* 29(2): 176–183.

Moen, Bob. 1999. Yellowstone sewage system overwhelmed. *Missoulian* 11 July: B-5.

Montana Off-Highway Vehicle Program, Project Application and Grant Program Information. 1998. Helena: Montana Department of Fish, Wildlife and Parks.

Montana Trail Users Survey. August 1994. University of Montana Institute for Tourism and Recreation Research.

Montgomery, D.R. 1994. Road surface drainage, channel initiation, and slope instability. *Water Resources Research* 30(6): 1925–1932.

Morrison, P.H., J.W. Karl, L. Swope, K. Harma, T. Allen, P. Becwar, and B. Sabold. 16 September 2000. Assessment of summer 2000 wildfires: History, current condition and ownership. Pacific Biodiversity Institute. Available online: http://www.pacificbio.org/Projects/fires2000/fire2000.htm [24 January 2001].

Motto, H.L., R.H. Daines, D.H. Chilko, and C.K. Motto. 1970. Lead in soils and plants: Its relationship to traffic volume and proximity to highways. *Environmental Science and Technology* 4(3): 231–238.

Murdoch, T., and M. Cheo with K. O'Laughlin. 1991. *Streamkeeper's Field Guide: Watershed Inventory and Stream Monitoring Methods*. Everett, WA: Adopt-a-Stream Foundation.

Nash, R. 1967. *Wilderness and the American Mind*. 1982. 3rd ed. New Haven, CT: Yale University Press.

National forest system facts. Available online: http://www.fs.fed.us/news/roads/factsheet.shtml [18 July 2000].

National Forests for All Uses . . . Keeping Natural Resource Quality . . . Building the Right Road. 1986. U.S. Department of Agriculture, Forest Service, Eastern Region.

National Management Strategy for Motorized Off-Highway Vehicle Use on Public Lands. January 2001. Washington, D.C.: U.S. Department of the Interior, Bureau of Land Management.

National Wildlife Refuge System Improvement Act of 1997 fact sheet. January 1999. U.S. Department of the Interior, Fish and Wildlife Service, Division of Refuges, Arlington, VA.

Neumann, P.W., and H.G. Merriam. 1972. Ecological effects of snowmobiles. *Canadian Field Naturalist* 86: 207–212.

Nez Perce Tribe: Ensuring Our Future Honoring Our Past. Undated publication. Lapwai, ID: Nez Perce Tribe.

Nijhuis, M. 1998. A county in Nevada assaults a river. *High Country News* 14 September. Available online: http://www.hcn.org/servlets/hcn.Article?article_id=4434 [1 November 2001].

1999 Status of the Nation's Highways, Bridges and Transit: Conditions and Performance, Report to Congress. Appendix E: Condition and Performance of the Transportation System Serving Federal and Indian Lands, ppE-1–E-15. Washington, D.C.: U.S. Department of Transportation, Federal Highway Administration, Federal Transit Administration.

Nixon, R.M. August 1970. *Environmental Quality: The First Annual Report of the Council on Environmental Quality.* Washington, D.C.: U.S. Government Printing Office.

Norling, B.S., S.H. Anderson, and W.A. Hubert. 1992. Roost sites used by sandhill crane staging along the Platte River, Nebraska. *Great Basin Naturalist* 52(3): 253–261.

North Fork Boise River watershed inventory. 1998. Unpublished report. Bozeman, MT: Roads Scholar Project, Predator Project (now Predator Conservation Alliance).

Noss, R.F. 1995. *The Ecological Effects of Roads, or the Road to Destruction: Road Ripper's Handbook.* Missoula, MT: Wildlands CPR .

Noss, R.F., H.B. Quigley, M.G. Hornocker, T. Merrill, and P.C. Pacquet. 1996. Conservation biology and carnivore conservation in the Rocky Mountains. *Conservation Biology* 10: 949–963.

Off-Highway Vehicle Environmental Impact Statement and Proposed Plan Amendment for Montana, North Dakota, and Portions of South Dakota. January 2001. Missoula, MT: U.S. Department of the Interior, Bureau of Land Management Montana State Office and U.S. Department of Agriculture, Forest Service Northern Region.

Off-Highway Vehicle Record of Decision and Plan Amendment for Montana, North Dakota, and Portions of South Dakota. January 2001. Missoula, MT: U.S. Department of Agriculture, Forest Service Northern Region.

Off-Road Montana! A Summary of OHV Laws, Regulations, and Tips for Responsible Off-Roading. Undated pamphlet. Helena, MT: Montana Fish, Wildlife and Parks.

Off-Road Recreation Vehicles: U.S. Department of the Interior Task Force Study. 1971. Washington, D.C.: U.S. Department of the Interior.

Olsen, J. 1970. Bad show out in the snow. *Sports Illustrated* 16 March: 28–35.

Oregon: Siuslaw NF closing roads. 1997. *Road-RIPorter* 2(3): 8.

ORV ban may aid plovers. 1989. *Environment* 31(1): 23.

Oxley, D.J., M.B. Fenton, and G.R. Carmody. 1974. The effects of roads on populations of small mammals. *Journal of Applied Ecology* 11: 57.

Palmer, C. 1997. *Environmental Ethics.* Santa Barbara, CA: ABC-CLIO.

Parks, forests, and public property. 2000. *Code of Federal Regulations* 36 CFR §219.19, 36 parts 200 to 299, revised as of 1 July 2000 p. 79.

Payne, J.F., and I. Martins. 1978. Crankcase oils: Are they a major mutagenic burden in the aquatic environment? *Science* 200 (21 April): 329–330.

Pease, C.M., and D.J. Mattson. 1999. Demography of the Yellowstone bears. *Ecology* 80(3): 957–975.

Perry, D.A. 1988. Landscape pattern and forest pests. *Northwest Environmental Journal* 4(2): 213–228.

Perry, D.B. 1995. *Bike Cult: The Ultimate Guide to Human-Powered Vehicles.* New York: Four Walls and Eight Windows.

Pinchot, G. 1947. *Breaking New Ground.* New York: Harcourt Brace Jovanovich. Reprinted 1972 edition, Seattle: University of Washington Press.

Platt, T.M. 1993. Cabinet-Yaak grizzly bear ecosystem: 1992 Forest Service road closure program compliance inventory. Unpublished report. Missoula, MT: Alliance for the Wild Rockies.

Poet, A. 2001. Blue Ribbon Coalition: Big corporate dollars. *Home Range* 11(2): 18.

Policies and issue summaries. Available online: http://www.funoutdoors.com/policy.html [20 June 2001].

Poll: Most Montanans support roadless plan. 2000. *Missoulian* (AP) 31 March: A-4.

Power, T. 1988. *The Economic Pursuit of Quality.* New York: M.E. Sharpe.

———. 1995. The economics of Wilderness preservation in Utah. Testimony for the U.S. House of Representatives, Committee on Resources and the Environment. *Southern Utah Wilderness Alliance Newsletter* [insert] 1995 (winter): 1–8.

———. 1996. *Environmental Protection and Economic Well-Being: The Economic Pursuit of Quality.* New York: M.E. Sharpe.

Preston, H.L. 1991. *Dirt Roads to Dixie: Accessibility and Modernization in the South, 1885–1935.* Knoxville: University of Tennessee Press.

Primack, M. 1992. The plovers' paradise. *Sanctuary* 31(6): 9–10.

Profiles: Oh, hawk of mercy! 1948. *New Yorker* 17 April: 31–45.

Project file for West Fork Squaw Creek road obliteration (subsequently renamed West Fork Waw'aatamnima [Fishing Creek]), viewed at Clearwater Forest Supervisor's Office, Orofino, ID, 29 March 2001.

Promoting Ecological Restoration to the World as a Science, Art, and Conservation Strategy. 21 September 2000. Pamphlet. Tucson, AZ: Society for Ecological Restoration.

Proposed Rules, Revised Statute 2477 Rights-of-Way, 43 U.S.C. §932 (RS-2477). 1994. As cited in *Federal Register* 59, no.146 (1 August): 39,216.

Public Land Statistics. Annual reports from 1949 to 1999. Washington, D.C.: U.S. Department of the Interior, Bureau of Land Management.

Public rewards from Public Lands 2000. Available online: http://www.blm.gov. nhp/pubs/rewards/2000/letter.htm [21 February 2001].

Purdy, P. 2001. Our scarred land: Monitoring ORVs not an easy job. *Denver Post* 11 February: G-1. Also available online: http://63.147.65.175/opinion/purdy0211.htm [1 November 2001].

Quammen, D. 1996. *The Song of the Dodo: Island Biogeography in an Age of Extinctions.* New York: Simon and Schuster.

Quigley, T.M., and H. B. Cole. May 1997. *Aquatic Strongholds and Areas of Predicted Foad Density: Highlighted Scientific Findings of the Interior Columbia Basin Ecosystem Management Project.* Portland, OR: U.S. Department of Agriculture, Forest Service, Pacific Northwest Research Station, General Technical Report, PNW-GTR-404; U.S. Department of the Interior, Bureau of Land Management. 34 pp.

Rae, J.B. 1965. *The American Automobile: A Brief History.* Chicago: University of Chicago Press.

Recreation agenda, The. September 2000. Available online: http://www.fs.fed.us/ recreation/recstrategy/rec_agenda_pm_pdf [21 November 2000].

Recreation, heritage and wilderness resources. Available online: http://www.fs. fed.us/recreation/fee_demo/fee_intro.shtml. U.S. Department of Agriculture, Forest Service [15 February 2000].

Recreation trail damage memo. 3 November 1998. Athens Ranger District, Wayne National Forest, Ohio.

Recreational Fee Demonstration Project: Progress report to Congress, fiscal year 1999. 31 January 2000. Available online: http://www.doi.gov/nrl/Recfees/ 2000R/2000Report.html. U.S. Department of the Interior and U.S. Department of Agriculture [15 February 2000].

Redwood National and State Parks. Available online: http://www.nps.gov/redw. U.S. Department of the Interior, National Park Service [13 December 2000].

Reed, R.A., J. Johnson-Barnard, and W.L. Baker. 1996. The contribution of roads to forest fragmentation in the Rocky Mountains. *Conservation Biology* 10: 1,098–1,106.

Refuge Roads Home Page, Scope of Improvements, U.S. Fish and Wildlife Service factsheet. Available online: http://bluegoose.arw.r9.fws.gov/roads/guidance/improvements.html [16 August 2000].

Report of the Chief. 1932, 1935, 1939, 1942, 1946, 1952, 1956, 1966, 1969. Washington, DC: U.S. Department of Agriculture, Forest Service.

Report of the Forest Service. 1985. Washington, D.C.: U.S. Department of Agriculture, Forest Service.

Report of the Forest Service. 1998. Washington, D.C.: U.S. Department of Agriculture, Forest Service.

Report to Congress on RS 2477: The History and Management of RS 2477 Right-of-Way

Claims on Federal and Other Lands. June 1993. Washington, D.C.: U.S. Department of the Interior. 55 pp.

Rich, A.C., D.S. Dobkin, and L.J. Niles. 1994. Defining forest fragmentation by corridor width: The influence of narrow forest-dividing corridors on forest-nesting birds in southern New Jersey. *Conservation Biology* 8: 1,109–1,121.

Richens, V.B., and G.R. Lavigne. 1978. Response of white-tailed deer to snowmobiles and snowmobile trails in Maine. *Canadian Field-Naturalist* 92: 334–344.

Riebsame, William. 1997. *Atlas of the New West: Portrait of a Changing Region.* NY: W.W. Norton.

Rieman, B.E., and J.D. McIntyre. 1993. *Demographic and Habitat Requirements for Conservation of Bull Trout.* Ogden, UT: U.S. Department of Agriculture, Forest Service, Intermountain Research Station and U.S. Department of the Interior, Fish and Wildlife Service.

Riley, L., and W. Riley. 1979. *Guide to the National Wildlife Refuges.* Garden City, NY: Anchor Press.

Riley, S.J. 1984. Effect of clearing and roading operations on the permeability of forest soils, Karuah Catchment, New South Wales, Australia. *Forest Ecology and Management* 9: 283–293.

Roaded Lands, Eroded Habitats: Findings and Implications of the Roads Scholar Project, 1994–1997. April 1999. Bozeman, MT: Predator Project (now Predator Conservation Alliance). 16 pp.

Roads in the National Forests. May 1988. Washington, D.C.: U.S. Department of Agriculture, Forest Service.

Roads in the Rocky Mountain Region. 1988. Washington, D.C.: U.S. Department of Agriculture, Forest Service.

Roaring from the past: Off-road vehicles on America's national forests. 1999. Available online: http://www.wildlandscpr.org/WCPRpdfs/RoaringFrom Past.pdf. Missoula, MT: Wildlands Center for Preventing Roads [1 November 2000].

Rolston, H. III. 1991. Life in jeopardy on private property. In *Balancing on the Brink of Extinction: The Endangered Species Act and Lessons for the Future,* ed. K. Kohm, pp. 43–61. Washington, D.C.: Island Press.

———. 1994. *Conserving Natural Value.* New York: Columbia University Press.

Romin, L.A., and J.A. Bissonette. 1996. Deer–vehicle collisions: Status of state monitoring activities and mitigation efforts. *Wildlife Society Bulletin* 24(2): 276–283.

———. 1996. Temporal and spatial distribution of highway mortality of mule deer in newly constructed roads at Jordanelle Reservoir, Utah. *Great Basin Naturalist* 56: 1–11.

Rosen, P.C., and C.H. Lowe. 1994. Highway mortality of snakes in the Sonoran Desert of southern Arizona. *Biological Conservation* 68: 143–148.

Rosenberg, K. 1994. *Wilderness Preservation: A Reference Handbook.* Santa Barbara, CA: ABC-CLIO.

Rost, G.R., and J.A. Bailey. 1982. Distribution of mule deer and elk in relation to roads. *Journal of Wildlife Management* 43(3): 634–641.

Rothman, H.K. 1989. A regular ding-dong fight: Agency culture and evolution in the NPS-USFS dispute, 1916–1937. *Western History Quarterly* 20 (May): 141–161.

RS 2477 bill would permit rampant roading. 1995. *Road-RIPorter* 1(1): 1–6.

Runte, A. 1984. *Trains of Discovery: Western Railroads and the National Parks.* Flagstaff, AZ: Northland Press.

——. 1987. *National Parks: The American Experience.* 2nd ed. Lincoln: University of Nebraska Press.

——. 1991. *Public Lands, Public Heritage: The National Forest Idea.* Niwot, CO: Roberts Rinehart in cooperation with the Buffalo Bill Historical Center.

Sax, J.L. 1970. *Defending the Environment.* New York: Knopf.

——. 1970. The public trust doctrine in natural resource law: Effective judicial intervention. *Michigan Law Review* 68: 473–566.

——. 1980. Liberating the public trust from its historical shackles. *University of California Davis Law Review* (winter): 185–194.

——. 1980. *Mountains without Handrails: Reflections on the National Parks.* Ann Arbor: University of Michigan Press.

Schmid, W.D. 1971. Modifications of the sub-nivean microclimate by snowmobiles. In *Proceedings of the Snow and Ice Symposium,* 251–257. Ames, IA: Iowa Cooperative Wildlife Research Unit, Iowa State University, Bureau of Sports Fisheries and Wildlife (Region 3).

Schubert, D.J. 1999. Petition to enhance and expand regulations governing the administration of recreational off-road vehicle use on national forests, submitted to U.S. Forest Service, 8 December 1999, on behalf of Wildlands Center for Preventing Roads and The Wilderness Society, with many other groups. Glendale, AZ: Schubert and Associates. Available online: http://wildrockies.org/WCPR/ [15 December 1999].

Sellars, R.W. 1997. *Preserving Nature in the National Parks: A History.* New Haven, CT: Yale University Press.

Seney, J.P. 1991. Erosional impact of hikers, horses, off-road bicycles, and motorcycles on mountain trails. Master's thesis, Montana State University.

Settlement reached in Pikes Peak suit. 15 April 1999. Available online: http://www.cnn.com/NATURE/9904/15/pikes.peak.cnn/ [1 June 2001].

Shaffer, M.S. 1998. Negotiating national identity: Western tourism and "See America First." In *Reopening the American West,* ed. H.K. Rothman, 122–151. Tucson: University of Arizona Press.

Shankland, R. 1951. *Steve Mather of the National Parks.* New York: Alfred Knopf.

Sheridan, D. 1979. *Off-Road Vehicles on Public Land.* Washington, D.C.: Council on Environmental Quality, U.S. Government Printing Office.

Show, S.B., C.A. Abell, R.L. Deering, and P.D. Hanson. 1941. A planning basis for adequate fire control on the southern Californian national forests. *Fire Control Notes* 5(1): 1–59.

Silent Majority: Public Attitudes toward Trail Use on the Gallatin National Forest. 1999. Bozeman, MT: Predator Project (now Predator Conservation Alliance). Available
online: http://www.predatorconservation.org/%20Media/PDF%20Files/The-
SilentMajority.pdf [29 October 2001].

Silver, S. 1997. From chainsaws to chassis: Motorizing the public lands. *Road-
RIPorter* 2(6): 1, 4.

Singer, P. 1974. All animals are equal. *Philosophia Exchange* 1(5): 213–257.

Slaughter, C.W., C.H. Racine, D.A. Walker, L.A. Johnson, and G. Abele. 1990.
Use of off-road vehicles and mitigation of effects in Alaska permafrost environments: A review. *Environmental Management* 14(1): 63–72.

Snook Fussell, L.M. 1997. Exposure of snowmobile riders to carbon monoxide.
Park Science 17(1): 1.

Snook, L.M. 1996. An investigation of driver exposure to carbon monoxide while
traveling in the wake of a snowmobile. Ph.D. diss., University of Tennessee,
Knoxville.

Snowmobilers seek legislative solution to access issues in Alaska's Denali National
Park. 31 May 2001. Available online: http://www.snowmobile.org/denali-
park.htm. Press Release, International Snowmobile Manufacturers Association [20 June 2001].

Snowmobiles will be tested in Yellowstone. 2000. *Missoulian* (AP) 15 January: A-2.

Soulé, M. 2000. Plenary session address, Annual Meeting of the Society for Conservation Biology, June 5–9, Missoula, MT.

South Rim transit. Available online: http://www.nps.gov/grca/transit/southrim.htm.
U.S. Department of the Interior, National Park Service [16 December 2000].

Sovada, M.A., C.C. Roy, and R.O. Woodward. 1998. Swift fox mortality in
grassland and cropland landscapes of western Kansas. In U.S. Geological Survey, Swift Fox Symposium: Ecology and conservation of Swift
foxes in a changing world. 18–19 February, Saskatoon, Saskatchewan,
Canada.

Spreiter, T.A., J.F. Franke, and D.L. Steensen. 1997. Disturbed lands restoration:
The Redwood experience. Paper presented at Annual Meeting of the Society
for Conservation Biology, 8 June, Victoria, BC, Canada.

Statewide Comprehensive Outdoor Recreation Plan. August 1994. Helena, MT: Montana Department of Fish, Wildlife and Parks.

Statistical Abstract of the United States 1998. 1998. Washington, D.C.: U.S. Department of Commerce, Economics and Statistics Administration, Bureau of the
Census.

Statistical Abstract of the United States 1999. 1999. Washington, D.C.: U.S. Department
of Commerce, Economics and Statistics Administration, Bureau of the Census.

Stebbins, R.C. 1974. Off-road vehicles and the fragile desert. Part 1, Part 2. *American Biology Teacher* 36(4): 203–208, 294–304.

Steen, H.K. 1976. *The U.S. Forest Service: A History.* Seattle: University of Washington Press.

Stone, C. 1972. Should trees have standing? Toward legal rights for natural objects. *Southern California Law Review* 45(2): 450–501.

——. 1987. *Earth and Other Ethics: The Case for Moral Pluralism.* NY: Harper & Row.

Stotter, D. 1996. *The Road-Ripper's Guide to the Bureau of Land Management.* Houghton, MI: ROAD-RIP (now Missoula, MT: Wildlands Center for Preventing Roads).

Strategic plan for Redwood National and State Parks: FY 2001–2005. Available online: http://www.nps.gov/redw/strategic_plan.html. U.S. Department of the Interior, National Park Service, Redwood National Park [13 December 2000].

Sumner, F. 1920. The need for a more serious effort to rescue a few fragments of vanishing nature. *Scientific Monthly* 10 (March): 236–248.

Sutter, P.S. 1997. Driven wild: The intellectual and cultural origins of wilderness advocacy during the interwar years (Aldo Leopold, Robert Sterling Yard, Benton MacKaye, Bob Marshall). Ph.D. diss., University of Kansas.

——. 1998. "A blank spot on the map": Aldo Leopold, wilderness, and U.S. Forest Service recreational policy, 1909–1924. *Western Historical Quarterly* 29 (summer): 187–214.

Swanson, C.S., and J.B. Loomis. March 1996. *Role of Nonmarket Economic Values in Benefit–Cost Analysis of Public Forest Management.* Portland, OR: U.S. Department of Agriculture, Forest Service, Pacific Northwest Research Station, General Technical Report, PNW-GTR-361. 32 pp.

Swihart, R.K., and N.A. Slade. 1984. Road crossing in *Sigmodon hispidus* and *Microtus ochrogaster. Journal of Mammology* 65(2): 357–360.

Table 54—Number of paid employees by occupational category for fiscal years 1992–1996. Available online: http://www.fs.fed.us/pl/pdb/96report/table54.html. U.S. Department of Agriculture, Forest Service [21 February 2001].

Tahoe Research Group. 26 February 1997. *Use of 2-Cycle Engine Watercraft on Lake Tahoe: Water Quality and Limnological Considerations.* Davis, CA: University of California–Davis.

Taylor, G.R. 1951. *The Transportation Revolution, 1815–1860.* New York: Rinehart.

TEA-21 fact sheet—Recreational Trails Program. Available online: http://www.fhwa.dot.gov/tea21/factsheets/rec-trl.htm. U.S. Department of Transportation, Federal Highway Administration [13 February 2000].

Thiel, R.P. 1985. Relationship between road densities and wolf habitat suitability in Wisconsin. *American Midland Naturalist* 113: 404–407.

Thompson, P.B. 1998. *Agricultural Ethics: Research, Teaching, and Public Policy.* Ames: Iowa State University Press.

Trails Management Handbook, R-1 Supplement. 10 January 1991. Forest Service Handbook 2309.18-90-1. Missoula, MT: U.S. Department of Agriculture, Forest Service.

Transportation Equity Act for the 21st Century: A Summary. 1998. U.S. Department of Transportation Publication No. FHWA-PL 98-038. Washington, D.C.: U.S. Department of Transportation.

Trombulak, S.C., and C.A. Frissell. 2000. Review of ecological effects of roads on terrestrial and aquatic communities. *Conservation Biology* 14(1): 18–30.

United States District Court, Western District of Washington at Seattle. 1996. *Washington Trails Association, et al. v. United States Forest Service, et al.* Filed 12 June 1996. Intervener-Defendent, No. C95-877R.

United States District Court, Western District of Washington at Seattle. 1999. *North Cascades Conservation Council, et al. v. United States Forest Service, et al.* Filed 31 August 1999. No. C99-889R.

U.S. Consumer Product Safety Commission. May 1987. CPSC Urges Caution for Three- and Four-Wheeled All Terrain-Vehicles. CPSC Document no. 540. Washington, D.C.: Consumer Product Safety Commission.

U.S. Department of Agriculture fact sheet on Clopyralid. Available online: http://fs.fed.us/foresthealth/pesticide/clopyralid.html [18 June 2000].

U.S. Department of Agriculture fact sheet on Picloram. Available online: http://fs.fed.us/foresthealth/pesticide/picloram.html [18 June 2000].

U.S. House. 1983. Committee on Interior and Insular Affairs Subcommittee on Public Lands and National Parks. *To Establish the Lee Metcalf Wilderness and Management Area in the State of Montana, and for Other Purposes: Transcript from Hearing on S. 96.* 98th Cong., 1st session, 17 May. Serial No. 98-3 Part IV, p. 67.

———. 1997. Committee on Agriculture. *Financing of Roads in the National Forest: Hearing before the Subcommittee on Forestry, Resource Conservation, and Research.* 105th Cong., 1st sess. 20 May. Serial No. 105-14.

———. 1998. Committee on Resources. *Future Maintenance and Repair of the Going-to-the-Sun Road in Glacier National Park: Field Hearing before the Subcommittee on National Parks and Public Lands, Kalispell, MT.* 105th Cong., 2nd sess. 21 September. Serial No. 105-115. 94 pp.

U.S. Secretary of the Interior Bruce Babbitt to Assistant Secretaries. 22 January 1997. Subject: Interim departmental policy on Revised Statute 2477 Grant of Right-of-Way for Public Highways, revocation of December 7, 1988, policy. Photocopied memorandum.

U.S. Senate, Committee on Interior and Insular Affairs, Document no. 115, "A University View of the Forest Service," 91st Congress, 2nd Session, 1970. (This report became more broadly known as "The Bolle Report," after its primary author, Arnold Bolle, who at the time was Dean of the University of Montana School of Forestry.)

Utah: RS 2477, again. 1997. *Road-RIPorter* 2(3): 8.

Van Dyke, F.G., R.H. Brocke, and H.G. Shaw. 1986. Use of road track counts as indices of mountain lion presence. *Journal of Wildlife Management* 50: 102–107.

Van Dyke, F.G., R.H. Brocke, H.G. Shaw, B.B. Ackerman, T.P. Hemker, and F.G. Lindzey. 1986. Reactions of mountain lions to logging and human activity. *Journal of Wildlife Management* 50: 95–102.

Varland, D.E., E.E. Klaas, and T.M. Loughlin. 1993. Use of habitat and perches, causes of mortality and time until dispersal in post-fledging American kestrels. *Journal of Field Ornithology* 64(2): 169–178.

Vaughan, R. 1994. *Endangered Species Act Handbook.* Rockville, MD: Government Institutes, Inc.

Vitousek, P.M., C.M. D'Antonio, L.L. Loope, and R. Westbrooks. 1996. Biological invasions as global environmental change. *American Scientist* (84): 468–478.

Vora, R.S. 1988. Potential soil compaction forty years after logging in northeastern California. *Great Basin Naturalist* 48: 117–120.

Walder, B. 1997. Money for motors from the halls of Congress. *Road-RIPorter* 2(3): 1, 3, 5.

———. 1999. Bulltrout rebellion?! Elko road rage erodes democracy. *Road-RIPorter* 4(6): 1, 4–5.

———. Undated pages. ERFO fact sheet. Missoula, MT: Wildlands Center for Preventing Roads.

Wanek, W.J. 1972. *A Continuing Study of the Ecological Impact of Snowmobiling in Northern Minnesota.* Research Reports for The Center for Environmental Studies, Bemidji State College, Bemidji, MN.

———. 1973. *A Continuing Study of the Ecological Impact of Snowmobiling in Northern Minnesota.* Research Reports for The Center for Environmental Studies, Bemidji State College, Bemidji, MN.

———. 1974. *A Continuing Study of the Ecological Impact of Snowmobiling in Northern Minnesota.* Research Reports for The Center for Environmental Studies, Bemidji State College, Bemidji, MN.

———. 1976. *A Continuing Study of the Ecological Impact of Snowmobiling in Northern Minnesota.* Research Reports for The Center for Environmental Studies, Bemidji State College, Bemidji, MN.

Ward, A.L., J.J. Cupal, G.A. Goodwin, and H.D. Morris. 1976. *Effects of Highway Construction and Use on Big Game Populations.* Washington, D.C.: Federal Highway Administration, Federal Highway Office of Research and Development Report, FHWA-RD-76-174.

Warren, L. 2000. Zion takes tourists out of their cars. *High Country News* 20 April. Available online:http://www/hcn.org/servlets/hcn.Article?article_id=5691 [1 November 2001].

Washington State bills to limit allowances for ORVs. 1999. *Backpacker* September: 15.

Weaver, T., and D. Dale. 1978. Trampling effects of hikers, motorcycles, and horses in meadows and forests. *Journal of Applied Ecology* 15: 451–457.

Webb, R.H., and H.G. Wilshire. 1978. *A Bibliography on the Effects of Off-Road Vehicles on the Environment.* U.S. Geological Survey, Open File Report 78-149.

———. 1980. Recovery of soils and vegetation in a Mojave desert ghost town, Nevada, U.S.A. *Journal of Arid Environments* 3: 291–303.

Webb, R.H., H.C. Ragland, W.H. Godwin, and D. Jenkins. 1998. Environmental effects of soil property changes with off-road vehicle use. *Environmental Management* 2(3): 219–233.

Wilkinson, C.F. 1989. The headwaters of the public trust: Some thoughts on the source and scope of the traditional doctrine. *Environmental Law* spring: 425–472.

———. 1992. *Crossing the Next Meridian: Land, Water, and the Future of the West.* Washington, D.C.: Island Press.

Wilkinson, C.F., and H.M. Anderson. 1987. *Land and Resource Planning in the National Forests.* Washington, D.C.: Island Press.

Wilkinson, T. 1998. *Science under Siege: The Politicians' War on Nature and Truth.* Boulder, CO: Johnson Books.

———. 1999. The Forest Service sets off into uncharted territory. *High Country News* 8 November: 8–12.

Willard, B.E., and J.W. Marr. 1971. Recovery of alpine tundra under protection after damage by human activities in the Rocky Mountains of Colorado. *Biological Conservation* 3(3):181–190.

Williams, T. 1996. Seeking Refuge. *Audubon* 98: 34–45.

Williams, W. 2000. The ghost cat's ninth life. *Audubon* 102(4): 70–77.

Wilshire, H.G., and J.K. Nakata. 1976. Off-road vehicle effects on California's Mojave Desert. *California Geology* 29(6): 123–132.

Wilshire, H.G., K.A. Howard, C.M. Wentworth, and H. Gibbons. 1996. *Geologic Processes at the Land Surface.* U.S. Geological Survey Bulletin 2,149, 1–41. Washington, D.C.: U.S. Government Printing Office.

Wilshire, H.G., G.B. Bodman, D. Broberg, W.J. Kockelman, J. Major, H.E. Malde, C.T. Snyder, and R.C. Stebbins. May 1977. *Impacts and Management of Off-Road Vehicles.* Report of the Committee on Environment and Public Policy. Boulder, CO: The Geological Society of America.

Wilson, C. 1979. Roadsides: Corridors with high fire hazard and risk. *Journal of Forestry* 77(9): 576–577, 580.

Winter Use Plan: Final Environmental Impact Statement for the Yellowstone and Grand Teton National Parks and John D. Rockefeller Jr. Memorial Parkway. 2000. Washington, D.C.: U.S. Department of the Interior, National Park Service.

Wood, K. 1998. Roads and toxic pollutants. *Road-RIPorter* 3(2): 10–11.

World Almanac and Book of Facts, 2000. 1999. Mahwah, NJ: World Almanac Books.

Yellowstone Science interview: Mary Meagher "The Biology of Time." 1997. *Yellowstone Science* 5(2): 16.

Yellowstone to get cleaner snowmobiles. 2000. *Missoulian* (AP) 13 December: A-5.

Zaslowsky, D., and T.H. Watkins. 1994. *These American Lands: Parks, Wilderness, and the Public Lands.* Washington, D.C.: The Wilderness Society/Island Press.

Zuckerman, S. 1991. Pitfalls on the way to lasting restoration. In *Helping Nature Heal,* ed. R. Nilsen, pp. 6–13. Berkeley, CA: Ten Speed Press.

Index